Stan & Jamie Robertson
674 Ravine Drive
Manistee, MI 49660

EXPLORING WILD NORTHWEST FLORIDA

D1569300

Wild Northwest Florida

1. Blackwater River State Forest
2. Blackwater River State Park
3. Big Lagoon State Recreation Area
4. Gulf Islands National Seashore
5. Rocky Bayou State Park
6. Grayton Beach State Park
7. Ponce deLeon Springs State Rec. Area
8. Florida Caverns State Park
9. Falling Waters State Rec. Area

10. Pine Log State Forest
11. St. Andrews State Park
12. St. Joseph Peninsula State Park
13. Three Rivers State Recreation Area
14. Torreya State Park
15. Apalachicola National Forest
16. Ochlockonee River State Park
17. St. Vincent National Wildlife Refuge
18. St. George Island State Park

19. St. Marks National Wildlife Refuge
20. Suwannee River State Park
21. Lake Talquin State Forest
22. Wakulla Springs State Park
23. River Bluff State Picnic Site
24. Hickory Mound Impoundment
25. Aucilla River Sinkholes
26. Apalachicola Bluffs and Ravines Preserve

EXPLORING
WILD
NORTHWEST
FLORIDA

GIL NELSON

PINEAPPLE PRESS
Sarasota, Florida

Dedicated to the memory of
Jim Hardison
whose exploring habit first led me
to many of the places described in this book
and
Inez Frink
whose enthusiasm inspired me
to seek out Florida's special places

Library of Congress Cataloging-in-Publication Data

Nelson, Gil, 1949–
     Exploring wild northwest Florida / Gil Nelson.
         p.   cm.
     Includes bibliographical references (p.   ) and index.
     ISBN 1-56164-086-7 (sc : alk. paper)
         1. Natural history—Florida.   2. Natural areas—Florida—
     Guidebooks.   I. Title.
     QH105.F6N445   1995   95-22760
     508.759′9—dc20   CIP

Inquiries should be addressed to:
Pineapple Press, Inc.
PO Drawer 16008
Southside Station
Sarasota, Florida 34239

Composition by Octavo
Printed and bound by Quebecor/Fairfield, Fairfield, Pennsylvania

10 9 8 7 6 5 4 3 2 1

CONTENTS

MAPS

ACKNOWLEDGMENTS

I would like to thank the many people who have offered their assistance to me throughout the writing of this book. Foremost among them are my wife, Brenda, and daughter, Hope. Each has been a consistent source of encouragement and I cherish their patience and love.

I would also like to thank Gayle Muenchow and Richard Hopkins for allowing me to use the photograph of them canoeing along Kennedy Creek for the book's cover. Their cooperation is much appreciated.

I would especially like to thank Dr. Walt Schmidt, Dr. Tom Scott, and Frank Rupert, all with the Florida Geological Survey, for their help in clarifying my understanding of Florida's geology. Their willingness to talk with me as well as to review and re-review parts of the manuscript is sincerely appreciated.

I owe a special thanks to Barbara Cook, Gail Fishman, Vic Heller, and Fritz Wettstein. All read and commented on parts of the manuscript. Barbara also helped with field work and provided significant information about Florida's three national forests, and Vic was a ready resource for information about Florida's wildlife management areas and native wildlife.

Others who assisted me with information and technical expertise about individual parks and natural areas include Robert Barlow, Tom Beitzel, Dana Bryan, Vernon Compton, Sandra Cook, Angus Gholson, Ann Harvey, Ronnie Hudson, Ann Johnson, Mary Jones, John O'Mera, Mark Milligan, Pamela Murfey, Dave Randall, Joe Reinman, Barbara Roberts, Albert Smith, and Robin Will. I would like to thank all of these individuals as well as the many rangers and staff at Florida's state parks, state and national forests, and natural preserves for the many helpful hints about the regions they serve and the parks they manage.

The line illustrations in this book were provided by Marvin

and Lee Cook and their staff at Wilderness Graphics, Inc. in Tallahassee. Their willingness to assist me with this project is much appreciated. Working with them is always a pleasure. David Simms provided all of the maps. His easy manner contributed to an enjoyable working relationship, and his penchant for quality work added considerably to the book.

I would also like to express appreciation to Su Jewell. Her outstanding book *Exploring Wild South Florida* provided the model after which this book is patterned and in many ways made the current book possible. I appreciated being able to share successes and challenges with her as this book progressed.

Last, but perhaps most importantly, I would like to thank June Cussen of Pineapple Press for offering me the opportunity to write this book. Her friendly style, cooperative spirit, commitment to quality, and excellent editing made writing this, as well as its companion volume, *Exploring Wild North Florida*, an especially enjoyable adventure.

INTRODUCTION

Northwestern Florida is a magnificent and enchanted land. With topography that ranges from rolling hills and sandy ridges to swampy flatlands and boggy meadows, it is an area replete with opportunities for outdoor exploration. It is also a region that draws residents and visitors alike into a fascinating world that encourages the pursuit of nature study and outdoor recreation as a rewarding and encompassing hobby.

Exploring northwest Florida can consume a lifetime. From the Suwannee River on the east to the Perdido River on the west, from the Georgia state line to the Gulf of Mexico, there are literally hundreds of locations that offer alluring glimpses of the Sunshine State's natural beauty. Many of these sites still reflect the way Florida may have appeared in more primitive times. Each has its own special attraction and can be revisited time and again with little fear of saturation.

The intense and recurring exploration of this relatively limited geographic area is the fundamental theme of this book. The more one visits northwest Florida's natural areas, the more one learns. Each field trip offers something new. Every revisit allows one to look at familiar places in new ways. With each visit comes closer observation that reveals new discoveries, offers new insights about our natural ecological systems, and fosters a deeper understanding of our native environments. The more familiar we become with the intricacies of our special places, the more clearly we come to understand the interrelationships that make Florida special, and the more we come to appreciate the state as a dynamic, integrated whole rather than a collection of unrelated geographic entities.

I
OVERVIEW

HOW TO USE THIS BOOK

This book is a study guide to the natural bounty of northwest Florida. Its central purpose is to encourage readers to explore, to discover, to learn, and to develop a more comprehensive understanding and keener appreciation of this distinctive region.

Chapter 1 begins with important tips for exploring the region, then outlines the precautions one should take for insuring enjoyment. Chapter 2 offers an overview of the Florida panhandle's landforms and topographic structure, and Chapter 3 provides a conceptual framework for better understanding the region's several natural habitats. Chapter 4 introduces the state's native wildlife, with special emphasis on the more interesting species. Chapters 5 through 7 describe 26 major field sites that represent the best of northwest Florida's special places.

Chapter 8 includes an annotated list of 20 additional field sites that also provide nature discovery opportunities, as well as several lists of the more common plant and animal species normally found in north Florida habitats. These lists help readers focus on the species that are likely to be seen on a particular field trip or in a particular area. These lists will help you use your other field guides more effectively, while the discussions of the various field sites will help you fit your understanding of these species into a larger frame of reference and a more meaningful context.

The reference list at the end of the book contains a bibliography for further study. Many of the books and publications listed there will lead you to new discoveries about Florida's natural areas. Some of these books are commercial volumes and can be found in bookstores or ordered from their publishers. Others are little-known government publications available only from the federal or state agencies which produced them or in the government documents sections of local libraries.

Whether you are a longtime Floridian, a new resident to the state, or a short-term visitor, this book will enhance your study of Florida's panhandle. Beginning and advanced amateurs alike will find its chapters broadening and its suggested field trips stimulating. It is hoped that you will find its pages rewarding reading and its content a ready reference to which you can return time and again.

PLANNING YOUR TRIP

Major Highways and Airports

Getting to northwest Florida is not particularly difficult. The area is crisscrossed by highways and served by several major airports.

For those driving to the Florida panhandle, two interstate highways provide the quickest access. Interstate 10 traverses the entire northern part of the state from Pensacola to Jacksonville and bisects the panhandle north and south. Interstate 75 skirts the eastern edge of the panhandle and intersects I-10 just east of the Suwannee River.

The interstates are the newest and most traveled of the panhandle's major highways. Though I-10 will get you near to your destination quickly and with little confusion, it discourages a more leisurely, "stop-and-go" travel agenda; it also bypasses much of what makes northwest Florida special. For explorers, the older roadways are by far the better choice.

The best of the traditional northwest Florida byways must certainly include US 98 from Pensacola to Fanning Springs. This highway hugs the western shore through much of the panhandle before moving only slightly farther inland as it skirts what locals call the Big Bend, that region of Florida that lies between Apa-

OVERVIEW

lachicola and Cross City and joins the panhandle to the peninsula. US 27 from the Georgia state line to Branford, US 231 from
the Alabama state line to Panama City, US 331 from the Alabama
state line to US 98, SR 85 both north and south of Crestview, and
US 29 from the Alabama state line to Pensacola are the best
north-south routes. Old US 90 is an east-west route that parallels
I-10 for its entire distance but is much less congested and more
reminiscent of north Florida as it existed 30 years ago, and SR 2
and SR 4 extend east and west across the northernmost reaches
of the panhandle.

Visitors arriving by air can choose from two major airports,
depending on which part of the panhandle they plan to visit.
The Pensacola airport is best for the western edge of the state,
and the Tallahassee airport offers the best access to the central
and eastern panhandle. Both airports are serviced by several
rental car companies. Since there are few organized tours and no
mass transportation to most of the places described in the following chapters, a rental car is a must.

Weather

North Florida's weather is more variable than that of the state's
more tropical regions. Though the average annual temperature
across much of the region is in the upper 60s to low 70s, during a
typical year the thermometer may fluctuate from winter lows in
the mid-20s to the mid- to upper 90s, or even the low 100s,
during June, July, August, and into September. Daily summertime temperatures average in the low 80s as they do throughout
much of the state, but daily winter temperatures average in the
40s, about 13 degrees lower than in the southern counties. Areas
in the northern panhandle may experience first frost near the
beginning of November in average years, about one month earlier than for regions nearer the central parts of the state. The
more northern counties also have at least 25 more frost days in
an average winter than do the central Florida counties.

Because of the mitigating influences of the Gulf of Mexico, the
temperature along the panhandle coastline is seldom quite as

hot or cold as more inland locations. However, the lack of breeze throughout the inland parts of northwest Florida can make a midsummer's day a wilting experience. Such days are often perfect for canoeing one of the region's spring-fed streams or tiny blackwater rivers.

Rainfall also fluctuates on an annual basis. The fall and early winter are typically the driest times of the year; late spring and summer the wettest. Annual rainfall varies radically from year to year but typically averages between 55 and 65 inches. The major rain events during summer are temporary (though often quite intense) thunderstorms that most often occur in mid- to late afternoon and last less than an hour. Winter rain events are more often associated with a passing cold front and often last an entire day or evening.

Fishing Licenses

State saltwater fishing licenses are required, with the following exceptions: 1) an individual under 16 years of age, 2) an individual fishing from a charter boat that has a vessel saltwater fishing license, 3) a Florida resident 65 years of age or older, and 4) a Florida resident fishing in saltwater from land or from a structure fixed to the land. Residents may obtain a ten-day, one-year, five-year, or lifetime license, and nonresidents may obtain a three-day, seven-day, or one-year license. Licenses are also required for freshwater fishing. The "cane pole law" allows a person to fish without a license in the county of his or her residence, with a pole not equipped with a reel, and using live or natural bait (catch and size limits still apply). Licenses may be obtained from county tax collectors' offices or from bait and tackle shops.

THE STATE PARK SYSTEM

The many state parks (including recreation areas, preserves, and reserves) are maintained to keep the lands in or restore them to their conditions when the first Europeans arrived. The historic sites preserve the cultural heritage. Fees are charged at most sites. People who plan to explore a number of parks, or who live near a park that they visit frequently, should consider buying an annual individual or family pass (available at any state park).

The parks are open from 8 AM to sunset every day of the year including holidays. The parks close at sundown, which means that the gate may close at an odd time. Parks with campgrounds generally allow check-ins after sunset. Primitive campsites have no facilities, and campers must pack out their trash. Pets are permitted only in designated areas and must be kept on a 6-foot (maximum) hand-held leash. Pets are not allowed in swimming, camping, beach, or concession areas. Guide dogs for the disabled are welcomed in all areas. Horses (where permitted) must have proof of a recent negative Coggins test.

THE NATIONAL WILDLIFE REFUGE AND NATIONAL FOREST SYSTEM

The National Wildlife Refuge system is composed of over 500 refuges across the country. Many, such as the one included in this book, were established to protect habitat for migratory birds, such as waterfowl. Unlike national parks and national forests, refuges are created solely for protecting natural resources. Only compatible activities are permitted. This is why some refuges offer few interpretive activities or public amenities. Many have educational facilities, such as a visitor center. Some offer guided tours. None of Florida's refuges permit camping. When you visit a refuge, come prepared with drinking water and anything else you may need. Pets may or may not be permitted (see separate entry or call the refuge to confirm).

The national forest system was originally established to provide renewable timber resources. However, through the years the U.S. Forest Service has expanded its objectives to include a multi-use approach to managing the lands under its control.

Hunting, fishing, camping, hiking, backpacking, and wildlife observation are encouraged in most national forests (including those in Florida), and a number of national forests provide protection for national wilderness areas and areas of special historical, geological, or natural significance.

Purchasers of a federal Duck Stamp (available at post offices and refuges; currently $15) are allowed free admission to all national wildlife refuges. Duck stamps are good for one year from July 1 to June 30, and non-hunters may purchase one. The funds from the stamps are used to buy habitat for more refuges.

Purchasers of a Golden Eagle pass (currently $25), good for one year from the date of purchase, are allowed free admission to any federal fee area. This includes all national parks, monuments, seashores, historic sites, and national wildlife refuges anywhere in the United States. Handicapped individuals may obtain a free Golden Access pass (good for free admission to any federal fee area). Senior citizens may obtain a Golden Age pass for a modest one-time fee, good for free admission to any federal fee area. All passes may be obtained at any federal fee area.

Maps

Several maps are useful for finding your way around the panhandle. The most comprehensive and compact is the state's official road map, which may be obtained by addressing a request to the Florida Department of Commerce, Collins Building, Tallahassee, FL 32304.

In addition to the official road map, the Florida Department of Transportation also produces detailed black-and-white maps for each of Florida's 67 counties. These may also be obtained by writing the department at 605 Suwannee St., Mail Station 12, Tallahassee, FL 32399-0415. There is a small fee for each map, but they are well worth the expenditure.

DeLorme Publishing Company produces the *Florida Atlas and Gazetteer*. It is an oversized softcover booklet that has color maps and is an excellent reference. It is available in many bookstores. For information, write to DeLorme Publishing Co., P.O. Box 298, Freeport, ME 04032.

Finally, many of the larger federal installations, such as the national forests, produce very good maps. Information about these maps is given with the descriptions of the areas.

LOCAL PRECAUTIONS

Snakes

There are six species of poisonous snakes in Florida, five of which are found in the panhandle. Of these, only three are widespread or commonly encountered.

The Florida cottonmouth is the most likely poisonous snake to be found in the wetlands. Older cottonmouths are typically dark in color and their bodies often appear encircled by even darker bands; younger snakes are much lighter and may appear patterned with regular, bronze-colored splotches or bands. Like most pit vipers, the cottonmouth has a narrow neck and a relatively large, triangular head. The sides of the head appear flattened, and each shows a wide black stripe running from the back of the head nearly to the nose. These wide black swabs often appear outlined below by a thin white line. Taken together, these latter characteristics provide an excellent field mark.

The eastern diamondback and dusky pygmy rattlesnakes are the more common poisonous upland species. The common name of the diamondback derives from the distinctive diamond-shaped markings along the center of its grayish back. The pygmy rattler gets its name from its small size; it seldom exceeds about 20 inches in length. The diamondback has an exceptionally large head and conspicuous "neck," and its tail is tipped with dark rattles. It is more often found in dry areas than the cottonmouth, and is most common in pine-palmetto flatwoods, near the edges of the wet areas. The pygmy is common in a variety of habitats and is noted for its disagreeable disposition. It will strike with little provocation and often lies coiled along the top of fallen logs or under the edge of native vegetation.

The eastern coral snake is the most colorful of our poisonous species. It is adorned with yellow, red, and black bands and is

Cottonmouth

easily confused with the scarlet kingsnake. The adages, "If the nose is black, it's bad for Jack" and "Red touch yellow, kill a fellow; red touch black, good for Jack" will help you remember two of the key distinguishing features between these species. The nose of the coral snake is black and its bright red and yellow bands are adjacent one another, while the nose of the king snake is red and its red and yellow bands are separated by wide black bands. The coral snake has the most potent venom of any of Florida's poisonous snakes, but is not as often encountered as the rattlesnakes or cottonmouth. In addition, it is not a pit viper and does not strike in the same way as these other species. Small coral snakes have relatively small mouths and must chew on their victims to inject their venom, though larger coral snakes can inflict serious bites without chewing. Most bites on humans are confined to areas between the victim's fingers or toes. The combination of arresting beauty and deadly venom make the coral snake a creature to be admired, but never accosted.

The state's least common poisonous snake is the copperhead. It is very attractive with dark brownish copper bands against a golden-brown or bronze-colored background. Its head is clear of markings but it has the typical neck and diamond-shaped head of a pit viper. The copperhead is limited in Florida to the bluffs and ravines region of the central panhandle, principally in Gadsden and Liberty counties.

Much has been made of the potential of snakebites, and most

of us have an unrealistic and unsupported fear of these reptiles. None of Florida's snakes are particularly aggressive, and none lie in wait for human intruders. The number of snakebites in Florida is quite few when compared to the number of people who visit the state's woodlands each year. You are much more likely to have an automobile accident on the way to your field site than a snakebite after you arrive. Nevertheless, it pays to be observant and to refrain from handling snakes if you are not sure of their identity. If you are bitten, it is important to remain calm, clean the affected area thoroughly, and seek competent medical help immediately.

Alligators

Whether because of their massive bodies or imposing appearance, alligators are one of those unfortunate animals that have developed a somewhat bad reputation. Like their reptilian relatives, the cottonmouth and eastern diamondback rattlesnake, they are often seen as sinister animals with an evil propensity for willingly and maliciously attacking unsuspecting humans. Also

like their reptilian relatives, much of this fearsome reputation is factually ungrounded and finds its basis mostly in a combination of myth and misunderstanding.

To be sure, alligators are powerful and effective predators with little desire, and perhaps even less ability, to discriminate between their targets. Their powerful jaws and seemingly indestructible digestive tracts have no trouble crunching and metabolizing full-grown deer, hogs, goats, dogs, and even the largest of hard-shelled turtles. Observing a ten-foot bull gator noisily ingesting a turtle—bones, shell, and all—is an awesome and inspiring demonstration of primitive power.

While most of a gator's natural predation goes unnoticed, those events that include human victims always create a stir of activity and apprehension in those of us who frequent the wetlands. However, since 1948, when the Florida Game and Fresh Water Fish Commission began keeping records, there have been fewer than 175 alligator attacks on human targets. No more than 15 of these altercations have been fatal, and it is suspected that at least six of these 15 attacks may have been directed toward victims who were already dead. Even with an estimated population of over one million alligators in Florida, the probability of attack, even upon avid outdoorspeople, is extremely low. The average Floridian is much more likely to fall victim to a bee sting, automobile accident, or household tragedy than to an alligator.

This is not to suggest that alligators are completely without threat. Nor is it to suggest that one should be unwary when in their company or lack vigilance when in their habitat. Gators will attack if provoked, particularly if the disturbed animal is a nesting female or a mother with newly hatched young. It is foolish to swim in waters where gators are known to occur or let children or pets venture too close to the edges of lakes where alligators live. It is also unwise to encourage an alligator's association with humans by feeding or molesting it. The most troublesome gators are those that have become accustomed to humans or have learned to associate humans with food. Alligators are, after all, wild animals that should be respected as such and left entirely to their own instincts and devices.

Insects and Ticks

Most of northwest Florida's insects are more appropriately considered nuisances than actual dangers. Mosquitoes, biting flies, no-see-ums, and chiggers have the potential to make a woodland outing tedious, but seldom impossible. For those susceptible to such critters, it may be wise to have a supply of repellant handy. It should be noted, however, that the use of commercial repellant is not guaranteed safe and has been associated with illness or even death in some instances. It should probably be used sparingly. Some outdoorspeople recommend nonrepellant products such as Avon's Skin-So-Soft and have used them with at least moderate success. Alternatively, wearing long sleeves and long pants, and taping the leg openings to the tops of boots, sometimes proves effective.

There are at least two types of insects that should be carefully avoided. The first type includes the wasps and hornets. A number of these flying insects have excruciatingly painful stings and can cause severe, or even deadly, reactions in those who are allergic to their poison. Many wasps are difficult to see due to their cryptic nests which are often well hidden among dense foliage. Canoeists who like to poke their canoes into the woodsy edges of slow-flowing creeks should be especially careful to check overhanging limbs before disturbing them. It is also probably wise to carry a supply of over-the-counter or prescription antihistamine in your first-aid kit.

The second troublesome insect is the fire ant. Fire ants are nonnative species that build sandy mounds up to one foot tall. They are easily provoked by unwary intruders and react quickly to disturbance. Their stings lend credence to their name, and the welts they inflict can stay with the victim for several days or weeks. Fire ant mounds are easily seen if one is observant. However, since many amateur naturalists spend a considerable amount of time looking ahead, or up, or through a pair of binoculars, the mounds are also easy to stumble onto accidentally. Suffice it to say that care should be taken when walking in any disturbed sandy site.

In addition to insects, north Florida's woodlands are noted for a number of tick species. While all of the species are known to attach themselves to humans and can cause an irritating sore if not quickly found and removed, only the deer tick has the potential for real danger. This tiny relative of the spider isn't much larger than the head of a pin; hence, it is difficult to find on the body. The deer tick is associated with lyme disease which has now been reported in north Florida. The best strategy for prevention of tick bites is to be observant while on an outing and then to take careful stock of oneself upon returning home. Ticks like places where clothes fit tightly, such as around the waist. They also seem to be drawn to underarms, the groin area, and the edges of the hairline at the back of the neck.

Poisonous Plants

Northwest Florida has only three plants that are likely to cause serious irritation on contact. These include poison ivy, poison oak, and poison sumac. The first two of these are by far the most

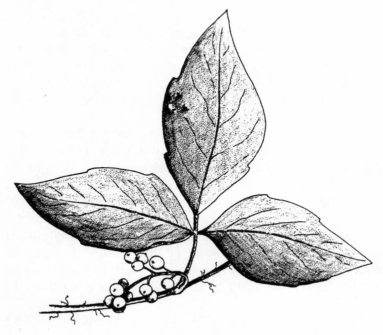

Poison Ivy

common and are so nearly similar that the average observer does not distinguish between them. Both are weakly erect shrubs or, more commonly, climbing vines that have compound leaves with three leaflets. The leaflets of both species are lobed on at least one side, though leaves of poison oak seem to display this feature more consistently. These plants are easy to identify because there are no other common woody vines that have alternate, compound leaves and only three leaflets.

Poison sumac is a seldom-encountered plant of swamps, bogs, bays, and wet woodlands. It has compound leaves with seven to 15 leaflets and reddish to tan twigs.

II
ORIGINS OF
NORTHWEST
FLORIDA'S LANDSCAPE

Of all there is to learn about northwest Florida's natural history, few things are more fascinating or intriguing than the Pleistocene origins of its geology and topography. A drive through the region's countryside leaves the impression that powerful forces have been at work in shaping its land. Gently rolling hills to the north give way to pine-studded flatlands and sandy inland dunes to the south. Large upland lakes and deep, rich soils of the uplands give way to a land dotted with swamps, springs, sinkholes, and scrubby woods near the coasts. Numerous rivers and streams thread their way through the landscape, dividing the geography into a series of natural drainage basins. Understanding the evolution of these landforms provides the underpinning for a full appreciation of the west Florida landscape as it exists today. Our floral communities, native habitats, and general ecology are all inextricably tied to and explained by the history of our land.

The story of the processes that have shaped Florida's topography necessarily begins with the history of a rising and falling sea. Several times during the last 1.6 million years, much of what is now the Florida mainland was sea bottom. As the earth alternately cooled and warmed, reacting to major climatic changes, the seas advanced and retreated in response. Massive glaciers expanded during the cooling periods, creeping down the continents, absorbing all available water and forcing the shoreline far out into what is today the Gulf of Mexico. During the warming periods the great ice sheets melted and the glaciers released their water to the rising sea, squeezing western Florida into a narrow strip that extended across what is today the northernmost extent of the state.

Four major glaciations and three corresponding interglacial periods dominated Florida during the ice ages (see Figure 2-1). Geologists say that a rise in sea level occurred during each of these interglacial intervals. During at least the Yarmouth period, and perhaps during the other two interglacials as well, the influx of water raised the sea to as much as 60 or 100 feet above its current level. Each of these seas left a mosaic of shorelines and eroding marine terraces for present-day scientists to unravel and interpret.

The currently accepted interpretation of these complex geological events recognizes the 60-foot terrace as the maximum extent to which the ice age seas encroached on present-day Florida real estate. The most convincing evidence for this comes from the extent and persistence of a landform known as the Cody Escarpment, a sudden drop in elevation that outlines much of northern Florida. Recognized by geologists as the most continuous topographic feature in the state, this escarpment had its origin as the shoreline of the Okefenokee Sea. It extends across much of north Florida, passing through Tallahassee and Gainesville and turning northward just before reaching Palatka. In places there is as much as 50 feet of relief from the crest of the scarp to its toe. In Tallahassee, a well-defined portion of the scarp separates the high rolling hills of the north from the flatlands to the south. The state's capitol building stands on one of the southernmost of these hills.

Each of the seas that followed the Okefenokee Sea was successively lower in elevation. None left a mark as clear as the Cody Scarp, and none are as easy to recognize in the landscape. Their identification and description is a task for geologists who study topographic maps, fossils, sedimentology, and geologic structure.

By the time of the Wisconsin glaciation, only 20,000 years ago, the sea had dropped to at least 300 feet (some say more than 400 feet) below today's level. This low stand of the sea pushed the shoreline well seaward of its current position. With the retreat of

PLEISTOCENE	Upper	Wisconsin Glacial
		Sangamon Interglacial
		Illinoian Glacial
	Middle	Yarmouth Interglacial
		Kansan Glacial
	Lower	Aftonian Interglacial
		Nebraska Glacial

Figure 2.1.

the glaciers, the water again returned, drowning both river valleys and freshwater springs, some of which still remain well beyond the present coastline. Our present sea level was attained about 3,000 years ago and has since remained relatively stable, though there is now documented evidence that it is once again on a slow, but seemingly constant rise. As a result of these past events, north Florida today is composed of a fascinating assortment of topographic features that offer outstanding opportunities for exploration. Figure 2-2 illustrates these landforms.

Extending east and west along the northern portion of the state are two large upland areas: the Western Highlands and the Tallahassee Hills. Taken together, these uplands were once part of a continuous feature that has now been bisected and lowered by a series of streams, rivers, and subsurface erosion. Bounded on the south by the remains of the ancient shoreline, these

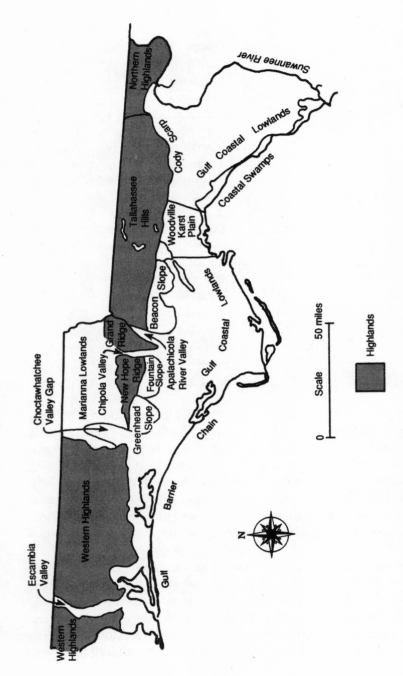

Figure 2.2. Adapted from maps provided by the Florida Geological Survey

highlands are composed of gently rolling hills with upland forests that are in some places reminiscent of the Piedmont foothills and in other places of more traditional upland pinewoods.

The western portion of the highlands, including particularly Escambia and Santa Rosa Counties, and to a lesser extent Okaloosa and Walton Counties, is unique for its surface and near-surface geology and the quality of its groundwater. In most parts of the state, the Floridan aquifer system, a thick limestone sequence, serves as an underground water storage system and provides most of northern Florida's drinking water. As the top of this subsurface limestone nears the western panhandle, however, it dips toward the southwest and plunges deep into the earth, eventually reaching a depth of nearly 2,000 feet. Above it lies a thick deposit of sand and gravel, consisting primarily of white to light brown quartz sand ranging to a depth of 1,000 feet. This so-called sand and gravel aquifer contains the softest water in the state.

The reason for this extremely soft water is explained by the action of underground water. Groundwater in the Floridan aquifer system increases in mineral content as it moves through and dissolves the limestone. Water that percolates down through the sand and gravel aquifer, on the other hand, encounters no limestone nor little other soluble material. It thus remains soft and virtually unmineralized.

These surficial sand deposits contribute to a somewhat uniform appearance of the rivers in the western panhandle. Flying over the area at 8,000 feet one is struck by the ribbons of yellowish brown water below. Each of the major streams west of the Choctawhatchee—the Yellow, Shoal, and to some degree even the Blackwater—all have the same characteristic color resulting from tannin-stained water flowing over white sandy bottoms.

The Tallahassee Hills region contrasts sharply with the Western Highlands. Beginning on the eastern banks of the Apalachicola River, these hills extend all the way to the western edge of the Withlacoochee River. The soils consist of yellowish orange clays, silts, and sands that support a lush natural vegetation. The pine-oak-hickory woods community still remains in many areas that have not yet been developed for agriculture or human habitation; but such areas are not likely to remain with us for the long term except in pockets of preserved public lands. There are few large streams within the hills region. The Ochlockonee is the only one of any size. Most rainfall either sinks directly into the ground or runs off into one of the area's large lakes.

The western edge of the Tallahassee Hills is often referred to as the Apalachicola Bluffs and Ravines. Though technically not a geologic sub-unit, the topography in this area is much different than in most other parts of western Florida. Characterized by steep ridges and deeply cut ravines, this region contains the greatest topographic relief in the state and offers some of the most unusual terrain to be found anywhere in the southeastern coastal plain. The hiking trails and campgrounds of Torreya State Park (see p. 181) offer a firsthand look at this magnificent and extraordinary setting.

Between the Western Highlands and the Tallahassee Hills lies a large area of erosion referred to as the Marianna Lowlands. That the area was once a highland itself is evidenced by two well-developed ridges on its southern and eastern flanks and remnant hills within its interior. Rock Hill, Orange Hill, High Hill, Oak Hill, and Falling Water Hill, the latter of which is the site of Falling Waters State Recreation Area (see p. 125), are all that is left of the central portion of this once-dominant landform. The remainder has been reduced to a well-developed karst plain, a common geologic feature in Florida that takes its name from a similar region in Yugoslavia.

A karst plain is an area in which subsurface limestone lies very near the surface, and which normally evolves from the interaction of two primary geologic processes. In the case of the Marianna Lowlands, the surface erosion resulting from the Choctawhatchee, Chattahoochee, and Chipola Rivers, coupled with the underground erosion of the limestone by groundwater, led to a generalized lowering of the land surface in this area. Today, the area is bordered on the south by the Holmes Valley Scarp, a northward-facing escarpment that originated with the development of the lowlands.

The Marianna Lowlands formed during a previous high stand

of the sea when the water table was much nearer ground level. As the sea receded, many of the underground cavities that were formed by and filled with water lay perched above the water table. Now filled with air, a sample of these cavities form the main attraction of the Florida Caverns State Park (see p. 126).

South of the Tallahassee Hills and Western Highlands lies a continuous strand of reclaimed sea bottom referred to as the Coastal Lowlands. In the far western panhandle, near Pensacola, these lowlands extend only a few miles inland, except in the valley of the Escambia River where they extend into Alabama. More easterly, the coastal lowlands reach their widest point as they near the Apalachicola River. This entire area—from just west of Panama City to Jefferson County—covers the remnant floor of the prehistoric Gulf of Mexico. Some geologists refer to this subsurface feature as the Apalachicola Embayment; others have termed it the Chattahoochee Embayment. The former name seems to be preferred by most authors. Though this feature lies deep within the earth and is not visible at the surface, it plays a role in determining the soils and vegetation that lie above it.

Much of the area overlying this ancient embayment is forested and is either owned by paper companies or contained within the nearly 600,000 acres of the Apalachicola National Forest. These forests are primarily of the north Florida flatwoods type, consisting of slash and longleaf pine overstory with a ground cover of saw palmetto, wiregrass, and over 200 species of shrubby and herbaceous plants.

Farther east still, the lowlands change character. Beginning on a line paralleling and slightly west of US 319 south from Tallahassee and through the villages of Crawfordville and Medart, the Woodville Karst Plain extends eastward to central Jefferson County. Somewhat similar to the Marianna Lowlands described above, the Woodville Karst Plain is composed of slightly younger limestone that in most places lies within 10 to 30 feet of the soil surface. Many of our more interesting rivers have cut their courses through this karst terrain, exposing the limestone along the way. The area is also noted for its numerous sinkholes, such as those along the Aucilla River (see p. 193).

Throughout its extent, northwestern Florida is unique. It offers abundance in its natural places, in its flora, and in its fauna. In many ways this abundance derives from, is dependent upon, and is explained by its present landforms and its more recent geologic past. An understanding of this past aids our exploration of this region and provides us with an organizational context into which we can fit our discoveries.

III

HABITATS AND NATURAL COMMUNITIES

The natural communities that make up Florida's landscape are as varied and interesting as the topography and geologic substructure that support them. At least 81 natural communities have been identified for Florida, all of which are subsumed within about 20 major ecosystems. All are readily identifiable in the field through a basic understanding of Florida's native plants. Learning the similarities, differences, and unique features of these several communities provides an important organizational scheme for exploring the state's natural endowments and for better understanding what makes its wildlands special.

SALTMARSHES

The Gulf coast of northwestern Florida is blessed with large stretches of protected saltmarsh. Long viewed only as mosquito hatcheries and waste places, saltmarsh communities are now recognized as important marine-life nursery areas and are heralded for their biological productivity.

To the uninitiated, the saltmarsh appears to be a monotonous, forbidding territory consisting of little variation. In some ways this is an accurate assessment. The several plant communities of the marsh are typically limited in species diversity and often cover large, unbroken expanses. But beneath the low canopy of each of these communities lies a veritable wilderness.

Typical *Juncus* Saltmarsh

Tiny nematode worms and herbivorous crustaceans consume both the juices and tissue of the living marsh grass. Snails graze on the abundant benthic algae. Bivalves consume the detritus suspended in the tidal influx. Together, these organisms constitute the lowest tier of an extensive food web that supports a surprising variety of reptiles, mammals, and birds.

The west coast of Florida contains some of the finest examples of irregularly flooded saltmarsh to be found anywhere in the world. Composed chiefly of black needlerush (*Juncus roemerianus*) and several species of Spartina, the largest area of Gulf coastal marsh stretches nearly continuously from just north of Tampa all the way to the mouth of the Ochlockonee River. West of the Ochlockonee, marsh areas are generally confined to the edges of inland bays and the landward sides of barrier islands.

One of the most striking features of the largest expanse of Gulf coast marsh is its proximity to open water. Whereas those saltmarshes west of the Ochlockonee are normally found in protected bays, lagoons, and estuaries, those from the Ochlockonee River southward lie immediately adjacent to the open Gulf.

This phenomenon is accounted for by the region's topographic structure. The northeastern quadrant of the Gulf of

Mexico is characterized by a relatively wide, gently sloping floor covered by an immense area of shallow water. With deep water lying well offshore and the area sheltered by the curvature of the coast, wave activity between Cedar Key and Alligator Point is reduced. In addition, the region contains few rivers large enough to provide significant quantities of sediment to the coastal shelf. With little sandy material from which to build islands and in a near-zero wave energy zone, beach and barrier development is discouraged in favor of the marsh.

ESTUARIES AND INSHORE MARINE ENVIRONMENTS

With more than 1,200 miles of saltwater shores and over two-thirds of its boundary bordering the Gulf of Mexico or Atlantic Ocean, it is not surprising that inshore marine environments constitute an important Florida resource. Shallow lagoons, salty bays, and brackish estuaries punctuate the coastline throughout the state and are counted among some of the world's most productive ecosystems.

Estuaries are essentially brackish environments that exist in the narrow zone where freshwater mixes with salt. Generally found near the mouths of major rivers, their salinity levels change dramatically throughout the year, contributing to their importance as a primary nursery ground for a variety of sea life.

Besides being extremely productive, estuaries are also extremely fragile. Perhaps more than any other natural community, they find their success in the ecological, biological, and geological interdependence they share with surrounding habitats. They rely on coastal barriers to protect them from the onslaught of ocean waves, and on rivers for freshwater input. The fringing saltmarshes trap nutrients and reduce erosion that might otherwise cloud the salty currents. Seagrass beds spread across the murky bottom, providing cover to a host of developing organisms. In various ways, the health of Florida's near-shore coastal environments is directly tied to the health of their supporting habitats.

Turtle Grass

The expansive seagrass meadows that are often associated with Florida's estuaries and inshore marine environments are some of the finest to be found anywhere in the world. Similar in appearance to the terrestrial habitats from which they take their name, these meadows are composed of an assortment of low-growing flowering plants that are uniquely adapted to life in a submarine environment. Although common in bays and lagoons on both coasts, they are most abundant along the gently sloping plane of the northeastern Gulf of Mexico where seagrass beds are known to extend several miles into the open Gulf, with no seaward protecting boundary.

Seagrasses are normally found in relatively shallow water. Like

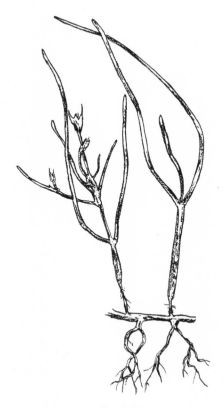

Shoal Grass

typical land plants, seagrasses depend on photosynthesis for energy production. For this reason, they cannot live in water that is either too deep or too dim to allow the penetration of sunlight.

Seven seagrass species inhabit Florida waters; only four are common and widespread. Probably the best known and most easily recognized of these four is turtle grass. Found in extensive meadows to a depth of about 60 feet, its leaves are up to 1 foot long and nearly 1/2 inch in width. It is easily distinguished and is the only one of our seagrasses with such wide, ribbonlike leaves.

Widgeon grass occurs in shallower waters and has threadlike leaves. It is most common in bays and estuaries and is equally at home in fresh and brackish waters. Widgeon grass meadows are one of the state's most ecologically valuable submersed aquatic plant communities, providing both food and cover for a variety of wildlife.

Shoal grass occurs in the shallowest of waters, though it is often found in quite deep water also. On extreme low tides entire beds of this species may be exposed to the air. The leaves of shoal grass are flat, very narrow, and tipped with three minute teeth. The three-toothed tip of an unbroken shoal grass leaf is a unique identifying feature.

The fourth of the most common seagrasses is manatee grass. Named, presumably, for its attractiveness to the manatee, or sea cow, it may be differentiated from the other common seagrasses by its cylindrical leaves. Manatee grass occurs at greater depths than the other three and is seldom found in very shallow waters.

Seagrass meadows are important components of our near-shore marine ecological system. In addition to providing nursery areas for much of Florida's most important and commercially valuable marine life, they provide both habitat and protection for a wide diversity of nongame organisms. A variety of fishes, crabs, snails, shrimps, and bivalves find shelter and food within the underwater meadows, while algae and tiny animals colonize seagrass leaves. All of these inhabitants are tied together in a dynamic food web that sustains and preserves both our near-shore and offshore marine environment.

BARRIERS, BEACHES AND DUNES

Florida's extraordinary panhandle coastline has long held a fascination for tourists and amateur naturalists alike. Its deep, white sand is so fine that the beach below you squeaks when you walk. Its seaward edge borders deep green and blue water, and supports a variety of crabs, snails, insects, and other near-shore marine inhabitants. Breaking waves run up on wide, sandy beaches against a backdrop of large sand dunes topped with a smattering of sea oats and ground-hugging morning glory. Atop and just behind the dunes lies an intriguing habitat that sup-

Sea Oats

ports a limited but interesting array of plants and animals. Unlike the saltmarsh regions discussed above, the seaward side of northwest Florida's sandy shoreline is distinguished by greater depth, stronger currents, increased quantities of sand, and higher wave energy. All of these features contribute to the formation of magnificent barrier islands, spits, offshore sand-bars, beaches, and dunes.

A cursory look at almost any state map will reveal any number of these intriguing coastal features along both of the state's northern coastlines. West of the mouth of the Ochlockonee River, for example, the map shows the Gulf coast lined almost

A Northwest Florida Beach Strip

exclusively with a swath of sandy beaches. In some areas these beaches form the outer edges of barrier islands and spits. In areas devoid of coastal barriers, they constitute the mainland shore.

Two primary types of coastal features fringe the west Florida coastline. Barrier islands are probably the most well known and easily recognized of the two. Completely surrounded by water and lined along their seaward faces by typical strands of Gulf coastal dunes, they offer some of Florida's most magnificent scenery.

Spits, or peninsulas, the other type of coastal landform, are similar to barrier islands in structure and function, but differ by being attached to the mainland. Stretching away from the coastline as relatively narrow ribbons of sand, they are more easily accessible than some of our islands and have become quite susceptible to the negative impact of overdevelopment and intense recreational use.

Compared with most landforms, Florida's islands and spits

have had a surprisingly short lifespan. Whereas much of geological history is measured in terms of epochs and eras, the history of our coastal barriers is measured only in centuries. Originating within the last 6,000 years, these landforms are the result of a combination of complex processes, some of which are still not well understood.

The short geologic history of most barrier beaches suggests that they are one of the world's most restless landforms. Their tendency to appear, disappear, or relocate—often changing dramatically even within the span of a single human lifetime—is legendary. Composed chiefly of shifting sands and subjected to the powerful forces of wind and water, they are anything but permanent. Those who have built cottages, and even entire cities, on barrier islands, only to watch the foundations wash away with time, can certainly testify to their transience.

Although much of Florida's coastal zone has succumbed to the destructive forces of residential and commercial development, it is still possible to find at least a few preserved examples of this once-extensive habitat. The panhandle coast, in particular, is bounded by an impressive assortment of coastal barriers, many of which benefit from public or private protection. Dog Island, St. George Island State Park, St. Vincent National Wildlife Refuge, St. Joseph Peninsula State Park, St. Andrews State Recreation Area, Henderson Beach State Recreation Area, Grayton Beach State Park, and Gulf Islands National Seashore all provide excellent opportunities for studying this fascinating terrain.

SAND PINE SCRUB

Sand pine scrub is a xeric, or exceedingly dry, sandy community with a rather sparse understory of shrubby, evergreen oaks and an overstory of its namesake, sand pine. During the late Pleistocene, when conditions were drier, scrub may have dominated much of the Florida peninsula. The largest expanses of Florida scrub are found in the central parts of the state. However, a narrow strip along the panhandle coast from about Franklin

Typical West Florida Coastal Scrub

County to the Alabama state line (see the description of Big Lagoon State Recreation Area, p. 111) also contains outstanding examples. In these latter areas the Florida rosemary, a sand-loving evergreen shrub, is sometimes a common constituent.

TEMPERATE HARDWOOD FORESTS

The temperate hardwood forest community finds the southern extent of its range along the wooded hillsides of Florida's uplands and is one of those systems that underscores the state's location at the overlap between climatic zones. Temperate forests are widely known to the north of the state and are considered the climax forest community for most of eastern North America. As might be expected, most of Florida's examples are chiefly confined to the northern parts of the state. Unlike in cooler climes, where temperate forests often stretch for thousands of uninterrupted acres, most examples of this community in Florida are found in localized pockets that are commonly referred to as hammocks.

Hardwood Hammock

The meaning of the term hammock is somewhat elusive; the word is generally applied to any area that is characterized by a diverse collection of both deciduous and evergreen hardwood trees. In south Florida parlance, *hammock* refers to the distinctive collections of tropical trees that dot the state's southern tip. In north Florida it denotes any one of several assemblages of primarily temperate hardwood species that typically occur in mixed stands and that may be found in a variety of soil situations.

As might be expected, not all north Florida hammocks are alike. Some are xeric in nature and are located on dry, sandy sites along the coastal strand or within ancient inland dune fields. Others occur in mesic uplands where the soil is rich and moist, such as the woodlands at Florida Caverns State Park (see p. 126), Falling Waters State Recreation Area (see p. 125), in and near Suwannee River State Park (see p. 174), and along the bluffs and ravines of the upper Apalachicola River (see p. 196). Still others are hydric and are confined to areas with poorly drained soils and high water tables. Examples of this latter type are evident along a number of Florida's spring runs as well as within our wooded coastal wetlands. The woodlands along the Wakulla and Wacissa rivers are prime examples of those found along spring runs.

Florida's temperate hardwood hammocks are best known for their diversity of broad-leaved trees and intriguing collection of herbaceous wildflowers. Southern magnolia, American beech, yellow poplar, spruce pine, American basswood, and several species of oaks, elms, and hickories make up the overstory in the more upland hammocks, while sweetbay, sweetgum, ironwood, sabal palm, diamond leaf oak, and loblolly pine are more representative of the lowlands. The ground cover is noted for such hard-to-find plant species as blood root, green dragon, jack-in-the-pulpit, and wild columbine.

FLATWOODS AND BAY SWAMPS

Northwestern Florida's pine flatwoods offer exhilarating opportunities to explore some of the state's most primitive and pristine lands. Wide expanses of this community are broken by twisted tangles of titi swamps and richly luxuriant forests. The sounds of one or more of Florida's numerous species of frogs and toads often echo through the stillness. Woodpeckers hammer out their mating drum rolls on the resonant boles of hollow trees, and Florida black bears hole up in the dense swamps, seldom making their presence known by more than tracks left in the mud or territorial scratch marks left on tree trunks. All of these combine to form a mysterious land visited only by a few adventurous souls who know the quietness and beauty of this extraordinary ecosystem.

Venturing into Florida's flatwoods–bay swamp ecosystem is an experience that no amateur naturalist should forego. Yet it is also a place one should not go unprepared. Trails are few and the thickets dense. Shallow pools of standing water often block the way. Wading is the standard mode of locomotion. But the wildlife is abundant and the plant communities intriguing. Opportunities for discovery are limitless.

Much of northwestern Florida is covered by pine flatwoods. Found on the mostly level, remnant sea bottom of the ancient Gulf, the most spectacular examples occur in the Apalachicola Coastal Lowlands of the central panhandle. These areas are characterized by a rather thick layer of fine sand overlying limestone. The sand retards the downward percolation of surface water, and the relatively flat terrain discourages development of major drainage systems. Because of these factors, the ground within the flatwoods is often wet and soggy.

The characteristic appearance and vegetation make the flatwoods an easy vegetational unit to recognize. The overstory typically consists of slash pine, long leaf pine, or a mixture of the two. Rarely, pond pine will also be dominant or included in the overstory. The shrubby understory is composed primarily of saw palmetto but often includes gallberry, fetterbush, staggerbush, and sweet pepperbush.

Although a panoramic view of a well-developed flatwoods gives the impression that it is all pines and palmetto, a closer inspection reveals numerous additional species. One of the most interesting and dominant plants in the ground cover is wiregrass. Wiregrass leaves are narrow, wiry, about 2 feet long, and grow in dense, spreading bunches. On undisturbed sites, the bushy clumps grow so close together that they nearly cover the ground.

Due to low elevation and a water table that is very near the surface, swamplands occur in close association with flatwoods habitat. Swamps typically comprise thickets that are too small or too scattered to show on generalized vegetation maps. These communities frequently contain standing water and occupy the shallow depressions of what was once a gently undulating sea bottom.

Titi swamps occur across the entire northern portion of the state and are normally dominated by either of two shrubby trees. In the panhandle, from about Jefferson County westward, the black titi is most often dominant. In the more eastern portions of the panhandle the dominant species is swamp cyrilla.

Often there is no overstory associated with titi regions. In some instances, however, scattered pond and/or slash pines are present. Common shrub associates in both communities include the large sweet gallberry, fetterbushes and staggerbushes, and a variety of thorny smilax vines.

Titi swamps often grade into a more diversely populated

swamp community. Commonly referred to as bay swamps, bay-heads, or bays, not because they contain open bodies of water but because of the typical tree species inhabiting them, they provide magnificent areas for exploration and discovery. Some of these bay swamps are comprised of a clearly dominant species. Others consist of mixed communities. In the panhandle the dominant species is often the sweetbay.

In the extreme western panhandle and in moist woods and swamps associated with the Apalachicola and New River drainage basins, bay swamps are sometimes characterized by Atlantic white cedar trees. These white cedar stands often appear as mature forests with stately trees that offer a beautiful contrast to the more common panhandle swamp community. Atlantic white cedar is best known as a tree of the eastern seaboard. However, several disjunctive populations inhabit the southern coastal plain. Widely separated white cedar stands ranging from Marion and Putnam Counties in the northern Florida peninsula to the Catahoula and Pearl Rivers in southern Mississippi constitute populations far south of this species' normal distribution.

RIVERS, STREAMS, AND LAKES

Florida's surface water systems offer some of the state's most attractive recreational enticements. From large alluvial rivers and clear spring-fed runs to deeply tannin-stained backwater sloughs or attractive cypress-ringed lakes, all are important components of our natural environment.

Four types of rivers are found in northern Florida. Each can be distinguished by the color of its water and the type of land it drains.

Alluvial streams are those that receive the majority of their water from the surface runoff that originates in the silty-clayey soils of the uplands. Such rivers typically appear turbid or muddy due to the high concentration of suspended particulates and organic detritus. The Apalachicola, which begins in the sloping hillsides of northern Georgia and is considered the state's muddiest river, as well as the Choctawhatchee and Escambia, are some of the panhandle's best examples.

Blackwater streams are found in sandy lowlands, mostly in the panhandle and near the northeastern Gulf Coast, where fine-grained soils retard the downward percolation of precipitation. Such sands are often saturated with water that is only slowly released from below-ground into the channels of nearby rivers. Blackwater rivers are usually free of suspended particles due to the filtering action of the sand, but are reddish black in color from the high content of organic tannins that have been leached from decaying vegetation. Most have either sandy or limestone bottoms. The Blackwater, Shoal, Yellow, Sopchoppy, Aucilla, and Econfina Rivers are good examples.

Spring runs are clear, flowing streams that originate at the headwaters of Florida's best-known natural feature. Typically cool in summer and warm in winter, spring runs display a relatively stable temperature range throughout the year and are especially attractive to an assortment of plants and wildlife. Important native plants include wild rice, arrowheads, spatterdock, and tape-grass; native wildlife species include the Suwannee' cooter, American alligator, brown and red-belly watersnakes, and a variety of fishes and insects. The panhandle's best-known spring-fed streams include the Wakulla, Wacissa, and Chipola rivers.

The fourth type of stream in northern Florida is usually small and seldom navigable. Seepage streams originate at the foot of slopes and steepheads (see below for discussion of steepheads, p. 41). They are typically clear in color, constant in temperature, and are usually tucked away between the walls of steep ravines under the protective canopy of rich, temperate woodlands. They are best known for their assorted population of amphibians, including numerous frogs, snakes, and salamanders, and two species of amphiuma, or congo eel. Most of these streams, at least some of which have no generally accepted names, are found in the panhandle, particularly in the bluffs and ravines area of the Apalachicola River.

In many ways Florida is as well known for its lakes as for its rivers. And even though the majority of its nearly 8,000 lakes are located outside the areas described in this book, there are still enough in northwest Florida to keep lake explorers busy.

Most of Florida's natural lakes result from the solution of sub-surface limestone. Solution lakes are usually circular in outline, conical in cross-section, and are situated in locations where the limestone is buried under a relatively thick overburden. Many contain dark, tannin-stained water and are variously ringed or studded with cypress trees. In most cases they are directly con-nected to the subsurface drainage system, including neigh-boring lakes, and have no visible outflow at the surface.

A limited amount of north Florida's surface water is held in oxbow lakes which form when large, meandering rivers change direction, cutting off and sealing the mouth of a former channel with natural fill. Oxbow lakes are generally accessible from the river that formed them but no longer carry the river's current.

Florida's lakes are complete ecosystems that support a variety of life through a complex set of biological processes. Green plants produce food through photosynthesis and provide an energy source for an assortment of zooplankton, insects, fishes, turtles, and birds. Organic waste is decomposed and recycled by bottom-dwelling bacteria. Some animals, such as frogs and ducks, use lakes temporarily for breeding or foraging; others make bodies of standing water the primary habitat in which they carry on all of life's processes. At every level, the denizens of our lakes interact in a dynamic, self-sustaining, but ever-changing system that insures the health of the lakes themselves as well as the health of our lakes' inhabitants.

RIVER SWAMPS AND FLOODPLAIN FORESTS

Florida's largest rivers create their own unique and fascinating wetlands. Although similar in appearance to the bay swamps and hydric hammocks discussed above, they differ in the source of their water. Bay swamps and hydric hammocks are recharged with surface water runoff from the surrounding land. River swamps and floodplain woodlands, on the other hand, are peri-odically inundated from the overflow of their associated alluvial

River Swamp

stream. As a result, the soil of the floodplain and bottomlands is silty, very rich in nutrients, and supports a large assemblage of trees and vines, and an impressive collection of wildlife species.

Water oak, overcup oak, diamond-leaf oak, water hickory, sugarberry, several species of ash, American sycamore, and river birch are among the more commonly seen trees. Common wildlife includes several species of salamanders and snakes as well as the wild turkey, southern flying squirrel, great horned owl, eastern screech owl, barred owl, pileated woodpecker, gray fox, bobcat, and white-tailed deer.

The best examples of floodplain and bottomland forests in Florida occur in the panhandle along the Choctawhatchee and Apalachicola Rivers, and to a lesser extent the Ochlockonee, Escambia, and Yellow Rivers.

SAVANNAS

Two major areas of wet savannas appear in northwestern Florida, one in the southwestern corner of the Apalachicola

National Forest (see p. 76), the other along SR 87 just west of the Blackwater River State Forest in Santa Rosa County. Both are classified as part of the wet prairie ecological community and are exceedingly interesting habitats that support a wide variety of amphibious and reptilian wildlife as well as a fascinating assortment of low-growing herbaceous plants.

Savannas and the pinelands that border them are very similar; the absence of trees in the savanna is the most conspicuous difference. Some botanists and researchers consider the two to be phases of the same community, while others see them as distinct. Their more widespread existence in prehistoric times was likely due in large measure to the cycle of fire and drought that served to keep woody plants from becoming established within their interior.

The treeless terrain and magnificent show of spring, summer, and early fall wildflowers make northwest Florida's savannas a plant lover's paradise. Bog buttons, hat pins, swamp coreopsis, tickseed, roserush, rush-featherling, beakrush, verbesina, and an impressive assortment of terrestrial orchids dot these boggy meadows. A variety of carnivorous plants including sundews, thread dews, and pitcher plants also thrive in the nutrient-poor soil, depending for sustenance on trapping a generous helping of the numerous insects that frequent the wetlands.

In addition to the fascinating plant populations, wet savannas are also well known as important habitats for frogs and snakes. The little grass frog, southern chorus frog, spring peeper, southern cricket frog, southern black racer, cottonmouth, and yellow rat snake all thrive in this wetland habitat. The limited number of northwest Florida's remaining savannas is a chilling reminder of how we humans have altered the native landscape in the few years since our arrival.

BLUFFS, RAVINES, AND STEEPHEADS

The eastern banks of the upper portions of the Apalachicola River offers one of Florida's most unique and interesting habitats. High bluffs with majestic overlooks and mountainlike vistas tower above luxuriantly forested slopes that fall away with a steepness unparalleled in Florida. Mature temperate woodlands of elms, beech, hickories, American basswood, and a variety of stately oaks overshadow densely shaded ravines that support an astonishing array of interesting and uncommon plants. Jack-in-the-pulpit, green dragon, stinking cedar, Florida yew, wild ginger, pyramid magnolia, and the strongly scented star anise are only a few examples. Over 100 plants that grow here occur no other place in the state; nearly a dozen occur no other place in the world.

The area referred to as the Apalachicola bluffs and ravines occurs on the eastern edge of the Tallahassee Hills geologic province (see p. 19), a region that is noted for its elevation and relief. It is an area bisected by a number of clear, trickling rivulets that originate at the base of one of the many steephead ravines.

Steepheads are interesting landforms often said to create their own microclimates by a combination of factors that tend to mitigate changes in ambient air temperature from one season to another. They are not widespread in northwest Florida and are not found east of the Ochlockonee River.

At first glance the uninitiated observer would probably assume a steephead to be a spring. The cool, clear, flowing water appears to arise directly from the ground, then trails off downgrade in a narrow run that is sometimes large enough to be called a rivulet. In actuality, springs and steepheads are quite different.

Steepheads typically form in regions that have significant relief, are near larger rivers, and have deeper soils containing large amounts of impermeable clays. Percolating surface water drains easily through the typically sandy overburden until reaching the compact lenses of fine clay that impede its downward progress. In effect, these lenses become underground aqueducts that redirect the natural flow along the top of the intervening clay, in a drainage pattern that is nearly perpendicular to the slope of the land. Eventually, the layer of clay intersects with the surface of the slope and the waters seep out of the ground into a steephead stream. As the volume of water increases, the steephead ravine is undermined from below, causing the top of the ravine to slump and the ravine to grow headward, or upslope toward the source of its water. The fact that the massive Apalachicola River probably got its start as a steephead stream is an obvious testimonial to the sheer power of these erosional forces (see Three Rivers State Recreation Area, p. 179).

Florida's bluffs and ravines constitute a singular resource that underscores Florida's unique geographic location. They form the epicenter of several overlapping biotic communities that support a diverse collection of floral and faunal species. Plants and animals that normally inhabit more northern climes flourish alongside those more typically thought of as Florida specialties. Species commonly associated with the Atlantic Coastal Plain overlap at the western edge of their distribution with those that are more often found in the Gulf Coastal Plain.

The areas in and around Torreya State Park (see p. 181) and The Nature Conservancy's Apalachicola Bluffs and Ravines Preserve (p. 196) offer two of the best places to explore this community.

SINKS AND SPRINGS

Sinkholes are natural features found across much of Florida. They are common in regions underlain by limestone and form in response to the movement of underground water. Sinks serve as the earth's drainage spouts, collecting surface runoff as they recharge the underground aquifer that holds most of the state's potable water.

In one type of sinkhole a solution cavity forms within the earth as water dissolves the underlying limestone. Eventually, the cavity becomes so large that the cover material is no longer supported. The cover collapses into the cavity, leaving the water visible from the surface. The walls of these cover-collapse sinkholes are sometimes lined with exposed limestone.

Another type of sinkhole results from cover subsidence rather than cover collapse. Although less dramatic in origin, such sinkholes also involve the solution of limestone. In solution sinkholes, however, it is the surface water rather than the groundwater that is the culprit. Most often, such sinkholes occur where the limestone is at or very near the surface. Rainwater percolating downward through the thin veneer of soil erodes and dissolves the surface of the limestone before it passes through the subsurface cracks that carry it deeper into the ground. As the limestone surface dissolves, the soil above gradually sinks, forming a depression that collects increasing amounts of runoff. The more runoff that is collected, the more the limestone is eroded, and the farther the area subsides. Sometimes the runoff brings impermeable clays and sands that effectively seal off the sinkhole from further interaction with the groundwater, forming a lake.

Most sinkholes in the Woodville Karst Plain (see p. 21) are of the cover-collapse type. Solution sinkholes are most common along the northeastern edge of the Apalachicola Coastal Lowlands (see p. 21), in southern Washington County, and in the Marianna Lowlands (see p. 20) of Jackson County.

One fascinating area, combining both a karst plain river and a series of cover-collapse sinkholes, occurs along the middle portions of the Aucilla River. Just north of the road to Goose Pasture campground, a Proctor and Gamble Cellulose Corporation recreation area, the Aucilla River disappears into a swallow hole. After passing a short distance underground, it reappears as a series of sinkholes with magnificent limestone exposures. Some of the sinkholes are quite small. Others, which are sometimes referred to as karst windows because they expose long portions of previously covered cave segments, are up to a mile long. Almost all have water flowing through them. A well-marked section of the Florida Trail follows these sinks (as well as portions of the river) which makes viewing them a relatively easy and enjoyable task (see p. 193 for more information about this region).

If sinkholes are the earth's drainspouts, then springs are its faucets. While sinks recharge the underground water supply, springs act as flowing wells, responding to the tremendous artesian pressure of underground water storage systems and discharging excess liquid to the surface. In total, Florida's springs produce about eight billion gallons of water a day, a staggering figure that rivals the daily amount of water that is artificially pumped for human use.

North Florida is one of the best locations in the United States for spring lovers. Over half of the 300 or so of Florida's springs occur in the region covered by this book, including 10 of the 27 that are classified as first magnitude. Such panhandle locations as the Wacissa and Wakulla Springs, the latter of which is now protected as Wakulla Springs State Park (see p. 187), are legendary landmarks.

SUBTERRANEAN ENVIRONMENTS

Its seems unusual to associate Florida with subterranean cave systems. Indeed, our relatively low elevation and near-to-the-surface water table prevent such natural features in most parts of the state. In the northern panhandle, however, particularly in those portions of Jackson County that are within the Marianna Lowlands geologic province (see p. 20), a small system of limestone-lined caverns provides a unique opportunity to inspect Florida's underground environment.

Florida's cave systems (the best examples of which are preserved at Florida Caverns State Park, see p. 126) are remnant chambers that were once part of the near-surface aquifer. As the ice age sea receded to its current level, what were formerly the passageways for underground rivers lay perched above the water table as air-filled pockets in the limestone. Since that time, surface erosion and leakage from above have continued to shape and reshape these corridors in a never-ending process of evolution and alteration.

Caverns are important wildlife habitats for seldom-seen creatures. The endangered gray bat makes its home in several caves near Marianna, as does the more common eastern pipistrelle and southeastern bat. The exceedingly rare Georgia blind salamander and the difficult-to-find cave crayfish also live in some of the caverns' more remote sections. These latter creatures are pale white in color and have become so thoroughly adapted to their lightless surroundings that they have completely lost the ability to see.

Most of us are not likely to see many of these critters unless accompanied by an expert who knows their habits, identity, and location. Their fragile habitats are most abundant only in the less accessible and more undisturbed of Florida's caves, and are well protected from human intrusion.

IV
EXPLORING
NORTHWEST
FLORIDA'S WILDLIFE

For the amateur naturalist whose passion is wildlife, the Florida panhandle offers a varied assortment of faunal inhabitants that represent almost every level on the evolutionary scale. Stationing oneself in the predawn stillness of a woodland thicket, sitting quietly along the edges of a gurgling stream, or walking gently along a primitive trail can yield an abundance of observation opportunities.

REPTILES AND AMPHIBIANS

For the amateur herpetologist few places can match the abundance and diversity of northern Florida. Nearly all of its habitats offer a variety of reptiles and amphibians to discover and identify.

Snakes

Over 50 different species of snakes live in that portion of Florida that lies west of the Suwannee River. With the exception of the six poisonous species highlighted in Chapter 1, all are essentially harmless, though some will bite. All are also important components of our native communities.

The most commonly seen of our native snakes include the

black racer, red rat or corn snake, gray rat or oak snake, yellow rat or chicken snake, eastern hognose snake, and the banded and brown watersnakes.

Few things are more delightful than a glimpse of the season's first black racer. They are found in many habitats but are most often seen in open areas, along roadways and highways, and in generally brushy sites near water. They begin moving in early spring and are often seen darting across roads and rural highways.

The rat snakes, too, are found in a wide variety of habitats but are particularly partial to old buildings and trash piles. The red and yellow rat snakes are brightly colored and very attractive. The gray rat is less colorful, but is quite docile and easily handled.

As their names suggest, the watersnakes are generally restricted to rivers, swamps, lakes, ponds, and sinkholes and are often seen stretched out on fallen logs. They are typically drab in color, have a temperamental demeanor, and will bite if accosted. They are usually misidentified as cottonmouths, though they are easily differentiated by lacking the distinctive dark swab that is obvious along either side of the cottonmouth's head.

The eastern hognose is the most docile of Florida's snakes. When disturbed or threatened it will often put on quite a show by flattening its neck and head to resemble a cobra and by making a variety of swaying and menacing gyrations. However, if touched it usually turns on its back and feigns death. If turned right side up, it will immediately turn upside down again.

Alligators

Florida's most distinctive reptile is, undoubtedly, the American alligator. Found in a variety of wetlands throughout the state, this prehistoric creature is considered by some to be the most magnificent example of Florida's native fauna, and is certainly an animal that few of us tire of seeing.

There is little question that the lowly alligator is Florida's most primitive link with the ancient earth. Alligators, along with a variety of other, now extinct, crocodilians, ancient birds, and

American Alligator

thunderous dinosaurs, date from the Mesozoic Era, or about 230 million years ago. They are at least a hundred times more ancient than we humans, and constitute one of our closest connections to prehistoric life.

Much of the alligator's evolutionary success can be attributed to its position at the top of the food chain. Its large body, intimidating jaws, and powerful tail make it the Sunshine State's most respected predator, and it is virtually without natural enemies in adulthood. The only decline in the alligator's population came earlier this century when it became the target of humans, the only predators that have ever caused it harm. Before being placed on the nation's list of threatened wildlife, its population declined significantly. However, with its new regulated status, its numbers have recovered rapidly, offering further evidence of its natural staying power.

Although fearsome at maturity, the gator is not without enemies during other phases of its life cycle. Young gators, in particular, are not so insulated from danger as are adults. While still enclosed in their hard, leathery eggs, they provide choice morsels for raccoons, bears, opossums, and skunks, and as hatchlings they have little defense against predation. Less than 10 inches long when born, young gators are extremely vulnerable to small animals as well as large wading birds such as the great blue heron. The latter is known to relish young alligators and is especially adept at forcing them head first down its long, sinuous neck.

Alligator nests are composed of large, conspicuous mounds of decaying vegetation. They are typically constructed in late June or early July and can be up to about 3 feet high and several feet wide. The female lays up to 50 eggs in the center of the mound and depends on the heat generated by natural oxidation to incubate the growing embryos. The 3-inch-long eggs hatch in about 70 days, and the hatchlings are carried from their darkened birth chamber in their mother's mouth. The young remain together for at least a year and spend much of the winter in a den with their other siblings.

Young gators are quite good at sounding an alarm when danger approaches. On a recent trip in the Apalachicola National Forest I examined a number of gator holes for signs of new hatches. At one location I found a number of young, yellow-striped hatchlings sprawled along the edge of a small, muddy puddle. As I walked past the lethargic colony I began to hear a high-pitched croak reminiscent of a muffled bark. Almost immediately, the head of an adult alligator surfaced in the middle of the tiny basin as if to warn me that I had ventured too close for the mother's comfort.

Much has been made about the size of an average alligator. It is common to hear uninitiated observers report gators that exceed 12 feet in length. In reality, such sizes are not common. While the longest American alligator on record measured more than 19 feet, alligators longer than about 10 feet are not easy to find today and are not often seen by the normal outdoorsperson. The length of the average female does not exceed 9 feet; the length of the average male is usually less than 11 feet. There must be something about an alligator's form or general demeanor that makes it loom much larger in the imagination than in reality.

Frogs and Toads

Learning to identify our native frogs and toads is often more easily done by sound than by sight. More than 30 species are represented in northwestern Florida, all of which have distinctive and easily identifiable voices. Hardly a month of the year passes

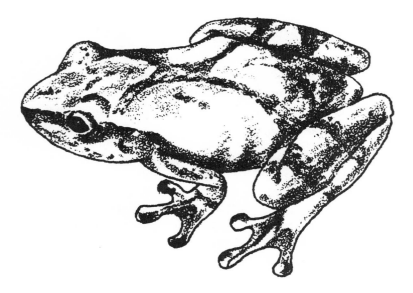

Spring Peeper

without hearing the distinctive call of at least one of these secretive critters. From the barking treefrog's houndlike chatter or the bullfrog's deep resonant drone, to the chuckling and clattering of the southern leopard frog or the high-pitched squeak of the familiar spring peeper, few things make north Florida evenings more delightful or more distinctive than the sounds of our frogs and toads. A complete accounting of those species native to the northern part of the state is included with the wildlife checklists found in Chapter 8.

BIRDS

Birdwatching has become a popular recreational pursuit for a wide range of nature enthusiasts. Increasing numbers of us spend at least some of our weekends visiting wildlife refuges, state parks, and other birdwatching hotspots, discovering the enjoyment that invariably comes with learning to identify our native birds.

Well over 300 species of birds visit northern Florida on a regular basis. Some of these are residents and may be observed at almost any time of year. Others are with us for only one season. Those that stay with us during the summer constitute our local breeding populations and normally spend their winters farther south. Conversely, those that overwinter usually have breeding grounds farther to the north.

A large number of birds pass through the panhandle only during their migration to or from their wintering grounds. Of these, some appear during both the spring and fall; others appear during only one of these seasons. While space does not allow a complete coverage of all of these species, a brief overview of some of the more common orders of birds will prove helpful, particularly if you are a beginning birdwatcher.

Herons, Egrets, and Ibises

The herons and egrets are probably the best known of Florida's marsh-loving birds. Heralded for their beauty and grace, they are most commonly associated with shallow waters at the edges of the wetlands. With heads outstretched and bodies erect, they are often seen standing motionless, gazing into the water in search of an unsuspecting frog or fish.

There are 12 members of the heron family in the continental United States. All of them can be seen at various times of the year within the confines of Florida.

Perhaps the most familiar of these splendid birds is the great blue heron. The great blue is a large bird with a slate blue body, a white face, and a conspicuous black stripe above its eye. A 7-foot wingspan easily makes it the largest of our native herons. When startled, the great blue ordinarily takes flight, uttering a harsh croaking call as if to emphasize its displeasure at being disturbed.

Another of our conspicuous large waders is the great egret. Only slightly smaller than the great blue, it is all white with a striking yellow bill and black legs. It is normally found wading slowly in shallow waters along the edges of marshes and ponds and can sometimes be seen stirring the water with its feet in an attempt to startle its prey into movement.

Great Blue Heron

More than one highway motorist has been amused at the sight of a cattle egret standing atop the back of a dairy cow in a roadside pasture. One of Florida's most prolific small herons, the cattle egret was a rare sight in the state until the early 1950s. Since then, it has rapidly expanded its range and is now a common resident in all parts of Florida. Its preference for dry, open, grassy feeding areas distinguishes it from our other heron species and probably helps account for its rapid expansion.

The little snowy egret is one of the most beautiful of our wading birds. Taken together, its dazzling white feathers and straight black bill distinguish it from all other members of its family. When in summer dress, it displays graceful plumes that curve upward from its head, neck, and back and form a strikingly beautiful array. The snowy's most unique feature, however, is the color of its feet. Referred to as the egret with the golden slippers, its bright yellow feet contrast sharply with its jet black legs.

The night-herons and bitterns are the most secretive members of the heron family. As their name implies, night herons feed primarily during the evening and early morning hours, preferring to spend the daylight hours roosting quietly in the branches of trees. Bitterns, on the other hand, feed by day but typically stay hidden deep in the marsh. They seem to favor the protection of dense stands of cattail and only rarely venture into open view.

North Florida also plays host to two members of the ibis family. Unlike the herons, ibises have long, down-curved bills and fly with their necks outstretched. They are most often seen crouching in the marshes, actively foraging for fish, crabs, crayfish, snails, and an assortment of aquatic insects.

The most commonly seen member of the ibis family is the white ibis. In adult plumage it is all white with black wingtips and bright pink legs and bill. It is equally at home in both fresh and brackish water and is often seen flying in "V" formations, reminiscent of the Canada goose.

The glossy ibis is one of north Florida's least-abundant long-legged waders. Although fairly common in the southern part of the state, it has only recently begun expanding its range northward. Although the glossy ibis was only rarely sighted in our area just a few years ago, the St. Marks National Wildlife Refuge now boasts a small resident flock of these birds. When observed closely, the breeding plumage of the glossy ibis is exquisitely beautiful. Its deep chestnut color is highlighted with tinges of glossy green and purple. At a distance or in poor light, however, the bird appears almost all black.

Ducks and Geese

Nothing conjures up a more pleasing vision of the coming winter than the sight of waterfowl winging southward on their fall migration. Long lines of high-flying ducks silhouetted against a wintry sky often recall pleasing fragments of our fondest childhood memories. The beginning of a new school year; the first cold front; crisp, cool mornings; and the colorful change of seasons are all associated with the spectacular migration of our ducks and geese.

Over 20 different types of ducks and two species of geese frequent the panhandle in winter. As early as September, migrants begin arriving from their northern breeding grounds. The blue-winged teal, northern pintail, American widgeon, and northern shoveler are among the first to appear. These are followed in rapid succession by the canvasback, gadwall, redhead, green-winged teal, American black duck, common goldeneye, buffle-head, snow goose, and three species of mergansers. By the onset of December, nearly all have reached their winter homes.

Learning to identify these cold-weather visitors is not as difficult as learning the identities of our smaller songbirds. Whereas songbirds normally stay hidden in the brush, or dart secretively among the branches of trees, the ducks and geese stay easily visible in wide, open spaces. Many spend their days diving and dabbling among shallow, freshwater ponds, or in near-shore coastal waters. This relatively sedentary feeding behavior allows extended observation of their habits and plumage.

Male ducks are easiest to recognize. Their bright colors and characteristic patterns make them conspicuous denizens of the marshlands. Each seems to have its own special feature. The green head of the mallard, the white forehead of the American widgeon, the spoon-shaped bill of the northern shoveler, the large white crescent on the face of the blue-winged teal—all are distinctive field marks.

Identifying female ducks, however, is more of a challenge. Usually attired in much drabber colors than the males, the females of different species often appear quite similar. Body shape, bill length, overall size, and the color of the wing patch are often the only characteristics available for distinguishing one female from another.

One of the most exciting duckwatching activities is following the gradual preparation for the spring migration and breeding season. Throughout the winter, the plumage of the males becomes more colorful with each passing week. By late January the birds enter a stage of migratory restlessness and courtship activity that foreshadows the coming of spring. Small groups of males band together in cavorting flight and aerial acrobatics in hopes of attracting a mate. Other males engage in ritualized postures, movements, and vocalizations that advertise their availability to interested hens. In some species, potential mates form bonds even before they migrate. These pairs can frequently be seen swimming together for several weeks prior to leaving on their northward flight.

Shorebirds, Gulls, and Terns

Birdwatchers distinguish three general types of coastal birds. Although representatives of each group are seen on north Florida shores, the collective name shorebirds is usually applied only to representatives of the plovers, oystercatchers, stilts, avocets, and sandpipers. More than 30 species of these birds visit north Florida's coastal areas. While a few stay hidden in the brush and are difficult to find or see, a larger number are quite visible among our dunes or along our beaches.

The sandpipers are by far the largest group of shorebirds found in north Florida. Ranging in stature from the sparrow-sized least sandpiper to the much larger willet, they are frequently seen on muddy or sandy beaches jabbing their bills into the soggy soil in search of insects.

Plovers are also birds of the open beach. More compact in appearance than sandpipers, they typically have short necks, short bills, round heads, and large eyes. They appear eternally hurried and race across the sand from point to point, stopping only briefly to search for food.

Two of our plovers are included on Florida's list of rare and endangered species. The snowy plover is probably the most imperiled. This small, pale-colored bird lives and breeds on dry open beaches where it builds no nest, preferring to lay its clutch of three eggs directly on the open sand. The increased use of its breeding habitat by humans and the desecration of its nest sites by domestic dogs and cats are among the chief causes of this tiny bird's decline. The piping plover is Florida's other threatened plover. It, too, is a small, pale plover that is usually found on sandy beaches. Its outline is more dumpy than that of the snowy plover.

The American oystercatcher is one of Florida's largest and most distinctive shorebirds. Also listed as a threatened species, it is the only member of its family in the state and is one of our easier shorebirds to identify. An adult oystercatcher is about the size of a small crow. It has a jet black head, a dark brown back, and a large, bright orange bill which it uses to pry open oyster shells and other mollusks.

To the uninitiated beachgoer, all large white birds often fall into the catchall category "sea gull." Such classification, however, is not technically correct. There are actually several species of gulls as well as a number of the usually smaller and more streamlined terns.

Gulls are typically wide-winged birds with stout, often hooked, bills and squared or rounded tails. Several species of gulls frequent north Florida. Our three most common include the ring-billed, herring, and laughing gulls. While laughing gulls normally prefer to remain within just a few miles of the coastline, herring and ring-billed gulls regularly venture farther inland and are often observed during winter frequenting shopping center parking lots, large neighborhood lakes, and sanitary landfills.

Terns differ from gulls in having pointed wings and bills and sharply forked tails. They are typically seen diving headfirst into the water after prey. As many as ten species of terns visit north Florida at various times of the year. Four species—the Caspian tern, royal tern, sandwich tern, and black skimmer—are listed as species of special concern by the Florida Committee on Rare and Endangered Plants and Animals. The smaller and more dainty least tern is considered threatened.

Raptors

The hawks, eagles, owls, falcons, osprey, and kites are the predators of the air. Their keen eyesight, sharp talons, and pinpoint

attacks make them some of the bird world's most feared aggres-
sors. Entire rafts of ducks take flight when a bald eagle or red-
tailed hawk circles, and songbirds dart for cover at the approach
of a Cooper's or sharp-shinned hawk. Their form alone seems to
incite a kind of frantic terror in their prey.

Red-tailed and red-shouldered hawks are probably the most
common of north Florida's resident birds of prey. Though they
differ in several respects and are relatively easy to distinguish,
many beginning birders have difficulty telling them apart. The
red-tailed hawk is the larger of the two and often soars high in
the sky. The combination of dark belly band, white chest, and
rufous-red tail easily sets it apart. Both of these species are often
seen perched atop dead snags or in the trees along highways and
interstates. This vantage gives them a good view of road shoulders, and their sharp eyes can easily pick out snakes and rodents
that might otherwise be hidden in the roadside grass.

North Florida's falcons include the peregrine, merlin, and
American kestrel. The peregrine and merlin are by far the least
common of the three. They visit in winter from about September
to May and are most often seen along the coast, particularly
during migration. Both species are regularly spotted at the St.
Marks National Wildlife Refuge as well as on St. George Island.

The peregrine was once common to nearly all of the world's
continents and was widely used for falconry. With the introduc-
tion of the pesticide DDT in the early 1950s, its population
plunged dramatically. Reintroduction efforts, pesticide regula-
tion, and close attention have stemmed the loss and its population is now increasing; it is likely that the species will be pro-
posed for delisting in the near future. Until then, the bird is still
listed as an endangered species and is uncommon enough to
make seeing it a birder's delight.

The bald eagle is another of our more special raptors. Once a
common nesting species throughout Florida, it, too, suffered
dramatic losses as a result of DDT, especially to the north of
Florida, and even disappeared from many locations in the
southern United States. Florida's population is slowly recov-
ering and the bird is much more commonly seen today than it
was 30 years ago. The St. Marks National Wildlife Refuge is a

good location for spotting the bird in the northwestern part of the state.

Many beginning observers confuse the bald eagle with the osprey, another coastal raptor. Both show white on their heads, but only the mature eagle has an all-white head; the osprey's head always shows a brownish stripe through the eye. The osprey also shows an all-white underside, which is never true of the bald eagle. Even very young eagles show only splotches of white on their bellies before taking on their dark adult plumage.

The osprey has historically been called the fish hawk by locals because of its efficiency as an airborne angler. It is not unusual to see a foraging osprey hovering excitedly over the shallow waters of a saltwater bay, then diving feet first into a school of fish. More times than not the bird is rewarded handsomely; it is common to see an osprey perched atop a dead snag or power pole devouring a large mullet or some other saltwater species.

MAMMALS

North Florida's terrestrial and freshwater mammals are not as great in number as its reptiles, amphibians, and birds. Only 50 to 60 species of native or established exotics are known to be present in the region. While some of these, such as the raccoon and white-tailed deer, are common and often seen, others, such as the several species of rodents, are well hidden and seldom encountered. At least a few deserve special mention.

River Otter

The river otter is one of the state's most delightful creatures. Its torpedo-shaped body and webbed toes are perfectly adapted to an aquatic lifestyle, and its dark brown to black, closely cropped fur gives it an exceptionally sleek appearance. Otters are found in an assortment of aquatic habitats from lakes, ponds, and artificial impoundments to alluvial and blackwater streams. They are most like the mink in general appearance; the two animals are quite closely related.

River otters are inquisitive and intelligent animals that seem genuinely interested in humans. They have been known to follow canoeists or swim along lake edges adjacent to hikers, intermittently poking their heads above the surface as if to stay abreast of the whereabouts of their intruders. Although they spend much of their time in the water, they also come ashore regularly and are often quite playful. Groups of otters will sometimes wet down a muddy bank, then use it as a sliding board, letting their body weight plunge them repeatedly into the water. Chancing unnoticed upon a group of otters at play is a rare but engaging adventure.

Florida Black Bear

The Florida black bear is one of Florida's largest land mammals, but is seldom seen. In historical times it was probably quite common in the denser woodlands throughout Florida and southern Georgia. Today, however, its population is much smaller. Its large black form is unmistakable and needs no description.

Florida bears are not pugnacious animals. Although most are powerful enough to inflict considerable damage, they are extremely shy, and there are no recorded reports of bear attacks on humans in the state.

The Florida black bear is a passive and highly secretive omnivore that avoids human contact whenever possible. Although classified a carnivore and known to occasionally feed on feral hogs, it is also fond of a variety of berries, young insects, and honey, including the fruit of the saw palmetto and the tender growing bud of the sabal, or cabbage, palm. It is essentially nocturnal and is most likely to be seen in the early evening or in the hour just before sunrise.

There are between 1,000 and 1,500 bears in Florida, and the northern part of the state harbors some of the species' largest and most successful populations. The swamps, bays, and dense woods of the Apalachicola National Forest and Eglin Air Force Base are two of its better-known haunts in the northwestern part of the state. There is also evidence that the Apalachicola popula-

Florida Black Bear

tion is expanding in number, a phenomenon that will likely continue given the Florida Game and Fresh Water Fish Commission's 1993 decision to prohibit hunting of the species.

Florida Panther, Bobcat, and Jaguarundi

Only three members of the Felidae, or cat family, inhabit
Florida's wildlands: the Florida panther, the bobcat, and the
jaguarundi. The Florida panther is the state's rarest mammal. Although often reported in northern Florida by amateur observers,
most wildlife-management professionals suspect that these reports are either misidentifications or sightings of captive-re-
leased animals. It is generally agreed that the northern part of the
state currently supports no naturally occurring panther populations. In recent years the Florida Game and Fresh Water Fish
Commission has conducted reintroduction experiments as part
of a comprehensive program to restore the animal as part of the
region's wildlife.

Unlike the panther, the diminutive bobcat is common in a
variety of north Florida habitats. Adults are two to three times
larger than a large house cat and are easily distinguished from

the latter by their short, stubby tail, triangular ears, and black spots on a reddish or gray background. Although common, they are not as easily seen as their abundance might suggest. Bobcats often move under cover of darkness, making them difficult to observe. Even when they hunt in the daytime, which they also commonly do, they are secretive and avoid crossing paths with humans. They are quite territorial and tend to inhabit the same general location for long periods of time if a stable food source is present. Finding a bobcat's foraging area usually insures greater success of regular sightings.

The jaguarundi is a medium-sized cat that is similar in general appearance to the bobcat except for its very long, bushy tail. Jaguarundis are known to be native to South America, Mexico, and southeastern Arizona. It is not known whether those seen in Florida result from natural range expansion or were introduced. In either case, they are not common and not often seen.

Bats

Florida is home to 16 species of bats, all but one of which occur in the panhandle; at least four occur only here. The southeastern bat; eastern pipistrelle; and yellow, red, hoary, and Seminole bats are among the most common.

Florida's bats are the butterflies of the night. They typically appear at dusk, seemingly from nowhere, and dart through the air, often too erratically for human eyes to follow. Their jerky, staccato flight is unmistakable and results from their method of gathering food. As they approach a flying insect, they cup their wings below them and literally scoop the unsuspecting prey into their open mouths. The entire process takes only a second or two, but is long enough to cause a noticeable pause in their flight pattern.

Bats are generally believed to live only in caves. Although this is essentially true for a handful of Florida's rarer bats, most spend their days hanging upside down from the ceiling of an old building or from the limb of a tree or shrub.

Finding a sleeping bat during the day is not impossible but not easy. They usually close themselves up tightly and often do not resemble an animal of any type. As a result, they often go unnoticed. They are also not easily aroused from their slumber when found, and ordinarily do not respond to anything less than the most severe intrusion.

West Indian Manatee

Along with the Florida panther, the West Indian manatee is one of the Sunshine State's best known and most loved animals. Its large, lethargic form is unlike that of any other of our marine mammals, and its exceedingly gentle nature sets it apart from nearly all of Florida's wild creatures.

Manatees are most often seen in winter when they congregate in warm coastal waters, around the headwaters of the larger springs, or near the mouths of the larger rivers. They are sensitive to cold and tend to seek warmer waters when seawater temperatures begin to drop. Although most of their range falls outside of panhandle waters, they are sometimes seen in the crystal clear waters of the Wakulla River, just up from its confluence with the St. Marks.

Manatees are strictly herbivorous and have no natural enemies. They are sometimes referred to as sea cows because they

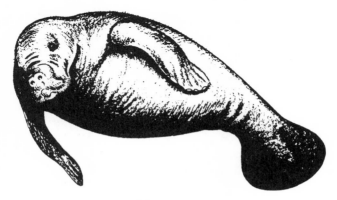

Manatee

61

graze on underwater vegetation and are absolutely harmless and defenseless. There are about 2,000 manatees in the state today, but their future is uncertain. Many show the telltale scars of collisions with motorboats; it is estimated that between 35 and 50 of the nearly 150 that are likely to die annually will do so as a result of accidents with motorboats. Although the state has taken a series of steps to protect the animal by enforcing speed zones in its most often used haunts, accidents still happen too frequently and there is grave concern about the creature's ability to survive in the long term.

BUTTERFLIES

Watching and identifying butterflies is fast becoming a popular interest for many of north Florida's amateur naturalists. A variety of these delicate winged creatures migrate through various parts of Florida each fall and spring and provide the basis for an intriguing pastime. Although particularly evident along the coastal strand, an equal number of butterflies also frequent more inland locations.

North Florida's most commonly seen species include the black, eastern tiger, spicebush, and zebra swallowtails, as well as the monarch, queen, viceroy, gulf fritillary, painted lady, long-winged zebra, and orange and cloudless sulphers. Most are attracted to one of several plants including lantana and saltbush, as well as several species of milkweed and beggar-ticks.

V
NATURAL AREAS:
FEDERAL LANDS

APALACHICOLA NATIONAL FOREST

The Apalachicola National Forest is one of north Florida's most impressive natural areas. Established in 1936, it currently contains nearly 600,000 acres that include a wide diversity of habitats and plant communities as well as more than 300 wildlife species.

Location, Mailing Address, and Phone

There are many entrances to the Apalachicola National Forest (ANF). Most are off one of seven highways: SR 20, SR 65, SR 67, SR 267, SR 375, and SR 379, and US 319. The forest is also crisscrossed by a variety of improved sand and clay roads. The official map of the Apalachicola National Forest shows all the main roadways and is a necessity for exploring the region.

Two ranger districts manage the forest. The address of the Wakulla Ranger District, which manages the part east of the Ochlockonee River, is: US 319, Route 6, Box 7860, Crawfordville, FL 32327. The headquarters for the Apalachicola Ranger district is located along SR 20 in the little town of Bristol. The mailing address is P.O. Box 579, Bristol, FL 32321. This office manages the area that lies west of the Ochlockonee River. Maps and information are available from both offices as well as from the Forest Supervisor, Woodcrest Office Park, 325 John Knox Rd., Building F, Tallahassee, FL 32303.

Facilities and Activities

Camping, hiking, backpacking, horseback riding, bicycling, birding, canoeing, botanizing, freshwater fishing, wildlife observation.

Camping

The ANF supports 15 campgrounds. Only two regularly require a user fee; the other ten are free. Camping is limited to 14 days per campground. Many campgrounds have volunteer hosts that can often provide useful information about the immediate area. It should be noted that all areas of the national forest are open for camping, except during the hunting season. Visitors who do not require facilities or prefer primitive conditions may choose from any available location.

Silver Lake

Silver Lake is the most developed of the ANF campgrounds and requires a fee for day use or camping. It is accessed by turning south off SR 20 onto SR 260, then east onto Forest Road 371. The entire access route is along paved roads. There are 45 campsites located in an attractive, sandy woodland. Restrooms and showers are scattered throughout the campground and there is a dump station. Several camping and picnic sites are accessible to the disabled. Silver Lake also offers a developed freshwater swimming area, a large picnic area with a covered pavilion, and a nice nature trail. The trail passes across a boardwalk along the edges of the lake, then through a variety of wetlands and sandy uplands.

Wright Lake

The Wright Lake campground is the other developed site that requires a user fee, but only for camping. It is located on Wright Lake in the extreme western part of the ANF near the Apalachicola River. It is reached by turning west off SR 65 on Forest Road 101, then northwest on 101-C. The area has a limited number of campsites, all of which are located in an open area under tall pines. There is a restroom and showers. Wright Lake provides an excellent base camp for exploring the western side of the ANF.

Hickory Landing

Hickory Landing is located on Owl Creek, just off the Apalachicola River. The landing is well developed and provides a launching point for canoes as well as motorboats. The landing is well used by both fishing enthusiasts and sightseers and is an interesting place to visit. Like Wright Lake, Hickory Landing is accessed by Forest Road 101, but is south of the road at the terminus of Forest Road 101-B. It contains a small number of separated campsites, pit-type restrooms, but no showers.

Porter Lake and Whitehead Lake

These two relatively primitive campgrounds are located close together on the Ochlockonee River. Porter Lake is located adjacent to Forest Highway (FH) 13 at the point where it crosses the river. Whitehead Lake is located at the terminus of Forest Road 186, a sand and clay road that turns off FH 13 just west of the Ochlockonee River bridge. Both are located on oxbow lakes that represent the river's former course. Together they offer only a handful of campsites.

Cotton Landing

This is another of the landings that offer access to the Apalachicola River. It has pit-type restrooms and only a few campsites, but is directly adjacent to Kennedy Creek. It has a developed landing that allows for launching both canoes and motorboats.

Camel Lake

The Camel Lake campground is quite nice and does not require a fee. It is located on a small lake that offers fishing, limited canoeing, a designated swimming area, and a small number of campsites. A few of the campsites are wooded and close to the lake; the others are more open. All have grills, a concrete table, and are suitable for tent camping. The Florida National Scenic Trail runs adjacent to the area. There is one restroom facility

Camel Lake Campground

with flush toilets but no showers (except the outdoor shower near the swimming area). Camel Lake is located in the extreme northwestern corner of the ANF. It is reached most easily by turning east onto Forest Road 105 off SR 12. The entrance to the campground is on the south side of 105, 2.1 miles from the highway.

Florida National Scenic Trail

Approximately 60 miles of the Florida National Scenic Trail cross the Apalachicola National Forest. Beginning at US 319 on the east and exiting the forest along Florida 12 at the ANF's north-west corner, this outstanding footpath traverses virtually all of the Apalachicola coastal lowland's native habitats. Turkey oak ridges, lush pine flatwoods, densely vegetated bays and swamps, longleaf pinelands, cypress ringed lakes, and mature floodplain forests are all touched by the trail's corridor.

Several sections of the trail make good day hikes. The stretch that runs along the Sopchoppy River from Forest Roads 329 to

343 is a particularly scenic route that offers an alternative to paddling for experiencing this little blackwater stream. The Bradwell Bay Wilderness Area section, which is described below, is the most rugged part of the path and is often covered with several inches of water. The section near Camel Lake passes adjacent to a number of attractive sandy lakes, and the sections along the eastern side of the Ochlockonee River near the FH 13 bridge allow close inspection of the river's bluffs and floodplain.

Woods Roads and Driving Trails

The ANF is criss-crossed by a network of sandy and improved clay roads that provide easy access to almost all of the more scenic areas. In addition, these bumpy thoroughfares also serve as important driving trails that are often bordered by densely vegetated wetlands and woodlands that are ripe for exploration. Visitors can leave their vehicles at almost any point along any of these roads, wander into the adjacent woodlands, and find unparalleled opportunities for nature study.

The roads are also good for those who prefer a driving or horseback riding tour to a hiking trip. Herbaceous wildflowers, blossoming trees, and an array of shrubs line the roadsides, and native wildlife is often evident. Driving the roads at sunup or sunset may result in opportunities for seeing white-tailed deer, raccoons, bobcats, a variety of songbirds, woodpeckers, hawks, and sometimes even Florida black bear.

All of the forest's main roadways are numbered, which makes them easy to follow. The official Apalachicola National Forest map, which can be obtained for $3 from any of the above addresses, is the most up-to-date source of information about these roads.

Best Time of Year

There is something of interest year-round. The summer months are usually hot and sometimes buggy. However, a number of plants are in bloom then, and it is a perfect time for canoeing.

Pets
Allowed in all parts of the forest.

WAKULLA RANGER DISTRICT
Facilities and Activities
Camping, backpacking, hiking, horseback riding, birding, fishing, botanizing, canoeing, nature study.

Leon Sinks Geological Area

Drive south on US 319 from Tallahassee for 7 miles, then turn west at the marked entrance. The U.S. Forest Service has future plans to install a permanent ranger station in the area to assist visitors and to insure the area's continuing preservation.

This area preserves one of the Woodville Karst Plain's most unique regions. Restricted to foot traffic only and laid out in nearly 6 miles of a circular trail that passes adjacent to 12 major sinkholes, the region has become an extremely popular recreation and visitation site.

The main attraction, geologically, is the massive Big Dismal Sink. It is a huge circular depression that is characterized by precipitous limestone walls that extend for at least 65 feet into the earth before reaching water level, and perhaps an equal distance below the water's surface. About 35 feet of limestone and 25 feet of loose sand are exposed along its steep-sided banks, and the outflows of several tiny springs trickle down its pockmarked walls, all of which can be easily viewed from the enormous cavity's upper rim. An overlook has been constructed on the sink's southern edge to make viewing easier. Big Dismal has consumed over three million cubic feet of rock and soil during its lifetime, making it comparable in size to the well-publicized Winter Park sink that first opened in 1981.

Hammock Sink also makes a good stopping point. An observation platform and wooden boardwalk extend along one side, which allows visitors an opportunity for close inspection. The water in the sink is often clear enough to see bottom, and the edges are clothed with native vegetation which provides cover for a variety of birds.

The Fisher Creek Rise area is another highlight of the Leon Sinks trail system. The trail crosses a small bridge over the narrow blackwater creek just below the point at which it surfaces from belowground. The creek then continues down a small valley until it is swallowed up again. A large population of wild azalea grows along the trail to the bridge. These large shrubs bloom in early spring and offer a spectacular show.

Bradwell Bay Wilderness Area

Accessed most easily from Forest Roads 314 and 329, at the trail markers.

Bradwell Bay is one of Florida's oldest national wilderness areas and is suited only for the most adventurous of naturalists. It is, in effect, a huge, densely vegetated swamp that covers nearly 25,000 acres and is bounded by a 7- by 7-mile square of forest service roads. The Florida National Scenic Trail passes through the bay's southern reaches and probably provides the most convenient access. Motorized access is prohibited.

Walking in Bradwell Bay is not a dry-foot experience, nor is it necessarily easy. During much of the year the water in the bay is quite deep. In many places it is more like wading than walking, and the surface of the water is often above the knees. In its heart, however, it is spectacular. Huge trees tower above a sparse understory, and large expanses of still water spread in all directions, offering awe-inspiring reflections of the forest canopy.

Bradwell Bay Wilderness is probably best known for what is locally called the "big tree area," one of the bay's more impressive endowments. Virgin slash pine still stand in this area as do exceedingly large specimens of black gum and ogeechee tupelo. One slash pine, which once had the distinction of being a national record, measures about 39 inches in diameter at breast height, and stands about 125 feet tall. Even the newest observer will recognize that there is something special about the size of this old tree.

Following the Florida Trail from the western trailhead, which is located on Forest Road 314, is the most direct route to the big tree area. However, the existing walkway does not pass immediately adjacent to the largest of the old pines, and leaving the trail to search for it can be risky without relying on a compass and marking your route with brightly colored flagging. It is easy to get lost here. In fact, it is probably not a good idea to enter any part of this wilderness area without map, compass, and some way to mark a trail. Although the trail is blazed with orange swabs of paint, it is not always easy to follow. It is important to keep your wits about you and to always be sure of the location of the next trail marker so you won't accidentally wander off the main path.

The trail through the eastern edge of Bradwell Bay Wilderness has a different aspect than its western counterpart. Though it, too, dips in and out of wet areas, it also crosses some particularly scenic areas of longleaf pine woodlands in which you are likely to see eastern bluebirds, red-cockaded woodpeckers, and Bachman sparrows. A short stretch of trail also traverses the banks of the Sopchoppy River before turning west.

Morrison Hammock Scenic Area

The access to Morrison Hammock is difficult to find. Although the area is clearly marked on the national forest map southwest of Sopchoppy, no trails lead into it and no roads provide direct access to its boundaries. The best way to enter is from SR 399 just south of its intersection with SR 22, a few miles west of Sopchoppy. The national forest map shows a block of public land (indicated in white) just to the northwest of the scenic area. This block of private land is bordered on the west and south by a firelane that makes good walking. However, the firelane stops at Cow Creek. Hence, venturing into the center of Morrison Hammock requires skill with map and compass and a generous supply of trail-marking tape so you can retrace your steps. The area contains some large trees, including at least one difficult-to-find cypress that is several feet in diameter at breast height.

Other trees include spruce pines, sabal palms, red maples, and hackberries. Stop at the ranger station in Crawfordville to ask for directions into the area before beginning your exploration.

Rock Bluff Scenic Area

Turn northwest on Forest Road 390, off SR 375, a few miles south of SR 20. Forest Road 390 leads to the small parking area at the edge of the scenic area.

The Rock Bluff Scenic Area lies at the bottom of a long bend on the eastern banks of the Ochlockonee River. A trail leads from the parking lot into the woodlands. When the water is low, it is possible to cross the ravine next to the trail and to enter the woodlands beyond it. High water requires skirting the end of the ravine.

Rock bluff is particularly noted for a number of plant species including hearts-a-bustin'-with-love, silverbell, pyramid magnolia, river birch, hickories, oaks, and a variety of other woody shrubs, trees, and vines. The woods beyond the ravine follow along a low bluff at the river's edge that eventually opens onto a vegetated levee that supports an open forest. The levee is generally clear of ground cover and allows easy passage to the water's edge. This portion of the river is a good place to watch for soaring hawks or to listen for the raucous, laughing call of the pileated woodpecker. The surrounding woodlands also support a number of songbird species.

Canoe Trails
Bradford Brook

Bradford Brook is a tiny, tannin-stained waterway that connects a series of cypress-ringed lakes in the northernmost parts of the forest, just southwest of Tallahassee. The passageways are marked and usually easy to follow. One entry point is along SR 263 just after it turns south toward the Tallahassee Airport off SR 371, or Capital Circle. The road crosses a small culvert; canoes can be launched most easily on the east side. Paddling west, back under the culvert, will take you to forest lands. The other entry point is off Aenon Church Road, which turns south off SR 20 less than 2 miles west of Capital Circle on Tallahassee's western edge. The pavement ends just before the little bridge that crosses the brook.

Sopchoppy River

Few rivers are as beautiful as the little Sopchoppy. Originating in national forest swamplands, less than an hour's drive from Tallahassee, it cuts its way for nearly 50 miles, first through a narrow crevice in the sandy pinelands, then through a boggy floodplain before finally emptying into Ochlockonee Bay. Precipitous banks rise as much as 20 feet on either side, and the tangled roots of ancient bald-cypress stretch along its white sandy edges. The pointed tops of cypress knees poke above the dark water against a backdrop of swamp lilies, wild azalea, and an interesting collection of other native plants. Prothonotary warblers, the golden-headed denizens of north Florida's wetlands, dart to and fro, disappearing into their well-concealed nests in the hollows of old tree stumps. Raccoons and bobcats prowl the river's fringe, leaving their telltale tracks in the soft white sand.

The Sopchoppy takes its name from the combination of two Creek Indian words: *Sokhe*, which means twisted or convulsive; and *Chapke*, which means "long twisted stream." Anyone who canoes for any distance along the upper river will appreciate the wisdom behind the name. Few stretches extend for even 100 yards without a curve, bend, or hairpin turn. As a result, canoeists often find paddling the river's upper reaches a challenging and somewhat demanding experience.

The lower river is a different matter. As the river nears Ochlockonee Bay, its appearance changes dramatically. Sharp, twisting turns give way to gentle meanders. Currents become slower; waters become deeper. The banks change from a series of sandy precipices to a succession of boggy floodplain swamps. Together, these changes contribute to an appearance that is radically different from the tiny river's more northern reaches. The view of the river from the bridge on US 319, just south of the town of Sopchoppy, is a stark contrast to the scene from Oak

Park or Trice Bridge, high up in the confines of the Apalachicola National Forest. One would not think these latter bridges even traverse the same stream as the one below.

Perhaps the Sopchoppy's greatest resource is its relatively unscathed natural state. The majority of the river lies under public ownership as part of the Apalachicola National Forest and St. Marks National Wildlife Refuge. No major cities are located along its course, and little development adorns its banks. The few cottages that dot the bluffs are limited primarily to areas near the tiny woodland community of Mount Beeser and the little town of Sopchoppy.

Above and below these lightly inhabited areas, the river flows largely through undisturbed Florida terrain. To the north, its corridor constitutes part of the Bradwell Bay National Wilderness Area; to the south, it skirts the eastern extreme of Thoms Island, a St. Marks National Wildlife Refuge Wilderness Area consisting of vast expanses of sawgrass marshes as well as scattered examples of sandy uplands and coastal hardwood hammocks (see p. 140).

The Sopchoppy also supports an interesting array of native flora and fauna. Nearly 20 endangered, threatened, or sensitive plants inhabit the area within a quarter mile of the river's channel. Salamanders, amphiumas, skinks, and snakes live in or around the dark red waters. Several species of frogs fill the shallows with their tadpoles throughout the summer, and at least 12 active nesting colonies of the endangered red-cockaded woodpecker reside in the longleaf pine woodlands closely adjacent to the riverine system. Populations of white-tailed deer and Florida black bear are also known to use the river for food, water, and shelter.

There are several places to access the portion of the river that flows through the national forest. The bridge on Forest Road 329 offers the best place to launch an exploration of the uppermost sections; the Oak Park Bridge on Forest Road 343 allows access to the middle reaches and serves as a good stopping point for a trip begun on 329.

More than one canoeist has been tempted to launch from

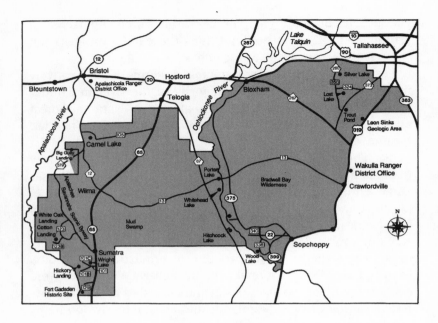

Apalachicola National Forest

Forest Highway 13. However, the river is densely vegetated just below FH 13, is not easily navigable, and has the propensity to turn a canoe ride into a hiking trip with a boat.

Lost Creek

Lost Creek is similar in aspect to the Sopchoppy. Its scenery includes white, sandy banks, cypress trees, wild azaleas, and similar wildlife. It is a short canoe trip but well worth paddling. Taking SR 368 (which eventually becomes Forest Highway 13) west from Crawfordville leads to a bridge across the river which is usually used as a take-out point. Just beyond the bridge, where the power lines cross the highway, is a turn-off to the right (north). This little road leads directly to a high bluff that over-looks the launch site. Be careful on this road. It is often wet and boggy, and the watery puddles it retains are sometimes much deeper than they appear. More than one paddler has become mired in the mud before ever reaching the river.

Ochlockonee River

The Ochlockonee River is one of the ANF's longest waterways and serves as the boundary line between the Wakulla and Apalachicola Ranger Districts. Most of its 64 miles pass through national forest lands, and there are a number of U.S. Forest Service-managed landings and campgrounds that provide access to the river's main channel. The Ochlockonee is bounded along much of its course by mature floodplain woodlands that are reminiscent of those along the Apalachicola and Choctawhatchee rivers. These mature woodlands offer outstanding scenery as well as important wildlife habitat. It takes three to four days to paddle the entire route.

The river's northernmost put-in point is at the bridge along SR 20, just west of SR 375. There is a fish camp here that charges a small launch fee but provides a nice parking area. You can see the Talquin dam from the bridge.

One of the first stops should be the Rock Bluff Scenic Area (see above), about 2 miles downstream. From Rock Bluff to Pine Creek Landing the river doubles as the Wakulla/Liberty county line and dips in and out of mostly undeveloped private land. The next two access points are Porter and Whitehead lakes, just off Forest Highway 13. Both make good camping spots. Whitehead Lake, which lies at the southern terminus of Forest Road 111, is a particularly secluded area but may be difficult to find from the river.

Revell, Mack, and Hitchcock landings also provide good camping spots but may be well used during hunting season. All are only a few miles from each other and not far south of Porter Lake. Day trips between these landings are easy to arrange and offer trips of varying distances.

The last of the designated national forest landings is at Wood Lake, on the east side of the river along Forest Road 338. Wood Lake is an oxbow that makes particularly good canoeing. Using a good aerial photo or topographic map, skilled canoeists can find their way upstream along a small backwater that heads northward from the lake, then into the river's main channel and back down river to the campground. The entire trip can last from two to several hours, depending how much exploring you do, and is an excellent paddling excursion. The campground at Wood Lake also makes a good overnight stop.

Horseback Riding

Any of the woods roads that criss-cross the Wakulla District are open for horseback riders and make very good riding trails. In addition, there are 30 miles of specifically designated horseback riding trails just off Highway 20, along the district's northern border. Signs pointing the way to the Vinzant Riding Trails are easily spotted from the highway.

Off-Road Cycling

There is a 7.5-mile off-road mountain bike trail along the forest's eastern edge. The Munson Hills Bike Trail is most easily accessed from the St. Marks Rail Trail which begins less than a mile south of Tallahassee's Capital Circle on SR 363.

APALACHICOLA RANGER DISTRICT

Facilities and Activities

The Wilma Savannas

In prehistoric times, before the days of human-induced fire suppression, much of the central panhandle was probably carpeted with boggy grasslands and wet pine savannas. Rapidly moving fires swept across the region often, ignited by one of the many thunderstorms that likely dominated much of the summer weather pattern. Today, the few remnants of these fascinating communities lie predominantly along the eastern edge of the Apalachicola River drainage basin, between the tiny crossroads villages of Wilma and Sumatra.

Two routes provide the best access to the Wilma savannas. The first is SR 65 which connects Hosford to Eastpoint. Several miles below its intersection with CR 12, SR 65 passes adjacent to several savannas that look somewhat like clearcuts. A few of these are marked with signs. These roadside savannas provide easy access to one of north Florida's most interesting assemblages of plants and make for great exploring. Walking in early fall or late spring through the boggy heart of any of these special places will reveal a number of orchids, asters, and carnivorous plants, such as the purple pitcher plant, that are difficult to find elsewhere.

The second route follows Forest Road 180 which turns west off SR 65 a little more than a mile past the CR 12 intersection. About 2 miles down 180, FR 123 turns off to the south then follows a long curve back toward the west. Just after the curve a large, open savanna will come into view on the north side of the road. The pineland that separates the savanna from the road, as well as the savanna itself, provide great places to study the plants. Continuing down 123 and onto 123A leads to additional savannas. However, 123A is not always in good condition, especially during wet weather, and care should be taken when driving it.

Apalachee Savannahs Scenic Byway

Portions of SR 12, SR 65, and SR 379 constitute the ANF's only national scenic byway. Designated in 1989, these picturesque roadways wind through a terrain that is filled with outstanding examples of flatwoods and bay swamps, as well as the savannas mentioned above. The shoulders along the byway are wide

Red-cockaded Woodpecker

enough for stopping, and several places support colonies of the endangered red-cockaded woodpecker. The latter can usually be found by looking for large pines encircled with a wide, white-painted band. These bands denote cavity trees and help the ANF's woodpecker technicians keep track of the colony's status; they also help visitors find likely spots to see this enchanting bird.

Mud Swamp/New River Wilderness Area

Accessed from SR 65 by taking Forest Highway 13 east. Carr Bridge, which is located on FH 13, is the northern limit of the narrow strip of wilderness that borders the New River. Continuing past the bridge to Forest Road 120, then southeast to Forest Road 170, then south to Forest Road 182 will lead to the northeastern corner of the wilderness area's main body.

The Mud Swamp/New River Wilderness Area is an 8,090-acre parcel that is composed chiefly of cypress, titi, and bay swamps. The area is densely vegetated, and no maintained trails lead into its interior. Hence, it is somewhat challenging to access on foot. During much of the year it is extremely wet. The New River is canoeable from Carr Bridge southward to Forest Road 182 but spreads out south of 182, particularly in wet weather, and can become difficult to navigate. Putting a canoe in the New River just west of the intersection of Forest Roads 120 and 164 is also possible. From this latter point you can paddle northward into the wilderness. However, the route is not always easy to follow and deserves caution.

Apalachicola River

The westernmost edge of the ANF lies along the eastern banks of the lower Apalachicola River. The creeks, sloughs, and junglelike tributaries of this outstanding waterway provide some of northern Florida's most intriguing flatwater paddling. Canopied waterways weave their way through magnificent wetland forests dominated by a variety of tupelo, ash, and titi trees. The buttressed bases of bald cypress line the swampy edges, supporting tall, straight boles that often extend high above the understory. A labyrinth of tannin-stained water stretches across an immense forested floodplain, crisscrossing, interconnecting, and diverging with such regularity that paddlers often find themselves plying the waters of several different streams as part of only a single, day-long excursion.

The Apalachicola River is located in the northwest Florida panhandle about 50 miles west of Tallahassee. Originating at the Jim Woodruff Dam in the little town of Chattahoochee, it flows freely for 107 miles before emptying into its estuary at the coastal fishing village of Apalachicola. For its first 20 miles the river flows along the edge of what geologists have called the Tallahassee Red Hills (see the sections on Torreya State Park and Apalachicola Bluffs and Ravines Preserve, pp. 181 and 196). Massive bluffs and beautiful wooded ravines line its eastern edge and its lower banks are studded with ancient limestone outcrops that were laid down eons ago when the sea level was much higher than it is today. As the river's channel leaves the uplands it gradually expands into an immense floodplain that eventually spreads over a 15-mile-wide expanse of wetland habitats that include majestic hardwood forests, dense wooded swamps, beautiful cypress backwaters, large expanses of open water, and a generous smattering of brackish and freshwater marshes.

Finding access to the lower Apalachicola's hidden treasures is not particularly difficult. A network of national forest-, county-, and state-owned roads provide passage to an assortment of entry points. Most of these byways are well maintained and easy to find off several of the more major highways.

All of the landings described below are located off SR 65 and SR 379, two lightly traveled thoroughfares that parallel the river's course. To reach these roads from I-10, turn west on SR 12 at exit 25. This will take you toward the rural hamlet of Bristol, some 21.4 miles from the interstate. At Bristol, SR 12 seems to dead-end but actually jogs west down US 20 for 0.3 mile before continuing south. SR 379 continues straight ahead and SR 12 turns off to the left about 14.5 miles south of Bristol. SR 379 eventually joins SR 65 about 27.5 miles past its juncture with SR 12. Following are seven of the most important of these landings. They are described below in the order in which they are approached when driving south on SR 379 and SR 65.

Big Gully Landing

Reached by turning onto Forest Road 133 which leads off to the west within the first mile after turning onto SR 379. Big Gully Landing is the ANF's northernmost access point to the Apalachicola River floodplain. It is also the landing that is farthest off the Apalachicola's main waterway. Like most of the U.S. Forest Service roads in the region, 133 is a well maintained sand and clay road that is denoted by a small brown sign with only its road numbers emblazoned in white on its otherwise unmarked face. It leads to a small, somewhat primitive landing that opens onto Big Gully Creek.

Big Gully Creek is more reminiscent of a route through a swamp than a well-defined waterway. A narrow access connects the landing to the creek. Paddling left from where the creek and access route intersect leads to a weaving passageway that winds through a forest of cypress trees. During much of the year, Big Gully's water spreads out in all directions, making the exact channelway somewhat difficult to follow. Paddlers new to the region must keep their wits about them to stay on course. Although Big Gully Creek is an interesting and beautiful area, it is probably best to begin one's exploration of the lower Apalachicola River floodplain at one of the more easily followed routes described below.

White Oak Landing

Turn off SR 379, approximately 11.1 miles south of the turn-off to Big Gully. Forest Service Road 115 angles off to the right at this point and is marked only by a small sign bearing its road number. The landing itself is situated off 115 on the banks of River Styx, a meandering stream that connects the narrowing floodplain with the main channel of the Apalachicola.

Several round-trips begin at White Oak Landing. One of the shortest and most interesting involves paddling west from the landing toward the Apalachicola River. About 0.25 mile upstream from the confluence of River Styx and the main river, Jinx Slough turns off to the north. There are actually two creeks that turn off at nearly the same location. Jinx Slough is the second, or westernmost of the two. Jinx Slough winds its way through magnificent woodlands and floodplain swamps for 3 to 4 miles before rejoining the Apalachicola. Turning left on the Apalachicola brings you back to the mouth of River Styx, and then back to the landing. The point at which Jinx Slough enters the Apalachicola is just above and across the river from a huge sandbar that is lined on its landward edge with willow trees. This sandbar is at a major bend of the river and is an outstanding place for primitive camping. Such sandbars are common along much of the river and offer a unique and interesting way to enjoy the river's backcountry.

Two one-way trips also begin at White Oak Landing, each of which terminates at Cotton Landing on Kennedy Creek. Both begin by first paddling west to the mouth of River Styx, then downstream on the Apalachicola. The easiest route to follow continues down the Apalachicola for nearly 9 miles to the mouth of Kennedy Creek. This route takes paddlers past two large ox-bow lakes off the eastern side of the river as well as past the mouth of the spring-fed Chipola River, one of the Apalachicola's major tributaries. So-called Kennedy Lake angles off to the east about 1.5 miles below the Chipola. The real entrance to Kennedy Creek turns off Kennedy Lake to the right about 0.25 mile upstream from the Apalachicola. It is probably wise to use the Wewahitchka and Kennedy Creek USGS topographic quadrangle maps mentioned below to insure making the appropriate turns.

Another route to Cotton Landing follows Shepard Slough which turns off the east side of the Apalachicola just south of the mouth of River Styx, then follows a twisting route to Kennedy Creek. After passing initially through a narrow, canopied channelway, the slough opens into several sections of wider water. Referred to as lakes on the map and by locals, they are actually enlarged sections of the creek that provide a brief respite from the dense, junglelike edges of the upper and lower portions of the slough. It is important to follow the current to find the way into and out of the lakes.

The passage through Shepard Slough is not for beginning explorers. The route is not always easy to find and the potential for taking a wrong turn is high. It should not be paddled except by those competent in map reading and familiar with finding their way in swampy terrain.

Cotton Landing

Forest Road 123 crosses SR 379 some 2.4 miles beyond the turn-off to River Styx. It is a semi-circular road that eventually returns to the highway 2.5 miles farther south. Both intersections of SR 379 with Forest Road 123 are marked with large forest service signs and are easy to find. Several other Forest Service roads turn off 123; 123-B leads to Cotton Landing and Kennedy Creek.

The trip down Kennedy Creek is one of the nicest on the lower river. Beginning high up on the watershed, the narrow, cypress-lined channel weaves its way, twisting and turning, through some of the region's most beautiful woodlands. The delicate branches of stiffcornel dogwood intermix with those of locust, cypress, and tupelo trees along the creek's perimeter, providing an appropriate overstory for the small patches of endangered spider lily that dot the wetlands. The yellow-gold heads of prothonotary warblers contrast sharply with the rich black waters as the tiny birds make their way into and out of their well-hidden nesting cavities. The occasional hooting of a barred owl or the loud laughter of the pileated woodpecker make the scene complete.

This trip is one of the longer and more varied day trips on the lower Apalach. Beginning at Cotton Landing, paddlers can follow Kennedy Creek for several miles to its intersection with Kennedy Lake. From this point it is only a short paddle to the left to reach the Apalachicola. From here paddlers can follow the Apalachicola to Owl Creek about 3.6 miles downstream. The only point of confusion along the big river is the turn-off to Brushy Creek. It is the only large turn-off before reaching Owl Creek.

Hickory Landing

Hickory Landing is located on Owl Creek and is accessed by taking Forest Road 101, then 101-B off SR 65.

Owl Creek is one of the lower river's most diverse waterways. At and below the landing, the creek is a wide expanse of rich, black water bordered on either side by the dark green leaves and overhanging boughs of ogeechee tupelo trees. In many places these overhanging limbs provide enchanting passageways that are separated from the main channel and allow paddlers to explore the watery edges. Above Hickory Landing, Owl Creek narrows and eventually becomes a tiny, twisting ribbon of black that finds its way through the swampy backwoods.

Hickory Landing is the beginning or ending point for a variety of possible adventures. Located only a short distance from Owl Creek's gaping mouth, it provides one of the shortest paddling distances to reach the Apalachicola's main channel. From this one beginning point paddlers can continue downstream on the big river and turn back into the floodplain at Fort Gadsden Creek or make the much longer journey to the northern terminus of either the East or St. Marks Rivers. Trips begun at Hickory Landing can last from only a few hours to as much as several days. Beginning upriver at either Cotton or White Oak landing allows a similar paddling opportunity with Hickory Landing as the termination point.

The paddle from Hickory Landing to Ft. Gadsden Creek is one of the shorter one-way trips on the lower Apalach and is easily paddled in less than three hours. Taking one's time, however, allows the opportunity to explore, relax, and make a leisurely visit to Ft. Gadsden State Historic Site, the location of an old British fort that serves as an interesting reminder of west Florida's history.

The trip begins by paddling down Owl Creek to the Apalachicola, then turning downstream toward Ft. Gadsden. The historic site occupies a bluff on the east side of the river and is serviced from the water by a small dock. Just beyond the old fort, Ft. Gadsden Creek turns off to the left and eventually leads to the landing. The only spot that is potentially confusing occurs about

2 miles upstream where Ft. Gadsden Creek's south prong angles off to the right. Paddlers should bear left to reach the landing.

Fort Gadsden Creek

Ft. Gadsden Creek passes under SR 65 at a small but obvious bridge. The landing is well off the highway at the end of a primitive, sandy, two-lane road. The unmarked access turns off SR 65 to the west just a few yards south of the bridge. At about 0.4 mile the access road diverges at an obvious fork. The road to the left appears more traveled, but the road to the right leads to the landing.

Ft. Gadsden Creek begins as a narrow waterway that quickly widens into a tupelo-lined blackwater stream. Paddling left from the landing and bearing right at the confluence with Ft. Gadsden's south prong eventually leads to an intersection with the Apalachicola. A short but strenuous paddle upstream on the Apalachicola leads to the Ft. Gadsden State Historic Site described earlier. A downstream paddle on the Apalachicola will lead to East River and either Graham Creek or Gardner Landing.

Graham Creek

The landing on Graham Creek is one of the Apalachicola's easiest to find. Located directly adjacent to SR 65, its parking area is an obvious landmark and the name of the creek is permanently engraved in the concrete banisters of the bridge that crosses it.

Launching at Graham Creek allows several miles of paddling on backwater creeks as well as access to the main river. Paddling left from the landing will immerse you immediately in an enchanting blackwater stream that begins as a relatively wide waterway and continually narrows to its confluence with the northern reaches of East River.

Turning right onto East River at the end of Graham Creek leads upstream against the current through a series of narrow passageways that skirt around fallen logs and other natural debris. The point at which East River meets the Apalachicola is directly across the river from a huge sandbar that often serves as a primitive riverside camping area much like the one described above for Jinx Slough.

Turning left at the end of Graham Creek will lead down East River, away from the Apalachicola, and toward Gardner Landing. Gardner Landing is actually located on an oxbow lake, slightly removed from East River's main body of water. Paddlers must be observant for a small watercourse leading off to the left several miles below the turn from Graham Creek.

Gardner Landing

Gardner Landing is part of the Apalachicola River Wildlife and Environmental Area and is not part of the National Forest. It is also one of the lower Apalachicola River's more out-of-the-way put-in points. Located on the banks of East River, it is reached by turning west off SR 65 just south of the point at which the Apalachicola Northern Railroad crosses the highway. A two-lane sand road leads away from the main thoroughfare, crosses the railroad track again, then terminates at a widened parking area.

In addition to the trip described above that originates at Graham Creek Landing and terminates at Gardner Landing, there is also a relatively long, circular trip that allows for paddling much of East River as well as a long portion of the Apalachicola. Paddling right from the landing leads up East River, in reverse to the direction described above for Graham Creek. For much of its course prior to the intersection with Graham, East River is a relatively wide stream with little or no current. Above this confluence, however, the channel narrows, the current intensifies, and the paddling becomes more strenuous for the final stretch to the Apalachicola.

Turning left where East River meets the Apalachicola will carry canoeists downriver with the gently flowing waters, offering a long respite from the brief upstream pull. Continuing downstream for just under 2 miles leads past the huge mouth of the Brothers River, which tumbles into the Apalachicola from the west. The mouth of the St. Marks River is an easily recognized tributary leading off to the east slightly more than 1.5 miles farther on. The St. Marks leads south, then east through a series of twisting hairpin turns before converging with East River about 0.5 mile south of the turnoff back to Gardner Landing.

Maps, References, and a Note of Caution

Knowing your way can be one of the lower Apalachicola River's most exciting challenges. So many of its creeks interconnect, diverge into smaller watery passageways, or trail off into swampy dead ends that it is easy to find oneself disoriented. Even what appear to be major waterways often pass through sections of ill-defined creekbeds or angle off into directions that are easily missed by the unobservant paddler. All of these potentialities require both reasoned caution and a significant degree of skill with map and compass. Newcomers to the territory must take care to study the maps diligently and then confine their sojourns to the more conspicuous and easily followed routes. For those who become experienced with backwater exploring, this magnificently endowed riverine system offers an outstanding opportunity for extended nature study, exploration, and discovery.

The most important general access map of the region is the official Apalachicola National Forest map mentioned above. It shows the roads as well as all of the landings and campgrounds, except for Gardner Landing (the latter is not on ANF lands). It can be used only as a general paddling guide to the major waterways but is not detailed enough for more intensive exploring.

Several U.S. Geological Survey topographic maps are the most helpful. Since many of the backwater creeks and sloughs along the lower Apalachicola floodplain interconnect in myriad ways, "topo" maps are extremely useful for insuring that paddlers stay on course. The most valuable quadrangles are Jackson River, Forbes Island, Fort Gadsden, Kennedy Creek, Orange, Wewahitchka, Dead Lake, and Estiffanulga. All of these quadrangles, plus any others that are included within the boundaries of Florida's three national forests, may be purchased from the Forest Supervisor at the address on p. 63; they may also be purchased directly from the U.S. Geological Survey by writing USGS Map Sales, Box 25286, Denver, CO 80225.

GULF ISLANDS NATIONAL SEASHORE

Its not easy to summarize the Gulf Islands National Seashore. Though its name conjures up images of sun, surf, and sun-bathing, the landscape and habitats it preserves are actually much more diverse than this. There are, of course, generous examples of rolling dunes, sandy beaches, and green Gulf waters. But there are also outstanding examples of pine-studded flatlands, freshwater marshes, sand pine scrub woodlands, magnificent hardwood hammocks, and extensive barrier island meadows.

This national seashore is actually a collection of several non-contiguous holdings spread along the Gulf coastal strand from just west of Destin, Florida, to just south of Biloxi, Mississippi. Established in 1971, its preservation came in the nick of time for much of the Florida panhandle. Since the early 1960s, the development in this entire coastal region has expanded dramatically, converting much of what was once miles of unspoiled beaches into hotels, amusement centers, restaurants, golf courses, and other nonnatural tourist attractions. As a result, the areas protected by the national seashore are important remnants of a disappearing natural endowment.

Location, Mailing Address and Phone

There are six land entrances to the natural areas of Gulf Islands National Seashore within the Florida District, three of which have visitor centers. The Naval Live Oaks Area is located on the south side of US 98 just east of Gulf Breeze. The Fort Pickens Area is located on Fort Pickens Road at the western end of Santa Rosa Island; the Santa Rosa Area is located near the center of Santa Rosa Island. Both of these latter two areas can be reached by taking SR 399 (via a toll bridge) south from Gulf Breeze to the island, then turning west or east, respectively. Fort Barrancas is accessed by taking the main entrance to the Pensacola Naval Air Station, which is located about 1 mi. south of SR 292 (Barrancas Ave.) on SR 295 (Navy Blvd.). The Perdido Key Area is located southwest of Pensacola on Johnson Beach Road, just off SR 292. The Okaloosa Area is located on the north side of US 98 between Destin and Ft. Walton Beach at the eastern end of Santa Rosa Island.

Superintendent, 1801 Gulf Breeze Pkwy, Gulf Breeze, FL 32561; (904) 934-2600. This address and phone is for all parts of the park located in the Florida District.

Facilities and Activities

Camping, nature trails, interpretive trails, visitor centers, book and gift shops, bike trails, birding, botanizing, saltwater fishing, boating, wildlife observation, ranger-led interpretive tours of Ft. Pickens and Fort Barrancas.

Naval Live Oaks Area
Visitor Center

This is a small visitor center but it looks large because it also houses the park's administrative offices. It is well worth the time to stop here. The staff and volunteers who work the desk are eager to provide information about the area and are equipped with a large number of brochures, maps, and leaflets that provide important information about the area's history, natural setting, and wildlife. There is a particularly good brochure describing the wildflowers and plants of barrier islands as well as a complete (and quite extensive) bird list. There is also a book store that offers guides to native plants and animals as well as general reading about the area.

Nature Trails

The Naval Live Oaks Area encompasses over 1,300 acres with more than 5 miles of walking trails on the north side of US 98, and another 2 miles west of the visitor center.

The trails on the north side of US 98 may be reached by one of two roads. The first is a paved park road that turns off the highway just west of the visitor center; the other is Bayshore Road which borders the area's eastern boundary.

The site of the old Pensacola–St. Augustine road parallels US 98 for approximately 2.2 miles and is the longest foot trail in this part of the park. It is also one of the last remaining remnants of Florida's first highway. The old road was originally constructed in 1824 to connect what were then two of Florida's most important centers of commerce. Today it passes through an interesting collection of coastal habitats that include sand pine scrub, longleaf pine woodlands, and hardwood hammocks characterized chiefly by live oak, southern magnolia, and pignut hickory. All of these habitats are substantially unchanged from the days when the old road was first constructed.

Several additional trails lead off Bayshore Road and crisscross the eastern end of the area. The habitats here are similar to those along the Pensacola–St. Augustine Highway, except for the area near the old beaver pond which harbors a small collection of wetland species. All make nice walking.

It is also worth exploring the beach strand along Pensacola Bay. The huge dunes there are quite arresting. They are large enough to be seen from the 3-mile bridge that crosses the bay when driving west from Pensacola and are likely the remains of ancient beach ridges that formed during a higher stand of the sea.

The Naval Live Oaks Area is historically significant for a number of reasons. Not only was it the site of the old highway, it also supported an important population of Florida Indians dating back 5,000 years. In 1829, President John Quincy Adams designated it as the country's first federal tree farm. The huge live oaks that grew there were reserved for use in the construction of wooden warships in the early- to mid-1800s, hence the name Naval Live Oaks. The trees that grow there today are descendants of the original virgin forest.

Santa Rosa And Okaloosa Areas

The Santa Rosa Area is traversed by a 7.2-mile stretch of beach road that bisects a narrow barrier island. Most people visit here to swim and enjoy the shore. Near the center of the area (about 7 miles east of Pensacola Beach and 4 miles west of Navarre Beach) the National Park Service has constructed a picnic pavilion with an exhibit room, snack shop, a number of picnic shelters, restrooms, and several boardwalks. Swimmers, snorkelers, and beachcombers have much to keep their attention. For nature lovers, the area is a good stopping place to begin an exploration of the barrier island ecosystem, one of Florida's most dynamic landforms.

The Okaloosa Area is a small picnicking and bayside facility located near the eastern tip of Santa Rosa Island. It is well separated from other parts of the national seashore and is used primarily by water sports enthusiasts. There is a picnic area and a small skiff and sailboat launch onto Choctawhatchee Bay.

Several suppositions have been advanced to explain the formation of Florida's Gulf coast barrier islands. One of these, the so-called submergence theory, maintains that during the last period of extreme low sea level, a little over 20,000 years ago, a system of ridges and swales developed along the panhandle coast, much like those that exist there today. Subject to the powerful forces of wind and waves, the same processes that influence our current beaches, these early coastal ridges became the highest points in the landscape while the terrain landward of the beaches remained relatively low and flat. As sea level rose, water inundated the lowlands, leaving only the tops of the ridges and dunes exposed above the surface. These newly formed islands became the forerunners of present-day barriers and the submerged areas landward of the islands became sounds and lagoons.

It is probable that Santa Rosa Island formed in this way. Stretching for nearly 50 miles between Destin and Pensacola, this thin ribbon of sand is actually more a continuation of the coastal strand that originates just south of Port St. Joe than it is an offshore island. Its relatively straight to slightly concave shape indicates that it has long been a coastal feature and has long fronted directly on the Gulf. In a lower stand of the sea it was presumably continuous with the mainland and was separated only by a narrow stretch of lowlands. As the sea returned, the lowlands were inundated and the Santa Rosa Island and Sound complex was born.

Fort Pickens Area
Facilities and Activities

Visitor center, camping, hiking, bike trails, historical and natural interpretation, swimming, snorkeling, picnicking, museum; a fee is required.

Visitor Center

The visitor center is housed in part of old Fort Pickens. Since a major interest here is history, the visitor center contains a large selection of history books that reflect the Spanish and Union influence on the area as well as the area's role during the Civil War. However, there is also a large selection of books about the park's natural endowments, including selections that focus on birds, marine life, insects, plants, and the park's several ecosystems. Another of the historic buildings contains a small museum with exhibits about the region's natural and cultural history.

Camping

There is a 200-unit campground nestled in one of the more woodsy areas. Camping is first-come, first-served and the campground fills up fast during spring and summer. Reservations are not accepted. Length of stay is limited to 14 days between March 1 and October 1, and 30 days the remainder of the year. A camp store is located near the entrance to the campground. A camping fee is charged in addition to the general entrance fee.

Hiking and Biking Trails

Several hiking/biking trails are scattered throughout the area. One of the best trails connects the campground to the fort and museum area. This trail starts at the edge of the parking lot next to the visitor center and runs along the route of an old narrow-gauge railroad bed. It is hardpacked oyster shell and may even be suitable for wheelchairs, though it is quite rough. It runs through typical sand scrub much of the way; myrtle oak, sand live oak, Florida rosemary, and sand pine are common. A side trail leads to the bayside beach.

The blackbird marsh trail is an interpretive walkway that

begins in the campground between campsites 15 and 16 in Loop A. It is a short trail that contains a boardwalk through a sawgrass marsh as well as along the sand ridges that surround it.

Birding and Wildlife Observation

Like many of the Gulf coast's migrant traps, the Ft. Pickens area can be outstanding for both birds and birdwatchers. The beaches contain shorebirds, gulls, terns, herons, and pelicans throughout the year; northern gannets, loons, and a variety of ducks are present in winter.

The fort area's grasslands, bayside beach, and bike trail are the most prized areas for birding, particularly during spring migration and winter. Winter wrens as well as lark and white-crowned sparrows are commonly seen, and groove-billed anis are sometimes known to winter here.

The blackbird marsh trail described above can be very good for spring migrants as well as wintering songbirds. Warblers and vireos are often seen in the low-growing oaks that are scattered throughout the area.

In addition to birds, a number of other wildlife species can be observed in the Fort Pickens area. The nearby woods and scrub support a variety of mammals, including the armadillo, opossum, skunk, and raccoon, and the surrounding ocean waters harbor the aquatic Atlantic bottlenose dolphin, the park's largest and most fascinating mammal. Associated saltwater fishes include the flounder, pompano, mullet, and sheepshead. There are also 16 species of snakes on Santa Rosa Island; only four are poisonous. The latter include the eastern diamondback rattlesnake, pygmy rattlesnake, cottonmouth, and eastern coral snake.

Perdido Key And Johnson Beach

The Perdido Key and Johnson Beach area is visited mostly in summer, and mostly by beachgoers. The area contains picnic shelters, restrooms, showers, and a snack shop.

The road into the area goes for only about 2 miles. However, the park extends for another 5 miles beyond the end of the road, terminating at the watery pass that separates Perdido Key from Santa Rosa Island. Although there is only one short nature trail in the developed part of the key, the undeveloped end of the island can provide a nice walk in winter and an opportunity to explore another of the Florida panhandle's outstanding barrier beaches. Primitive camping is allowed on this end of the island but requires that all supplies be carried in. No facilities are available beyond the parking lot and no vehicles (except boats that arrive from offshore) are allowed. Primitive campers who desire to leave a vehicle overnight in the parking lot must obtain a camping permit before beginning their hike.

Fort Barrancas

This is primarily a historical site located within the confines of the Pensacola Naval Air Station. Fort Barrancas, the main attraction, was built by the United States in the early 1840s on the site of what was once the Spanish-controlled Fort San Carlos. The fort was later occupied by Confederate soldiers after Florida seceded from the Union. Today, the area also contains a visitor center, a book store which specializes mostly in historical literature, a picnicking facility, and a short nature trail. The 0.5 mile nature walk passes through a good example of sand pine woodlands, similar to those at nearby Big Lagoon State Recreation Area (see p. 111), and is an interesting place to explore.

Best Time of Year

Spring and fall are best for birding; summer is best for water sports. Winter is best if you desire to explore a desolate beach in cool temperatures with little interference from others.

Pets

Pets are permitted throughout the park (including the campgrounds) except on the beaches and inside any structure. Leashes are required.

ST. MARKS NATIONAL WILDLIFE REFUGE

A St. Marks sunrise is a wondrous event. Overlooking the light-house pool on a crisp fall morning, the first light reflecting the colorful new plumage of wintering ducks is an experience no Florida explorer should forego. Whether you are interested in birds, mammals, frogs and toads, snakes, alligators, wildflowers, or just walking quietly in the woods, the St. Marks National Wildlife Refuge offers a generous variety of family and individual field trips and a continuing opportunity for exploration and discovery.

The St. Marks National Wildlife Refuge is one of the refuge system's oldest installations. It was established in 1931 and currently encompasses over 65,000 acres on land as well as nearly 32,000 acres of open water in adjacent Apalachee Bay. More than half of the refuge's lands are classified as wetlands, but there are also sizable tracts of forested uplands. St. Marks is divided into three management units: the St. Marks, Wakulla, and Panacea. Each offers its own unique habitats, wildlife, and activities, and each is treated separately below.

Location, Mailing Address and Phone

The St. Marks Unit is accessed from the village of Newport by turning south from US 98 onto Wakulla CR 59. The Wakulla Unit is reached by turning south off US 98 onto the Wakulla Beach Road, which is located about 3.4 miles west of the US 98 and US 363 intersection; or by turning south off 98 onto SR 365, then south to SR 367 and SR 367A. The Panacea Unit is reached by turning west off US 98 onto SR 372A in the middle of the little town of Panacea or by taking SR 372 between US 98 and Sopchoppy.

Refuge Manager, P.O. Box 68, St. Marks, Florida 32355; (904) 925-6121.

ST. MARKS UNIT

Facilities and Activities

Hiking, birding, canoeing, boating, bicycling, fresh and saltwater fishing, butterfly watching, botanizing.

Visitor Center

Your first stop in the St. Marks Unit should be the visitor center which is located on the right side of the road just past the fee station. It is the central repository for information on all parts of the refuge. The St. Marks Refuge Association operates a book-store and gift shop in the visitor center which is stocked with a

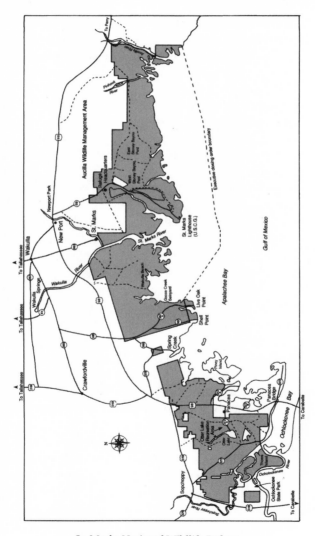

St. Marks National Wildlife Refuge

good supply of field guides that will help you identify the local plants and animals. There is also an outstanding collection of exhibits that orient visitors to the refuge, its purposes, the habitats and wildlife it protects, its history, and how it is managed. Volunteers and refuge staff are usually available to offer more immediate information, and a sightings log is maintained that will alert you to the location of any rare or special birds (or other wildlife) that might be in the area. The observation deck and Plum Orchard Pond Nature Trail, both of which are located out the rear entrance of the visitor center, are also well worth a visit.

Lighthouse Road

CR 59, or Lighthouse Road, is the refuge's main artery. It extends from the refuge entrance to the lighthouse (approximately 7 miles from the entrance) and is the only road on the St. Marks Unit that is open for driving. It is also the most visited part of the refuge and provides many excellent stopping points. The numerous pools along the road's edge offer glimpses of large wading birds as well as ducks, grebes, mergansers, and coots. Bald eagles often perch in the dead trees that dot the marshes, or fly low across the pools. A variety of raptors, including an occasional peregrine falcon or merlin, also frequent the pools.

About 2 miles beyond the visitor center, the Aucilla Tram Road (so named because it is an old logging tram that eventually leads to the banks of the Aucilla River) turns off to the left. It serves as the starting point for many miles of hiking trails that lead in some places through dense woodlands, in other places out along the dike roads that border the waterfowl impoundments. Be sure to obtain a map of these roads at the visitor center; the routes are sometimes confusing.

The next three stops along Lighthouse Road also lead out to the dike roads; each has a parking area. The first is locally referred to as the twin dikes because the two paths parallel each other for a short distance before becoming one. The second is marked by an observation deck on the west side of the roadway. Looking east from the deck out over Mounds Pool insures a good chance of seeing eagles. Looking west exposes a large expanse of

Juncus saltmarsh. The last of these three stops is a single dike that goes only a short distance before intersecting with another. Ducks often congregate in Mounds Pool #3, just beyond the intersection.

The next important stopping point is the easily accessible Mounds Nature Trail that begins near the restrooms and encircles Tower Pond. From the back side of the trail you can stand atop an observation deck and watch the activity of the pond, or gaze out over the *Juncus* marsh toward the coast. Deer are sometimes seen along the sand flats that lie within the marsh just off the trail's southeastern vista. It is also possible to cross over into the marsh across from the pond, if you don't mind getting your feet wet. This is one of the easiest places to find direct access to the saltmarsh and sand flats ecosystem.

The last stop on CR 59 is the parking lot that overlooks Apalachee Bay, Lighthouse Pool, and the St. Marks Lighthouse. The bay is a good location for shorebirds, saltwater ducks, brown pelicans, and an occasional reddish egret. The 28-acre pool is good for a variety of freshwater ducks, American coots, common moorhens, long-legged waders, an occasional American bittern, and American alligators. The lighthouse was built in 1829 and has been in near continuous operation since. It is 80 feet tall and was originally staffed by a lighthouse keeper whose only access was by boat. It was automated in 1960 and is currently under the control of the U.S. Coast Guard. It is open for tours only once or twice a year.

Dike Roads and Hiking Trails

For enterprising observers the many dike roads that crisscross the freshwater impoundments provide access to the more remote sections of the refuge. There are over 25 miles of walkable roadways in this levee system, all of which are easy to get to.

The dike roads are actually management tools that allow refuge biologists to control water levels and maintain an appropriate balance between the aquatic vegetation that serves as food for the wintering waterfowl and the weedy plants that will take over if not controlled. The dikes can be accessed on foot from any of the locked gates off the main Lighthouse Road and are open for hiking and nature study year-round. Although they are often hot and buggy in summer, in fall, winter, and spring they offer some of north Florida's most enjoyable walking. The map distributed at the visitor center shows all of these routes.

One section of the dike roads doubles as part of the route of the Florida National Scenic Trail. Stretching for more than 15 miles in the St. Marks Unit alone, the trail begins deep in the Refuge near the Aucilla River, then passes through several areas of enchanting wetlands including a magnificent portion of Swamp Hammock before joining the road to Deep Creek. There are several designated primitive campgrounds along the route of the trail. However, only end-to-enders, those hiking across all three units of the refuge, are granted camping permits. No other camping is permitted on refuge lands.

Birding

The primary purpose of the St. Marks Refuge is to provide suitable habitat for wintering waterfowl. Nowhere is this more obvious than on the St. Marks Unit. As early as September the cold-weather visitors begin to arrive. By the first of December at least 19 species of ducks and two species of geese are using refuge habitats. Throughout the winter, blue and green winged teal, mallard, canvasback, gadwalls, black duck, pintail, northern shoveler, American widgeon, redheads, buffleheads, wood ducks, ring-necked ducks, scaup, and an occasional flock of snow geese offer close-up lessons in waterfowl identification. Less-common species include the ruddy duck, black scoter, old squaw, cinnamon teal, common goldeneye, and Eurasian widgeon.

Wintering waterfowl constitutes only part of the refuge's bird life. The wetlands also support a variety of long-legged waders and shorebirds, and the many woodlands and thickets support an astonishing number of sparrows, warblers, vireos, and other songbirds.

With such an array of birdlife, it is no wonder that the refuge is visited by so many birdwatchers. An ordinary, though somewhat hardworking birder who visits the refuge regularly during all of its seasons can hope to see over 200 bird species during an average year. In addition to the winter waterfowl season, spring and fall are particularly good times for birdwatching. At these times migration is in full force, and many species find St. Marks an adequate rest stop along their journey, which increases the number of birds that can be seen.

Other Wildlife

Good wildlife habitat is nondiscriminatory. While the refuge may have been set aside initially to provide winter homes for migrating waterfowl, many other species also find its protected marshes, hardwood hammocks, pine flatwoods, and freshwater impoundments suitable places to live and to raise their young. In addition to the over 300 bird species that have been recorded within the refuge boundary, at least 50 different kinds of mammals and over 100 species of reptiles and amphibians—including snakes, turtles, lizards, salamanders, frogs, and toads—also inhabit the refuge.

The refuge is also host to a small population of Florida black bears (most of which are on the St. Marks Unit and are only rarely seen) as well as sizable populations of bobcats, white-tailed deer, and both grey and red foxes. Occasionally, a jaguarundi, a bobcatlike animal with a long instead of stubby tail, is spotted.

For many visitors the alligators still provide the main attraction. Most often seen sunning on the banks of one of the freshwater impoundments, these long-tailed, scaly-backed crocodillians appear sluggish and lethargic. On land they lumber along awkwardly, able to move quickly for only very short distances. Underwater, though, they move with speed, agility, and grace. Once listed as an endangered species, these animals have made a tremendous comeback and only recently have been removed from protected status. Refuge biologists estimate that there are now over 2,500 gators on refuge lands. However, this figure should not be taken as a precise reflection of the population. Because of their propensity to stay hidden below the surface or

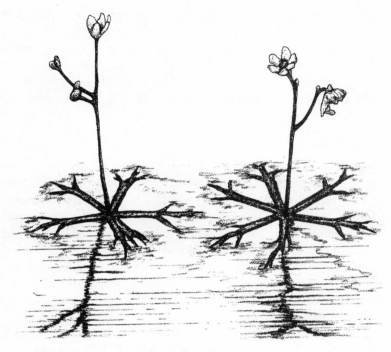

Bladderwort

in their underground caves, alligators are extremely difficult creatures to census. The refuge may harbor many more than the current estimate.

Wildflowers

For the wildflower enthusiast the refuge offers numerous opportunities. In spring, both Aucilla Tram and Port Leon Roads (the latter is near the visitor center) offer an array of flowering plants. Duck potato, colic root, grass-pink, blue flag iris, canna lily, wild indigo, lizard tail, and several varieties of wild hibiscus and milkweed are the more obvious flowering plants. In early spring both white and blue violets pop out along each of these roads and the reddish tint of red maple fills the forest canopy. A number of the insectivorous butterworts and bladderworts bloom along or in the shallow ditch just inside the Aucilla Tram Road gate.

For fall flowers the best areas are the dike roads. Yellows, blues, and purples predominate with several species of golden-rods, blazing stars, and mist flowers in full splendor. Butterflies are often abundant on many of these flowers during both spring and fall. The refuge's annual wildflower day usually occurs in April or May and offers a good way to learn about the native flora.

Butterflies

Increasing numbers of visitors come to the St. Marks Unit in fall and spring to see the plethora of colorful butterflies that migrate through the area. The brightly adorned monarch is probably the most abundant species. The monarch arrives in large enough numbers to attract butterfly researchers who capture, tag, and release the delicate creatures in an attempt to learn more about their habits and migration routes. Other species include the Gulf fritillary, zebra, several species of swallowtails, queens, painted ladies, and a number of skippers, sulphurs, and buckeyes. The refuge also offers regular annual events (usually in the fall) that feature butterflies and butterfly identification programs and field trips. For individual field excursions, the dike roads are your best choice.

WAKULLA UNIT

Facilities and Activities

Hiking, birdwatching, botanizing, wildlife observation.

North Line Road and the Florida National Scenic Trail

Reached by turning south off US 98 onto Wakulla Beach Road (see directions on p. 94). The entrance to North Line Road is located on the west side of Wakulla Beach Road and is marked by a parking area and a Florida Trail sign. The road is gated to prevent entrance by automobiles most of the year but is always open for walking.

Portions of the Florida National Scenic Trail lead in two directions from this parking lot. The trail's North Line Road section, the longer of the two, heads west, and a shorter, but equally interesting section turns east.

North Line Road borders the Wakulla Unit's northern boundary and is an outstanding walking path. The road is a dry walkway through an otherwise lowland terrain and is bordered by a hardwood forest that is in some places moist, in other places extremely wet. The Florida National Scenic Trail and the roadway share a common path for about 2 miles before the trail leads off to the southwest. The trail traverses the entire Wakulla Unit, leaving refuge land at the intersection of SR 365 and SR 367.

After leaving North Line road the trail passes through an exceptional hardwood–oak–cabbage palm forest. Some particularly nice ironwood line this trail, as do a number of loblolly pine and a variety of other tree species. Less than 3 miles after leaving North Line Road, the trail crosses another road. Just beyond this intersection, a blue-marked trail leads off to the left to Shepard Spring, a small, circular, beautiful, clearwater spring that forms the headwater of Shepard Spring Creek, which eventually empties into Apalachee Bay. Due to its alligator population and pristine nature, Shepard Spring is not a swimming or diving area. During the rainy season the area around Shepard Spring can be wet and boggy; prepare to get your feet wet.

Immediately west of Shepard Spring the trail passes through a dense stand of bamboo. From here to its intersection with CR 367 (about 2.5 miles) it weaves through several areas of upland woods and pine forests where it is sometimes possible to see large herds of white-tailed deer.

The North Line Road portion of the trail is a good place for seeing a variety of small songbirds including the prothonotary and black-and-white warblers, an occasional woodcock (if you are patient and lucky), and white-tailed deer. Remaining on the road, instead of turning onto the trail, also offers good walking conditions and will offer plenty of opportunity for studying the Wakulla Unit's woodlands.

The trail east of Wakulla Beach Road is a 3 mile jaunt that terminates at the refuge boundary, about 0.25 mile from the Wakulla River. (In reality, the trail continues on at this point but passes into private land. Only users of the Florida National Scenic Trail may hike beyond the fence line.) This portion of the trail supports some very interesting examples of mature hardwood forests and a variety of wildlife.

Wakulla Beach

Located at the end of Wakulla Beach Road (see above for directions).

Wakulla Beach is a good place to see saltmarsh, the Apalachee Bay, and some good examples of coastal hardwood hammock. Although used mostly by locals for swimming and saltwater recreation, referring to the area as a beach seems to stretch the definition of the word for many visitors.

For plant enthusiasts, the area adjacent to the beach provides a great place for studying saltmarsh flora. Large areas of saltwort, glasswort, and saltgrass meadows border expanses of needlerush marsh, and the narrow strip of beach supports a number of the coastal zone's woody shrubs. The delicate blue saltmarsh aster and yellow-flowered sea oxeye are both found here.

Wakulla Beach is also known as a good birding location. The mud flats that are exposed at low tide are often covered with large numbers of shorebirds and long-legged waders, the surrounding marshes harbor sharp-tailed, seaside, and swamp sparrows, and the live oak woodlands attract an assortment of passarines during migration. Woodcocks are also a regular occurrence at dawn along the roadway.

PANACEA UNIT

Facilities and Activities

Hiking, birdwatching, canoeing, freshwater fishing, botanizing, wildlife observation.

Otter Lake

Turn west on CR 372A from US 98 in Panacea. Otter Lake is at the end of the road.

Otter Lake is a 136-acre lake that receives the bulk of its water from tiny Otter Creek. A boat launch and parking lot is located on the east side of the lake and offers easy access. The lake supports a large congregation of cormorants that use it as a roost site. Wood stork have also roosted here historically, but their numbers have dwindled so dramatically in recent years that

refuge biologists say that the lake is no longer considered to have
a roosting population. Large numbers of ospreys also nest in the
taller trees surrounding the lake; their scraggly nests are easy to
spot and are evident year-round. The lake's swampy edges support a diverse collection of songbirds including a variety of warblers, vireos, and kinglets during spring migration.

Walking Trails

*Park at the sandy crossroad that intersects CR 372A about 0.2 mile
inside the refuge boundary. Two trails begin here. The Otter Lake
Loop is a 9-mile walk marked in blue; the Piney Ridge Loop is 5
miles long and marked in yellow.*

These trails circle through the Panacea Unit, cross Otter
Creek and Levy Ditch, and pass through or adjacent to a variety
of habitats including hardwood hammocks, pine uplands, and
wetland woods. Levy Ditch, which was originally constructed in
the 1800s to aid farmers in controlling and diverting surface
runoff, leads to a refuge-maintained green tree reservoir. This
designation refers to an area that is inundated with water
during part of the year but dry the remainder of the year. Today
the area around the ditch is a rich woodland with a generous
acorn crop and is managed by refuge biologists as a wood duck
nesting area.

The Panacea Unit is a good area for birdwatchers. The low
oaks and proximity to water provide good habitat and attract a
number of songbirds, including spring migrants. The area
around the lake is good for wood ducks, though the latter are
secretive and may be difficult to see.

Thoms Island

*Most easily accessed by canoe from the narrow beach adjacent to
the swimming area at Ochlockonee River State Park (see p. 145).
Paddling right (south) from the swimming area, then left (east)
into Dead River takes you along the island's northern border.*

Thoms Island has been a nationally designated wilderness
area since 1975. It is largely a marshy island that is surrounded
by a combination of the Sopchoppy, Ochlockonee, and Dead
Rivers. The island's western tip, which is the only high and dry

section, can be reached from the state park in less than 20 minutes of paddling. The western end is bordered on the northern edge by a bluff that leads to a nice woodland where gopher tortoise burrows dot the ground. The eastern end is low, marshy, and crisscrossed by several twisting streams that allow access to the island's interior. The muddy banks and marshy shallows along these streams support an assortment of wildlife including marsh wrens, soras, otters, raccoons, and a large number of wading birds. One of the best of these streams turns into the island off the Ochlockonee a little more than 0.5 mile below its intersection with the Dead River. This creek traverses most of the island's eastern end before emptying into the Sopchoppy River just below its confluence with the Dead River's eastern terminus. It is probably best to use a topographic map or aerial photograph to find your way through this channel.

Pets

Allowed, but must be on leash at all times. It should be noted that alligators have occasionally attacked pets that ventured too close to the edges of the pools.

Best Time of Year

Fall, winter, and spring are best for birding and hiking. Summer activities are more restricted due to heat and insects. However, opportunities for observing alligators are abundant during summer, and canoeing along the coastline is also enjoyable.

ST. VINCENT ISLAND NATIONAL WILDLIFE REFUGE

St. Vincent Island lies along the westernmost boundary of Apalachicola Bay. Teardrop in shape, it is nearly 9 miles long, 4 miles wide, and encompasses 12,358 acres. It has been wholly owned by the U. S. government since its 1968 entry into the National

Wildlife Refuge System, but once served as a privately owned hunting and wild game preserve for nonnative animals. Stories allege that zebras, elands, and several other exotic species once roamed freely on the island. A small but well-established sambar deer population, a large deer imported from India, is about all that is left of this experiment.

St. Vincent is a late Holocene barrier island that began developing about 6,500 years ago. It is part of a unique collection of offshore beach formations that line the Florida Gulf coast from about Port St. Joe to Carrabelle. The island is a favored study area for coastal sedimentologists and geologists because of its well-preserved topographic features. Twelve sets of successive dune lines, which include about 180 individual ridges, traverse the island from east to west, effectively charting the island's formation and development. Many of these ancient ridges are easily discernible along the island's several sandy roadways. Walking from north to south leads hikers over one ridge after another and progresses from the island's oldest to its youngest sediments.

St. Vincent also supports a surprising array of habitats for so small an island. As might be expected, estuarine and Gulf coast beaches line the island's northern and southern edges, but the interior contains dense wetland tangles, freshwater lakes, coastal hardwood hammocks, sand scrub, open pinelands, and freshwater marshes. A large number of plants and animals are represented in these communities; exploring them completely can take years.

Location, Mailing Address and Phone

The headquarters and visitor's center is located in Apalachicola. Access to St. Vincent Island is by boat only. The shortest and most direct route is across Indian Pass which separates the island from Indian Peninsula. Indian Pass may be reached by traveling SR 30 from US 98 and then east on SR 30B. The Indian Pass area is complete with a boat landing that is less than 0.25 mile from the narrow end of the island. The refuge is open to the public only during daylight hours.

Refuge Manager, St. Vincent National Wildlife Refuge, PO Box 447, Apalachicola, FL 32329; (904) 653-8808.

Facilities and Activities

Wildlife observation, hiking, shelling, birding, swimming, sea kayaking, visitor center.

A visitor center and exhibit area is located in the quaint coastal village of Apalachicola. It is worth stopping here for information and to learn about the island.

Although St. Vincent contains numerous roads and U. S. Fish and Wildlife Service personnel regularly transport government vehicles to the island, there are no public ferries and no privately owned vehicles are allowed. It is sometimes possible to arrange delivery to the island with local fishing guides, but this cannot be guaranteed.

There are no visitor facilities on the island and no access to fresh water. Due to the drying effects of the salty air, open sun, and rugged conditions, visitors should bring plenty of water—about one gallon per person for day-long excursions.

The best way to reach the island is by motorboat across Indian Pass. Sea kayakers should have little difficulty paddling to the island, and even canoeists have occasionally made the relatively short trip. However, paddlers should be cautioned that Indian Pass is subject to strong, and potentially dangerous, currents during tide change. These currents can become a formidable obstacle for canoeists and kayakers, and can even sweep them out to sea. Paddling should be avoided on incoming or outgoing tides and should be restricted to days with good weather and quiet winds.

Although it is permissible to land a boat at any point along the island's perimeter, it is usually advisable to land motorboats on the bay side to insure protection from the breaking waves and higher winds of the Gulf. There is a docking facility, but it is restricted to official use only. Kayakers and canoeists should bring gear for chaining and locking their crafts to a tree.

An extensive system of sandy service roads crisscrosses St.

Vincent Island and provides over 80 miles of hiking trails from which you can see most of the refuge. A map of these roadways is available from the headquarters and visitor's center.

The east end of the island contains a number of freshwater lakes open for use seasonally that are favored fishing spots as well as good locations for seeing wildlife. Most of the lakes are accessible from Apalachicola Bay or St. Vincent Sound but require a boat; only electric motors are permitted in the lakes. Hikers may make the 6 to 9 mile walk (depending on destination) to the lakes but must be sure to allow time to return before sundown.

St. Vincent is excellent for wildlife. A variety of mammals, reptiles, and birds live on or visit the island at varying times during the year. White-tailed deer are common throughout the interior of the island, and a large variety of gulls, terns, and shorebirds are found along the coast. Migrating songbirds and shorebirds visit the island during both spring and fall, and ospreys nest near the freshwater lakes on the island's eastern end. The western tip of the island is sometimes covered with shorebirds including a variety of sandpipers as well as black skimmers and least terns. Snakes are also abundant on the island, including a large population of cottonmouths and pygmy rattlers. Endangered and threatened species, or species of special concern found on the island include the bald eagle, indigo snake, wood stork, peregrine falcon, and gopher tortoise.

The island is also a nesting site for the threatened loggerhead sea turtle. The huge, square-headed females of the species, which climb up on the beach in summer under cover of darkness to lay their eggs in a shallow nest, are more likely to be seen than the males, but the secretive nature of these creatures makes sightings of either sex extremely rare.

The most obvious and dominant beach animal is the ghost crab, a pale-colored crab of the upper beach. It is chiefly a scavenger that feeds on the remains of decaying animals but is also known as a fierce predator with claws strong enough to crush small crustaceans. It is typically nocturnal but is also likely to be seen in the daytime.

Ghost crabs live in burrows under the sand. The exits to these burrows are often about 1 inch in diameter and are quite easy to recognize. Although ghost crabs are primarily terrestrial creatures, they still must return to the water periodically to wet their gills and are often seen scampering across the sand.

The Puerto Rican mole crab is another of St. Vincent's interesting beach animals. At first this small crab looks more like a large insect than a crustacean. It is oblong to oval in shape and has two feathery antennae. It is found in the swash of breaking waves where it buries itself under the sand, leaving only its antennae exposed to filter out particles of food.

Most of west Florida's beaches are so overrun with people that shell hunting is futile. This is not the case at St. Vincent. The wide beaches here are difficult to access and seldom visited, making the Gulf side of the island a shell-hunter's paradise. Probably the best time to look for shells is in the winter after fall storms have churned up the seas, though most any time of year is good. The most common snail shells found include scotch bonnets, lettered olives, lightning whelks, and apple murex. Bivalve shells include the giant Atlantic cockle, angel wing, channeled duck, and several of the tellins.

For history buffs, the bay side of the island has well-preserved kitchen middens. Early Florida Indians used the island as a hunting and fishing site during certain parts of the year and left huge mounds of oyster shells behind as evidence of their labor. Pottery shards literally litter the beach near these middens and

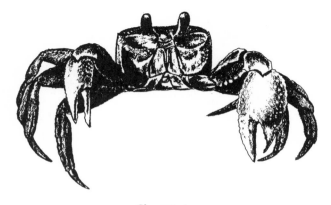

Ghost Crab

are interesting links to the panhandle's more primitive and pristine days. Searching for or removing artifacts is illegal.

Best Time of Year

Cold winter days are best for walking the trails but offer fewer hours of daylight. Birding is best in spring, summer, and fall. Shelling and wildlife observation are good year-round.

Pets

Not allowed.

VI
NATURAL AREAS:
STATE LANDS

BIG LAGOON STATE RECREATION AREA

It's not difficult to understand how this park got its name. Its entire southern face is bordered by a huge lagoon that is separated from the open waters of the Gulf of Mexico by the narrow strip of sandy land that makes up Perdido Key. The park is not large—less than 700 acres—but it offers a good opportunity to explore several of the panhandle's coastal habitats. There are a number of easy-to-access areas of coastal scrub along the main park road, and the portion of the park that lies north of the campground, though it has no trails, contains a particularly good example of sand pine woodlands.

Location, Mailing Address, and Phone

Off SR 292A southwest of Pensacola and the Pensacola Naval Air Station.

Big Lagoon State Recreation Area, 12301 Gulf Beach Highway, Pensacola, FL 32507; (904) 492-1595.

Facilities and Activities

Camping, picnicking, nature trails, swimming, birding, boating (including a boat ramp with dock on the Intracoastal Waterway), fishing.

View from the observation deck

Camping

The campground offers more than 75 campsites in several loops in the center of the park. There are electrical hookups as well as a dump station. Some sites are separated by natural hedges or thickets; others are more open. A few are grassy; most are sandy. A boardwalk connects the campground to a beach area on the Intracoastal Waterway.

Nature Trails

Almost all of the three nature trails in this park are located atop boardwalks to protect the fragile vegetation. All pass through similar habitat that includes such plants as myrtle oak, sand live oak, yaupon holly, gallberry, beach elder, and lowbush blueberry, as well as large populations of both the minty and Florida rosemaries. A few interpretive signs along the trails help visitors understand both the natural and cultural significance of the region.

Two trails allow exploration of the Big Lagoon side of the main park road. The yaupon trail begins at the Governor's Pavilion and passes through typical open coastal woods before reaching the shore of Big Lagoon and circling back to its beginning. Near the end of the main park road another circular trail leaves the parking lot along an elevated boardwalk. This trail crosses the entrance to Grand Lagoon twice on footbridges and includes a well-constructed tower. The tower offers a nice vista of the Gulf of Mexico across the Perdido Key section of Gulf Islands National Seashore, as well as an impressive view of the lagoon and park. Both of these trails also include several covered picnic shelters.

The Grand Lagoon trail leaves the north side of the main park road adjacent to the parking lot for the amphitheater. It follows footpaths and boardwalks to the edge of Grand Lagoon in one direction and along the edges of Long Pond in the other. Both directions offer covered platforms that provide unobstructed views of Grand Lagoon. The Long Pond portion of the trail also leads back to the campground. Due to their proximity to both fresh and brackish water as well as sandy ridges, the boardwalks that make up the Grand Lagoon/Long Pond trails traverse a greater diversity of plant communities than do the other two trails.

Birding

The park boasts an extensive bird list that includes a number of spring and fall migrants. More than 20 warbler species have been recorded in the park as well as a large number of shorebirds, gulls, and terns. Since this area is well protected, it is often used by migrants as a final resting place before heading south in the fall, or as a landing spot on the return trip in spring.

Best Time of Year

Fall, winter, and spring for birding and walking the trails; summer for swimming, boating, and fishing; spring, summer, and fall offer a wide variety of colorful wildflowers.

Pets

A leash is required where pets are allowed; pets are not allowed in the campground or on the beaches.

BLACKWATER RIVER STATE FOREST

The near-surface geology of the western panhandle is unlike that of any other location in the state. Rolling hills of deep quartz sands dominate the landscape and contribute to a scene that is both reminiscent of and cryptically different from similar regions in other parts of Florida.

One of the most subtle differences is the lack of limestone at or near ground level. Unlike most of Florida, the top of the limestone in the western panhandle is covered by over 1,000 feet of coarse, gravelly sands, the topmost layer of which is the ground-up rubble left behind by a series of Pleistocene glaciers. Though the surface sands are obvious landmarks that signal one's entry into Walton, Okaloosa, and Escambia Counties, the subsurface sediments and deeply buried limestone are hidden from view and known only to the geologists and naturalists who have carefully studied the area.

More obvious differences between western Florida and other parts of the state include the area's extremely soft water, a result of the unmineralized sands through which it flows, and the handful of plants that exist at or near the eastern edges of their generally more western or northern ranges. The large leaves of the dog banana, striking red flowers of scarlet basil, tall straight trunks of Atlantic white cedar, strong-scented leaves and stems of minty rosemary, and relatively limited range of the Arkansas oak are testimony to the singular nature of the region.

The Blackwater State Forest lies in the center of this fascinating terrain. Composed of 183,670 acres and divided into seven subunits, the Blackwater is Florida's largest state forest and one that is particularly conducive to nature study and outdoor recreation. The area within the forest was originally purchased by the federal government in the 1930s, then leased to the state for management purposes in 1938. It was finally transferred to state ownership in the mid-1950s. Due to this longtime public ownership, much of the forest's natural resource base reflects little disturbance, and there are many places that have emerged relatively unscathed from the 20th century's preoccupation with rampant and unbridled development.

Pitcher Plant

Several examples help make this point. The Blackwater River and Juniper Creek are considered Outstanding Florida Waters and constitute two of the state's most pristine natural water supplies. Several thousand acres of the forest's longleaf pine–wiregrass woodlands are contiguous with and part of the world's largest remaining expanse of this critically endangered ecosystem. And the soggy pitcher plant, herb, and frog bogs that dot the region contain a generous variety of threatened or endangered native species and are among the finest such places to be found anywhere in the southeastern United States.

Location, Mailing Address and Phone

West of Crestview; SR 4, SR 191, and SR 189 are the major highways that access this forest.

Blackwater Forestry Center, 11650 Munson Highway, Milton, FL 32570; (904) 957-4201.

Facilities and Activities

Blackwater Forestry Center, camping, hiking, canoeing, horseback riding, swimming, birding, botanizing, wildlife observation, picnicking, fishing.

Blackwater Forestry Center

On SR 191, less than 0.5 mi. south of SR 4.

This should be your first stop (weekdays only). It is the headquarters of the Blackwater State Forest and is a good place to pick up maps and other written information. The rangers here are also helpful and are often available to answer questions. On weekends there are usually rangers available at Krul Recreation Area.

Camping

Ten general purpose campgrounds are scattered across the Blackwater State Forest, only five of which have developed facilities. Together, the ten contain 175 campsites, nearly one-half of which have electrical hookups.

Krul Recreation Area

On SR 4, just west of its intersection with SR 191.

Krul Recreation Area is one of the oldest and most used of the Blackwater's campground and day-use areas. It was built by the WPA in the 1930s and is the only day-use area on the forest that charges a usage fee. There is a small, six-acre lake with a designated swimming area and paddleboat concession, and an old grist mill to whet the appetites of history buffs. Summer weekends are particularly crowded at Krul due mostly to the swimming area. However, during mid-week in the fall and winter the place can be deserted; the latter is an outstanding time of year to use Krul as a base camp from which to explore the area.

The 66-unit camping area is situated atop a hill overlooking the lake and amid an open forest of black tupelo and several species of upland oaks. Most sites offer electricity, and there are restrooms, tables, and a scenic walking trail along and over Sweetwater Creek that connects Krul with Bear Lake.

Bear Lake

North of SR 4, just east of Krul Recreation Area.

Bear Lake has 40 improved campsites, only six of which have electricity. A dock and boat ramp provide access to the lake for

1. The low-growing, carnivorous purple pitcher plant is one of the panhandle's more common pitcher plants.

2. Typical pine flatwoods, though seemingly clothed exclusively with pines and palmetto, often harbor as many as 200 different herbaceous plants.

3. Early morning is an excellent time to paddle one of west Florida's numerous cypress-ringed ponds, like this one at Lake Talquin State Forest.

4. Marshes, palm trees, and slash pine characterize the open spaces at Hickory Mound Impoundment.

5. The showy flowers of the insectivorous thread dew are lesser known but much more eye catching than the plant's sticky, cylindrical leaves.

6. The Alum Bluff area of The Nature Conservancy's Apalachicola Bluffs and Ravines Preserve is one of the state's most important botanical and geological treasures.

7. Oystercatchers, which nest along the Big Bend coast, use their long, sturdy bill to pry open oysters, hence their common name.

8. The showy purple flowers of low-growing drum-heads add a touch of ground color to west Florida's bogs, savannas, and wet pinelands.

9. The restless, shifting sands of barrier islands can rapidly undo the work of humans; this mostly covered boardwalk at St. George Island State Park is a good example.

10. Sea oats can grow to great depth as they help bind beach sands to stabilize dunes and reduce erosion.

11. An overnight stay in the wilderness preserve at St. Joseph Peninsula State Park usually ends with a beautiful sunrise over St. Joe Bay.

12. The rose-colored flowers held on slender stems make the somewhat infrequent Barbara's buttons an exciting find.

13. A group of amateur naturalists enjoys lunch on a natural limestone ledge along the upper reaches of the Apalachicola River at Torreya State Park.

14. The long-legged waders, like this great blue heron at St. Marks National Wildlife Refuge, are some of Florida's most magnificent and easy to learn bird species.

15. West Florida's wet pine savannas and herb bogs, like this one along Highway 65 in the Apalachicola National Forest, support an amazing variety of herbaceous plants including a wide number of asters, grasses, sedges, and insectivorous species.

16. It's not difficult to see why insects might be attracted to the gaping mouth of the blue butterwort.

17. Several active heron rookeries are located along the Big Bend coast, like this one just west of the St. Marks National Wildlife Refuge.

18. The golden-club, a frequently seen aquatic, recognizable by its showy flower stalks, is one of the panhandle's most beautiful wetland plants.

19. White pelicans frequent several locations across northwest Florida during winter and spring.

20. The tannin-stained waters of the Aucilla River are typical of many northwest Florida streams.

21. This limestone-lined sink is typical of the Aucilla River's lower reaches.

22. The cypress-studded edges of Kennedy Creek.

canoeing and fishing. Swimming is not allowed here, but the 107-acre lake offers some of the best freshwater fishing in northwest Florida. There is a dining hall and pavilion as well as an interesting nature trail that connects Bear Lake to Krul Recreation Area.

Hurricane Lake

In the northeastern part of the forest off numbered Forest Roads 30, 24, and 31.

Hurricane Lake is a 354-acre artificial impoundment that was opened for fishing in 1973. Though not considered primitive, the campgrounds located on both the north and south sides of the lake are not as developed as those at Krul and Bear Lake. Running water, flush toilets, picnicking, and a boat landing are among the facilities. Fishing is one of the lake's major attractions.

Karick Lake

On numbered Forest Roads 38 and 42, east of SR 189.

This 58-acre lake is primarily a fishing lake. Two campgrounds, one each on the north and south sides of the lake, offer running water, flush toilets, a dump station, picnic area, and boat landing.

Coldwater Recreation Area

Located at the terminus of Forest Road 1, four miles south of SR 4, and west of the East Coldwater Creek bridge.

This area is provided primarily for horseback-riding enthusiasts. There is a dining hall, pavilion, 65 campsites with water and electricity, enough stables for 72 horses, and enough kennels for 124 dogs. There are many miles of scenic horse trails here, and the waters of Coldwater Creek provide outstanding opportunities for swimming and canoeing.

Other Sites

Juniper Bridge, Kennedy Bridge, Red Rock Picnic Area, Bryant Bridge, and Camp Lowry are primitive campgrounds scattered

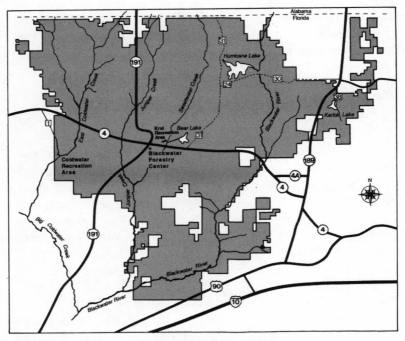

Blackwater River State Forest

throughout the forest. None have running water, flush toilets, or electrical hookups.

Hiking

There are many walking opportunities within this forest. Two developed trails and a large number of two-lane woods roads provide many miles of enjoyable hiking.

The 21.5-mile Jackson Red Ground Trail is the longest footpath in the forest and also one of the best known. Its eastern terminus is at the southeastern corner of Karick Lake, and its western terminus is at the Red Rock Picnic Area on Juniper Creek. The trail follows the historical trading route charted and cleared by the armies of Andrew Jackson, one of the state's earliest and perhaps most ruthless governors.

118

The Jackson Trail passes through all of the forest's major cover types. Blueberries and shrubby oaks line the trail along some parts of its route, pines along other parts, and cypress in the wetter areas. A wide variety of wildflowers bloom during spring, summer, and fall and add a variety of color to the ground cover. Two shelters, each about 6 miles apart, are available for overnight campers. Water is available only at the two end points and at Krul Recreation Area, the latter of which requires traversing the Sweetwater Trail described below. Campfires are permitted only at Karick Lake, Red Rock Picnic Area, and the two shelters.

The 4.5-mile Sweetwater Trail is more of a lengthy nature walk than a hiking trail and may be accessed at Krul Recreation Area, Bear Lake Recreation Area, or off the Jackson Trail just north of its intersection with SR 4. At Krul the trail leads off the eastern end of the campground, then crosses Sweetwater Creek on a suspension bridge before continuing to Bear Lake. Just beyond the bridge the path crosses an old woods road and enters one of the trail's more interesting areas. A seepage slope with a variety of bog plants dominates this area and can be beautiful in spring and fall. The large, dark brown heads of rayless sunflowers are particularly evident here in mid-fall.

There is also a particularly nice trail around Bear Lake. This 4-mile trail winds its way through several native communities including longleaf pine–wiregrass uplands, Atlantic white cedar wetlands, and pitcher plant bogs, and even crosses over a beaver pond. The Bear Lake Trail is directly accessible from the Sweetwater Trail.

Canoeing

Blackwater State Forest offers many canoeing opportunities with outstanding scenery. The several lakes that dot the area more than meet the needs of stillwater paddlers, and the area's several rivers offer unsurpassed beauty for those who like to feel the tug of gently tumbling currents.

The Blackwater River is, by far, the most paddled of the forest's waterways. The headwaters of this magnificent stream lie in the Conecuh National Forest in southern Alabama, but the river is hardly navigable before it dumps over the state line into Florida. The Blackwater has been protected from run-off and pollution since at least the 1930s and is one of the cleanest rivers in the state. Only a few acres of its upriver banks are privately owned; over 95 percent of its course above I-10 passes through publicly owned lands that are managed, in part, to insure the river's integrity.

The Blackwater's name is somewhat misleading. Though it is darker than many of its tributaries, it certainly does not exhibit the rich black color associated with many of Florida's tannin-stained waterways. Along much of its route the river is almost clear, leaving its white sand bottoms visible even to a depth of several feet.

Large sandbars are evident along many of the Blackwater's bends. These make excellent campsites as well as temporary respites. Many of these locations are overshadowed by the tall, straight boles of Atlantic white cedar, an uncommon tree in Florida that enjoys a rather disjunctive distribution in the state. Many people confuse this stately plant with the red cedar, though the two are easily distinguished by their cones, the shape of their branchlets in cross-section, and the manner in which their branchlets are disposed from their supporting branches. The reddish brown bark that often spirals around the trunk is also a good field mark on the large specimens that line the Blackwater.

There are a number of canoe access points to the Blackwater River. The crossings at Kennedy Bridge, Florida 4, Bryant Bridge, and Blackwater State Park are the better put-in spots.

Coldwater and Juniper Creeks are tributaries of the Blackwater; Sweetwater Creek is a tributary of Juniper. All three are relatively shallow, clear, fast-flowing streams that pass over sandy bottoms and adjacent to sugar-white sandbars. In many respects they are much like the Blackwater, though generally smaller, faster, and more likely to have logjams and obstructions.

It is best to begin a paddling adventure on Coldwater Creek no father north than SR 4. It is nearly 20 miles from SR 4 to SR 191, but there are at least two landings between these two locations. Only the bridge on SR 4 and at Coldwater Creek Recreation Area are within the state forest.

Juniper Bridge on SR 191 just south of SR 4 is a good put-in point for Juniper Creek. It is about 5 miles from here to the Red Rock Picnic Area, and another 6 miles to the terminus at Forest Road 86. Many people combine their trip on Juniper Creek with one on Sweetwater Creek. It is possible to access the Sweetwater near the bridge on Forest Road 121, just south of the intersection of SR 4 and SR 191. The confluence of the two creeks is about 2 miles south of this launch site. For those who want a more challenging and more pristine experience, it is possible to put into Sweetwater Creek at SR 4. The river is little used for the 2 miles before it reaches Forest Road 121 (the normal landing), and its canopied corridor engenders a sense of wilderness for nearly the entire route. However, on low water there can be many obstructions along this section which can require a number of pull-overs or short portages.

Botanizing

At least five plant assemblages inhabit various portions of this state forest: longleaf pine–turkey oak uplands, slash pine lowlands, hardwood swamps, Atlantic white cedar wetlands, and wet savannas. All provide good opportunities for studying the area's native plants.

A number of trees and shrubs inhabit these typical communities. The more common include black titi, sweetbay, yellow poplar, several species of ash, red maple, sand post oak, black tupelo, American holly, fetterbush, American beautyberry, and southern magnolia. Several wild azaleas, including the Florida flame azalea, are also found here, as are the Florida anise and mountain laurel. The latter two plants typically bloom in early spring; the azaleas bloom from spring through summer, depending upon the species. A variety of herbs also inhabit the region, including green eyes, blue curls, partridge berry, bachelor's buttons, liatris, lobelia, angelica, verbena, showy crotolaria, rayless sunflower, agalinis, bandana daisy, and cypress vine. Rare, endangered, or threatened plants include the white-topped pitcher plant and panhandle lily. Two good pitcher plant savannas are found along Forest Road 64 (the Spanish Trail), less than 1 mile west of its intersection with SR 191. Needless to say, a good shrub, tree, and wildflower guide is a necessity when visiting this forest.

Wildlife Observation

A variety of wildlife is also found in this forest. The more common and likely to be seen animals include white-tailed deer, opossum, raccoon, cottontail rabbit, skunk, wild turkey, and both the red and gray foxes. There is also a sizable population of red-cockaded woodpeckers; much of the forest is managed to insure the success of this federally endangered species. Other, more rarely seen endangered or threatened species include the gopher tortoise, gopher frog, tiger salamander, pine barrens tree frog, American bald eagle, Florida black bear, and Florida sandhill crane.

Summer birding can be outstanding here. Mississippi kite, wood thrush, chuck-will's-widow, blue grosbeak, indigo bunting, prothonotary warbler, Louisiana waterthrush, yellow-breasted chat, brown-headed nuthatch, Bachman's sparrow, red-cockaded woodpecker, and the elusive Swainson's warbler all nest here. The road to Karick Lake is a good place to look for the Bachman's sparrow; an easily accessible red-cockaded woodpecker colony is located on Forest Road 13 less than 1 mile south of its intersection with Forest Road 64 (also known as Spanish Trail). Look for the white-banded trees that mark the colony.

Best Time of Year

There is something of interest year-round here.

Pets

Generally allowed. Must be on a 6-foot leash at designated recreation areas; not allowed at the Krul, Bear Lake, or Bone Creek recreation areas, at Camp Pauquette, or at the training center.

BLACKWATER RIVER STATE PARK

In most ways, the 590-acre Blackwater River State Park is an extension of the Blackwater River State Forest (see p. 114). The sandy uplands, gently rolling terrain, characteristic plant communities, and resplendent river seem to dissolve the boundaries between these two outstanding west Florida landmarks. When paddling the lively currents that thread their way between the Blackwater River's charming banks, it is difficult to tell where one of these installations ends and the other begins.

Location, Mailing Address and Phone

Located off US 90 in the western panhandle, about halfway between Milton and Crestview.

Blackwater River State Park, 7720 Deaton Bridge Rd., Holt, FL 32564; (904) 623-2363.

Facilities and Activities

Camping, picnicking, canoeing, nature trails, birding, botanizing, fishing, boating.

The Blackwater River is the park's major attraction. Whether interested in canoeing, swimming, fishing, boating, or just walking quietly along one of the two riverside nature trails, most people who come here do so for the water.

The Blackwater is an outstanding and well-used canoe trail (see the description in the section on Blackwater River State Forest, p. 119), and the state park provides an often-used terminus for those who begin their paddling excursions farther upstream. However, it is possible to launch a canoe at the park, paddle upstream until the current tires you, then just drift back down to the starting point. Canoe access is from the parking lot on the northwest side of the bridge.

There are also two designated hiking trails at this park; each follows along the river for at least part of its course. The shorter trail leads away from the southern edge of the westernmost campground loop, then drops almost immediately to the river. A boardwalk takes you across the edge of a cypress backwater, then to a large sandbar on the river's edge. Campers use the trail primarily to access one of the river's many swimming sites, but the footpath continues upriver, sometimes behind a natural levee, before encircling a small lake and returning to the starting point. The other trail leads off the eastern side of the paved highway just south of the bridge (a parking lot for this trail is available on the west side of the highway). This trail is much longer than the first and forms a complete circle without the need to retrace steps. Part of the trail passes along the river; another part leads through both low-lying and upland areas. For skillful observers, white-tailed deer, bobcat, wild turkey, and the playful river otter can be seen along parts of these trails.

Amateur botanists will enjoy identifying the range of plants that are found here. Common persimmon, sweetgum, dogwood, red maple, sycamore, magnolia, and several species of holly are the most common tree species; shrubs include several species of blueberries as well as wax myrtle, saw palmetto, gallberry, and three kinds of wild azaleas. Even the river supports an assortment of vegetation. Look for the papery-thin leaves and yellowish, tightly closed, rounded flowers of spatterdock, or the beautiful white flowers and shieldlike leaves of white water lily. Both are common in the quieter waters of the river's edges, sloughs, and oxbows.

Camping is available in the 30-site campground located on the north side of the river. All sites have electric hookups, and there is a restroom and shower facility central to most sites. The picnic area is located near the river, off a large parking lot at the terminus to the park's entrance road.

Best Time of Year

Spring, summer, and fall are the busiest times. Weekdays and winter weekends are usually less crowded and are excellent times to paddle and explore.

Pets

Allowed on a 6-foot leash; not allowed in swimming areas, campground, or tied to structures, plants, or trees.

FALLING WATERS STATE RECREATION AREA

There is something highly suspicious about the idea of a water-fall in Florida. How can a state known for its beaches, surf, and exceedingly flat terrain ever be suspected of including anything that even approaches a bona fide waterfall?

Falling Waters State Recreation Area is a classic example of inland Florida's unique topography. Located in the state's Western Highlands geologic province (see p. 17), this relatively small, 155-acre park is situated atop one of several remnant hills that once constituted a ridgelike connection across the pan-handle's northern reaches.

The waterfall from which the park takes its name, the only such feature in the state, is a 67-foot cascade that drops precipi-tously into a cylindrical, 20-foot-wide, 100-foot-deep limestone cavern known as Falling Waters Sink. During rainy seasons the waters literally roar over the edge of the fall. It is difficult to imagine that the small stream leading to the cavern's rim could create such an enchanting spectacle.

Location, Mailing Address and Phone
Three miles south of Chipley; take SR 77 south from I-10, then 77A east to the park.
Falling Waters State Recreation Area, Rt. 5, Box 660, Chipley, FL 32428; (904) 638-6130.

Facilities and Activities
Camping, nature trail, botanizing, swimming, picnicking.

Falling Waters is a peaceful, out-of-the-way, lightly visited park that preserves an outstanding natural endowment. In addi-tion to its namesake waterfall, the park also harbors a variety of indigenous plants and animals, an enchanting campground, a small swimming area, and plenty of opportunity for unhurried nature study.

Several trails traverse the park. The most popular by far is the system of boardwalks that circle through the sinkhole region at the end of the park's main road. The lush forest that lines the walkway offers a close-up look at the mesic woodlands that once

125

blanketed the northern regions of the panhandle. A number of the region's native plants are found here. An overlook platform below the rim of the waterfall allows visitors to look deep into the sink and stand at eye level to the rushing waters. Just up from the falls, another trail leads to the swimming area, then on to the campground. The sparse pinelands that lie in the central parts of the park offer the opportunity to roam freely in the open under-story and enjoy the fields of wildflowers that appear in spring and summer.

The swimming area is located on a small lake at the conflu-ence of several small spring runs. A grassy yard adjacent to the lake offers a relaxing respite and an enjoyable place to spend an afternoon.

The 24-site campground is located on a hill in a planted pine woodland and is connected by footpaths to both the swimming area and waterfall trail. All sites have electrical hookups, grills, and tables. Reservations are not accepted but are usually not needed.

Best Time of Year
Any time of year is good for camping, though the summer can be warm; spring, summer, and fall are best for botanizing; summer for swimming.

Pets
Allowed on a 6-foot leash; not allowed in the swimming area, campground, or in any structure.

FLORIDA CAVERNS STATE PARK

A rush of cool, damp air meets your face as the ranger opens the huge metal door at the bottom of the rustic stairwell. The sound of your footsteps echoes from unseen and mysterious channel-ways that stretch away into the darkness as the beam of the ranger's flashlight bounces off colorful limestone formations. Calling your attention to points of interest along the way, he recounts the history of your surroundings, explains the differences between stalactites and stalagmites, and teaches you the names for the columns, rimstones, sodastraws, and draperies that surround you. He carefully explains how these caverns, the very place you now stand, were once filled to excess with the rushing waters that created them.

The 1,284-acre Florida Caverns State Park preserves one of the Sunshine State's most interesting and unique natural resources. Its massive system of limestone-lined passageways constitutes one of the most extensive cave ecosystems in the entire southeastern coastal plain, and has long served as an inviting attraction for school-day field trips and family outings, as well as scientific investigations.

Topographically, these ancient treasures lie in the Marianna Lowlands topographic province (see p. 20), a region of karst terrain where the top of the underground limestone lies only a few feet from the surface of the land. Formed in prehistory when the sea level was much higher than it is today, the caverns were once part of a vast network of interdependent, water-filled cavities that acted much like underground rivers. As the water moved through these stream channels it dissolved and eroded the limestone, enlarging and enhancing the watercourses. As the sea eventually receded to its current level, what were formerly underground rivers lay perched above the water table as air-filled pockets. Since that time, surface erosion and leakage from above have continued to shape and reshape these passageways in a never-ending process of evolution and alteration. Today, the largest and most accessible of the cavities form one of the park's main attractions.

Location, Mailing Address and Phone
Three miles north of Marianna on SR 166.

Florida Caverns State Park, 3345 Caverns Road, Marianna, FL 32446; (904) 482-9598.

Facilities and Activities

Camping, hiking, birdwatching, fishing, wildlife observation, botanizing, picnicking.

Visitor Center

The park's visitor center is located adjacent to a circular parking lot at the end of one of the main park thoroughfares. The building is a rustic stone structure that was constructed during the 1930s by the Civilian Conservation Corps. Today it serves as a repository of information and is well worth visiting. Tours of the caverns begin here, and a small museum housed inside tells the caverns' story through a small but well-done collection of exhibits and dioramas. One of the park's main nature trails begins just outside the building's entrance.

The visitor center contains a comfortable sitting area inside as well as a large, open-air porch off the rear of the building. Both provide convenient resting places following a walk on the nature trails. The porch overlooks a vegetated slope that contains many of the park's more special plants. Throughout the spring and again in the fall this slope can be quite colorful and is a good place to search for low-growing herbaceous species. The room below the porch houses vending machines and restrooms.

Caverns

For those who want an inside look at the caverns, the park staff conducts regularly scheduled guided walks. Tours begin at the visitor center and cost $2 for children 3-12 and $4 for visitors 13 and up. This fee is in addition to the park entrance fee. Offered daily between the hours of 9:00 AM and 5:00 PM, a typical tour begins with a 15-minute video orientation followed by a 45-minute excursion into some of the most interesting and easily accessible of the cavities. The activity is well worth the price of admission.

Wildlife

It is not surprising that such a unique landform would support an equally unique collection of animal life. Through the years, the Florida Caverns have become well known for an interesting assortment of creatures, some of which are specially adapted for living in their darkened surroundings. The endangered gray bat, for example, makes its home in several of the caves in and around the park, as do its cousins, the eastern pipistrelle and southeastern bat. Although the pipistrelle and southeastern bat are two of the state's more common and widespread bat species, the tiny gray bat is known in Florida from only a few locations, all of which are near Marianna. In typical bat fashion, these interesting mammals attach themselves to the ceilings of their subsurface homes during the day, then come out at night to forage on the abundance of flying insects that share their airspace.

The exceedingly rare Georgia blind salamander and the difficult-to-find cave crayfish also live in some of the caverns' more remote sections. These pale white creatures have become so thoroughly adapted to their lightless ecosystem that they have completely lost the ability to see.

Most of us are not likely to see many of these critters on a normal visit to the park. Their fragile habitats are more abundant only in the less accessible and more undisturbed caves, and are well protected from the interference of human intrusion. However, we can be content to know of their existence and of the key role the park plays in their preservation.

Birding is also good here. More than 110 species have been identified in the park, including all of the southeastern United State's thrushes, three species of owls, five species of hawks and kites, and more than 20 species of warblers. Spring and fall are probably the best times for birding due to the large number of species that frequent the park only during migration.

Plants

For many, the landscape surrounding the caverns holds as much attraction as the narrow crevices and passageways that lie within them. Plant enthusiasts, in particular, are drawn to the park for its plethora of rare and unusual species. The list of professional botanists who have visited its woodlands through the years reads like a litany of great names in science; pioneers such as Frank Chapman, Roland Harper, and J. K. Small all have found occasion to make exploratory sojourns to the region.

But it doesn't take a professional botanist to sense that there is something interestingly different about this place. Even novice plant lovers will immediately recognize the park's singular floristic composition. Wildflowers more often thought of as northern specialties bloom in juxtaposition to those of more southern charm. Bloodroot, Indian pink, wild columbine, rue anenome, wood nettle, and atamasco lily intermix in a lush and enchanting ground cover, forming a veritable carpet for a hard-wood forest dominated by the magnificent boles of hickories, southern magnolia, white oak, and American beech. There is no plant list for the park, but several of the rangers know about some of the more special plants and can direct you to the locations where you might find them.

Nature Trails
Exploring the park's woodlands is a relatively simple proposition. The well-kept and easily followed system of nature trails covers a large portion of the rock-studded terrain and passes through each of the park's characteristic habitats. Beginning at the visitor center allows you to traverse a beautiful beech/magnolia forest as well as walk along the upland edges of the Chipola River's rich floodplain and soggy bottomlands. One stretch of the footpath even allows walkers to pass through a natural, above-ground tunnel that offers the opportunity for a close-up study of its pock-marked, limestone ceiling. Other parts of the trail pass through regions dominated by ironwood, eastern hophornbeam, and Carolina silverbell. In many places wild columbine dominates the ground cover with an admixture of trillium and blood root.

In addition to the designated walking trails there are also horse trails and a number of gated park roads that provide good walking. Almost any of the roads between the entrance and the swimming area offer easy and fascinating day hikes. In dry weather it is possible to park adjacent to the point at which the Chipola River disappears under a natural bridge, then walk downstream along an old canal to where the river resurfaces. The woods along the canal and river are rich in diversity. The canal is the remains of a ditch cut through the natural bridge in the early 1900s to allow logs to be floated downstream.

Camping
In addition to the foregoing attractions, the park also supports an excellent campground. There are more than 40 campsites sit-

uated in an attractive wooded area. Restrooms with showers are available. The popularity of this park makes the campgrounds fill up quickly.

Picnicking and Swimming
There are several picnicking facilities and a developed, spring-fed, freshwater swimming area. Most picnic areas have at least one covered pavilion that is large enough to support a group.

Canoeing
The Chipola River passes through the park but goes underground at a natural bridge along one of the park's main roads. It is possible to put a canoe in here and paddle upstream for some distance. The Chipola's waters are generally clear, except following periods of heavy rainfall, and provide pleasant paddling.

Best Time of Year

Late winter and spring are best for seeing birds and flowering plants. Walking the trails and visiting the caverns are enjoyable activities any time of year.

Pets

Must be maintained on a 6-foot leash where allowed; not allowed in the campground, visitor center, swimming area, or inside any structure.

GRAYTON BEACH STATE RECREATION AREA

Tiny Grayton Beach State Recreation Area is an out-of-the-way park in an out-of-the-way corner of Florida. "It's not the kind of place visitors stumble onto by accident," says one longtime north Floridian who grew up near the area. "People who come here generally know exactly where they're going."

There may be less truth to this assessment than there once

was. In 1994 this little stretch of the panhandle coastline was selected by the director of the Laboratory for Coastal Research as the best beach in the United States. Those who have visited here would certainly agree with this accolade. The beaches are beautiful, the green Gulf waters enchanting, and the lifestyle extremely relaxed. There is no pollution, relatively few people, little development, and the shoreline looks much as it has for decades.

In addition to its aesthetic recognition, Grayton Beach also has an interesting geologic history and a topographic structure that is quite different from typical panhandle coastal landforms. Its sediments are older than most other west coast barriers and its freshwater supply has no visible outlet to the Gulf. Western Lake is blocked from ocean waters by what geologists call a bay-mouth bar, a sandbar that extends across the mouth of a brackish water sound. Such formations are often characterized by subsurface hydraulic action that actually provides an underground connection between the waters of the bay and sea. Though it appears to the casual observer that Western Lake is a land-locked freshwater pond, it is actually a brackish bay that trades water almost continuously with the open Gulf.

Though its base sediments may be older than many of its counterparts along the Gulf coast, the beach ridge that characterizes Grayton Beach is a relatively young and unstabilized landform. Many of the park's sand dunes are in rapid migration, as evidenced by the patches of partially covered vegetation that dot the landscape and by the inability of many typical dune plants to gain a toehold along their wind-rippled faces. A walk through the park gives visitors the sense that they are observing geologic history in the making—a rare opportunity in a science in which time is ordinarily measured in epochs and eons rather than in years and months.

Location, Mailing Address and Phone
SR 30-A, south of US 98, near Grayton Beach.

Grayton Beach State Recreation Area, 357 Main Park Rd., Santa Rosa Beach, FL 32459; (904) 231-4210.

Facilities and Activities

Swimming, bathhouse, camping, nature trail, boating, lakeside boat ramp.

Most people visit this park for swimming and sunbathing. The beaches are beautiful and ample facilities are available to entice beachgoers. There is a bathhouse, a boardwalk to the beach, and two picnic areas with tables for a lunchtime respite from the surf. There is also a small, 37-unit campground located in a sparse scrub area that provides overnight accommodations that include water and electricity.

In winter the shores at Grayton Beach can be almost deserted, providing an outstanding opportunity for birdwatchers to test their skill at identifying winter-plumaged shorebirds and gulls or for scanning the horizon for northern gannet as they dive head-first into offshore waters. Even for nonbirders, a winter walk on the beach can be enjoyable. There are usually more shells to investigate during this time of year, particularly after strong winter storms, and the water takes on an even more penetrating green.

For naturalists, the circuitous system of interlacing nature trails is a must. Near its beginning, the main trail follows behind the dune ridge and offers interesting lessons in naturally induced beach migration. There are places where only the crowns of pine, oak, and magnolia trees are visible atop the sands, evidence that the dunes are in a continuous state of flux. While it would appear that inundation by sand would result in the death of the plants that it covers, this doesn't seem to be the case. There are several instances along the Gulf coast where migrating beaches have buried, then unburied native vegetation as they moved past, leaving the plants apparently unharmed. The key to survival seems to be related to the length of time a particular individual stays covered. At Grayton Beach this time is often short.

At least some beach plants are well adjusted for this temporary inundation. The sea oat, for example, of which there are many representatives at Grayton Beach, generally has a deep stem that may reach several feet below the surface of the dune. As the dune continues to grow, this stems sends out vigorous, branching rhizomes at or just below ground level. These modified branches insure that the plant captures an adequate water supply from the porous sand while at the same time staying firmly planted in position. As dune growth continues, the sea oat branches again and again, each time sending out new rhizomes to hold the plant in place. As a result, an individual sea oat may reach to the very base of the dune that supports it and be held in place by an extensive labyrinth of rootlike structures.

Beyond the dunes the trail passes along the edge of Western Lake, then into a coastal pineland and an associated bay swamp. These woods can be outstanding for birdwatching during spring and fall migration, and the marshes along the lake are known for their resident population of seaside sparrows. A variety of warblers, vireos, woodpeckers, and other small songbirds frequent the area. A strong cold front in late spring can fill the trees with an assortment of brightly colored avians.

Best Time of Year
Summer is best for saltwater and beach activities; fall, winter, and spring are best for birds. Walking the nature trail is worthwhile during any part of the year.

Pets
Allowed on a 6-foot leash; not allowed on the beach, in the campground, or in the bathhouse.

HICKORY MOUND IMPOUNDMENT

In 1986 The Nature Conservancy brokered a deal that transferred approximately 60 miles of coastline and 65,000 acres of tidal saltmarsh and wet coastal hammock to public ownership. Dubbed the Big Bend Purchase because of its strategic location between the St. Marks National Wildlife Refuge and the protected mouth of the Suwannee River, the acquisition cost the Conservancy, and eventually the state of Florida, $20 million and was the largest purchase TNC had ever made east of the Mississippi River. It also provided valuable habitat for a variety of rare, endangered, or threatened animals including the manatee, Kemp's ridley sea turtle, green sea turtle, American bald eagle, reddish egret, and wood stork.

Hickory Mound Impoundment lies in the middle of this out- standing tract of land and provides one of the easiest access points for sampling the region's scenic beauty. Situated south of US 98 and east of the St. Marks National Wildlife Refuge, Hickory Mound is a 700-acre brackish marsh impoundment that has long been known as a haven for visiting waterfowl. It was severely damaged by Hurricane Kate in 1985 and suffered a major setback in its use as a wintering ground. It has since been revitalized by a cooperative effort which included funding from Ducks Unlimited and the Florida Game and Fresh Water Fish Commission, and in-kind contributions from Proctor & Gamble Cellulose. The impoundment's scenic drive and boat ramp were completely restored and a wildlife observation tower and sev- eral picnic areas added. Use by waterfowl has increased

Bald Eagle

135

dramatically since the completion of the marsh revitalization project, and the area is returning to its former productivity. Future plans call for a visitor center, marked hiking trails, and interpretive exhibits.

Hickory Mound Impoundment is included within the Big Bend Wildlife Management Area and is open for hunting during portions of the fall, winter, and spring. Care should be taken during these times of year.

Location, Mailing Address and Phone

Located south of US 98 in coastal Taylor County, a few miles east of the Econfina River bridge; turn south onto a hard clay road at the sign, then continue for about 7.6 miles to the marked entrance.

Florida Game and Fresh Water Fish Commission, 620 S. Meridian, Tallahassee, FL 32399-1600.

Facilities and Activities

Boating, fishing, hiking, scenic drive, wildlife observation tower, bicycling.

There are very few facilities at Hickory Mound, just lots of beautiful scenery and wildlife. The area is somewhat out-of-the-way for many visitors and seems to be most heavily used by anglers. Yet, its scenic drive, wide expanses of marshland, and dense cabbage palm hammocks can be major attractions for birders, naturalists, and outdoor enthusiasts.

The scenic drive is a several-mile loop that begins near the welcome sign at the entrance road's intersection with Swartz Tram Road. Continuing down the main road leads to a two-lane dike that extends out across the marsh. From the time the road leaves the woodlands, marsh vistas are a continuous companion. The left side of the road, which first faces east, then south, is mostly *Juncus* saltmarsh that stretches to the edges of Apalachee Bay. The impoundment is on the right, or north, side of the road and is mostly a combination of cordgrass meadows that form the edges of numerous open-water ponds and exposed mud flats. A variety of wading and shorebirds use the marshes including whimbrels, willets, clapper and sora rails, wood stork, and all of north Florida's herons and egrets, including the reddish egret. Alligators are often spotted plying the shallows and raccoons are commonly seen digging in the mud or making their way across the flats.

Several small picnic areas, most with only one or two tables, are scattered along the roadway, including one near a well-marked wildlife observation tower. The nearly 20-foot tower overlooks the main part of the impoundment but also affords a view of the bay beyond the dike road. This platform is an outstanding place to scan the marsh for birds and mammals. A variety of feeding areas are within view, including open water, mud flats, sparsely vegetated meadows, and dense marsh. A huge, active osprey nest adorns the top of a dead snag across the pond, and American bald eagles are sometimes seen over the marsh. The large pine behind the observation tower is a good perch for wood stork.

A little way past the observation tower there is a developed boat ramp that provides access to Apalachee Bay and the marshes of the Big Bend Aquatic Preserve. Canoes and sea kayaks as well as motorboats can be launched here. Paddling through the saltmarsh to open water, then along the edges of the bay, is an interesting excursion with many opportunities to see wildlife. However, those who have never paddled in such places should be particularly careful of their route. There are no landmarks in the marsh, and side creeks turn off regularly. It is sometimes easy to stand in your boat and see your intended destination, but difficult to find a passageway to take you there. Leaving brightly colored strips of engineering tape along your route, then retrieving them on your return trip, can be very useful.

Any number of places along the dike road provide good bank fishing, and the boat ramp provides access to the bay. Many anglers set up along the roadside near one of the picnic areas and spend the day testing their luck.

Just beyond the boat ramp the road turns northward. A small road to the right leads to the edge of the impoundment and makes a nice walk. Shortly thereafter the road leaves the marsh and reenters the woodlands just beyond a sawgrass pond on the right side of the road. The next major turn to the right is Swartz Tram Road which leads back to the entrance sign.

Swartz Tram follows along the edge of a mature cabbage palm hammock that supports a variety of trees including red maple, sweetgum, water oak, and a number of locust. There are no trails into this hammock but there are a number of places on both the north and south sides of the road that provide easy entry. Although it would be somewhat difficult to get lost here, those venturing deep into the hammock should probably carry a compass to help them keep their sense of direction.

The scenic drive is also good for bicyclists. The hard-packed roadway makes for easy peddling and the scenery is outstanding. The entire circle described above requires little energy for seasoned cyclists.

Visitors to Hickory Mound should write the Florida Game and Fresh Water Fish Commission at the above address and request the Hickory Mound Unit brochure. It includes hunting dates as well as a map of both the impoundment and the surrounding Big Bend Wildlife Management Area.

Best Time of Year

Winter is best for exploring the hammock and for seeing wintering waterfowl. Summer is good for observing wood stork, summer shorebirds, alligators, raccoons, and nesting osprey. Fishing, canoeing, and boating are good year-round.

Pets

Allowed.

LAKE TALQUIN STATE FOREST

Exploring Lake Talquin State Forest is more like visiting several parks than one. The forest's 14,175 acres is divided into seven self-contained units, each with its own boundaries and separate access. Located in Leon, Gadsden, and Liberty Counties, just west of Tallahassee, it is one of those special places where visitors can sample Florida's natural bounty within a stone's throw of urban and suburban neighborhoods.

The state acquired the majority of the Lake Talquin property in 1977 as a donation from Florida Power Corp. Soon after its acquisition the Department of Agriculture assumed management responsibilities for the site and currently administers 10,366 acres in cooperation with the Florida Game and Fresh Water Fish Commission. The remainder of the forest is administered directly through the Division of Forestry. In addition, the Game and Fresh Water Fish Commission has direct management responsibility for several thousand acres of the Joe Budd Wildlife Management Area.

Five of the forest's seven units are part of three separate wildlife management areas. As might be expected, hunting is permitted in most parts of the forest and the land is managed in part to insure this purpose. Nonhunting recreation is restricted to certain tracts and to those times when hunting season is closed.

Location, Mailing Address and Phone

West of Tallahassee off SR 263, SR 20, US 90. Directions to each subunit of the forest are given below.

Florida Division of Forestry, 1214 Tower Dr., Tallahassee, FL 32301; (904) 488-1871; Lake Talquin State Forest Office (904) 487-4250.

Facilities and Activities

Hiking, wildlife observation, botanizing, birding, fishing, boating, picnicking, canoeing, horseback riding.

There are few developed recreational facilities in this state forest and only one campground. However, each of the forest's units is easily accessible, contains numerous canopied woods roads that are open only to foot traffic, and offers outstanding opportunities for botanizing and wildlife observation. Camping

Budd Pond

is permitted by special use permit which may be obtained by contacting the forest office.

Talquin

On SR 20, approximately 3.5 mi. west of Tallahassee.

The Talquin section of the forest is a 2,834-acre parcel that is sandwiched between SR 20 and the southern shores of Lake Talquin. Like its counterparts, it encompasses several native communities, the largest expanse of which is sandy, upland, turkey oak–slash pine woodlands. The section is crisscrossed by a half dozen improved roadways, most of which are in good condition and easily driveable by most types of vehicles. However, there are some places with relatively deep sand, and at least a few low spots that can be muddy following heavy rains.

In addition to the driving trails, there are a number of overgrown roads that are closed to vehicular traffic but are open to walking. Each of these old roads is marked at its terminus with a small, white "No Vehicles Allowed" sign; all are easy to follow. A map brochure is available at the entrance but shows only the drivable roads.

The upland woods are a good place to look for wild turkey and white-tailed deer, two of the forest's most populous animals. These woods also support a surprising number of both woody and herbaceous plants. Sweetleaf, black cherry, chickasaw plum, sparkleberry, highbush blueberry, pawpaw, persimmon, and southern crabapple are the easiest shrubs to find, and the roadsides throughout the forest seem to change color with the season as the more tender herbs pass in and out of bloom. A succession of whites, blues, and yellows predominate from spring to fall as several species of blackberries and the large flowered pineland hibiscus give way first to ironweed, climbing butterfly pea, and a number of meadow beauties, then to several species of St. Johns-wort, rattlebox, and goldenrod.

Besides the uplands, there are also a number of densely vegetated creek and river swamps throughout the area. Most of these wetlands contain standing water during much of the year which makes them particularly attractive to wildlife as well as a haven for plants. The yellow poplar and swamp chestnut oak are easy to find here, as are sweetgum, water tupelo, hickory, ironwood, stiffcornel dogwood, and several species of wild grape.

One particularly interesting wetland lies along the northern arm of Beaver Dam Road as it approaches Poison House Road. A two-lane bridge that passes over a narrow darkwater creek marks the location. If the water is not too high, it is possible to wander off into the swampy terrain adjacent to the bridge and enjoy being enclosed in a shady wetland forest.

Another good location is the terminus of Hunting Camp Road. Although this area is heavily used on weekends during hunting season, there is little activity during other parts of the year. There are at least two canoe launch sites near the hunt camp that provide access to the lake. Paddlers can explore the swampy areas near the landing, and fishing enthusiasts will enjoy using these accesses as starting points for seeking out the bream and bass that have made Lake Talquin famous.

Just before intersecting Hunting Camp Road, Beaver Dam Road passes adjacent to a scenic magnolia forest. The road is sandy directly adjacent to this hammock and not conducive to parking, but becomes hardpacked again a few yards further along. This hammock is just upslope from the lake and is a good place to explore. There are no trails here so walkers should carry a compass if they plan to stray out of sight of the roadway.

North and South Ochlockonee

Both units may be reached from the intersection of I-10 and SR 263; for North Ochlockonee drive north on SR 263 to Stoneler Rd., then west on Stoneler for 0.9 mi. to the entrance; for South Ochlockonee drive south on SR 263 for 1.4 mi. to US 90, then west on 90 for 1.8 mi. to an obscure clay road that turns off to the north adjacent to a large metal powerline tower.

Together, the North and South Ochlockonee tracts encompass 2,685 acres that include a variety of woodlands from dry, sandy, turkey oak uplands and temperate hardwood forests to river swamps. Both tracts lie along the eastern edge of the Ochlockonee River and both offer interesting hiking and wildlife observation opportunities. The map for the Ochlockonee River Wildlife Management Area, which is available near the end of the entrance road to the northern unit or by writing the Florida Game and Fresh Water Fish Commission in Tallahassee, provides the best overview of the area.

The northern tract is the larger and more varied of the two and offers a larger number of walking paths. As with the remainder of the forest, the roads here are well marked and easy to follow.

One enjoyable hike begins at the point where the River Road is blocked from further vehicular traffic. Continuing beyond the gate leads to the road's intersection with a gas pipeline easement that crosses the forest. The easement is easy to walk and leads directly to a small bluff on the Ochlockonee River. Upland forest transforms into riverine woods as the trail nears the river and gives way to a smattering of river birch and willow trees. An unmarked trail leads southward along the river's edge on a natural levee that separates the river from the backwaters. Possum haw holly, green haw, willow, sweetbay, American holly, live oak, and sparkleberry line the trail and a narrow, sandy beach follows along the waterline. It is possible to see deer and squirrel here as well as cottonmouth and several species of water snakes. Frogs and toads are also abundant; the rasping call of the squirrel tree frog is common on early summer mornings.

Another attractive location in the northern tract is the cypress-ringed pond that lies at the end of Cypress Pond Road. Large, buttressed bases of bald cypress encircle the pond or stand surrounded by water well offshore. A small landing is suitable for a canoe or small boat. The pond is small, but paddling slowly among the huge tree trunks during early morning light is a refreshing activity.

The Southern Ochlockonee unit is smaller and has only one drivable road. The Lewis Loop passes through young, sandy, upland woods along its eastern and northern extents, then through somewhat more mature hardwoods along the west. Hickories, ironwood, dogwood, and loblolly pine are common along the latter route. The entire route is good for seeing white-tailed deer and wild turkey.

Both the northern and southern tracts have many roads besides those that are open for vehicles. These make outstanding footpaths. They are generally open enough to provide edge habitat that attracts wildlife, but sheltered enough to suggest a footpath. Even the hardwood stands in these tracts are generally open enough to allow easy walking. Carrying a compass and quietly following your own off-road trail can yield many opportunities for observing wildlife.

Joe Budd and Midway

Turn off US 90 onto SR 268 approximately 2.1 mi. west of the I-10/US 90 interchange, west of Tallahassee; the entrance to the Midway unit is at the terminus of Central Road, about 1.3 mi. after turning onto 268; the entrance to Joe Budd is located about 1 mi. past Central Road and is marked.

The Joe Budd and Midway units are both located on the north side of Lake Talquin, between Tallahassee and Quincy. Together, they comprise 8,415 acres, all of which are managed under the auspices of the Joe Budd Wildlife Management Area. Both units are similar to the locations described above and support similar plant and animal communities. Wild turkeys are abundant and often seen on both units, as are white-tailed deer. A variety of birds also use the unit's varied habitats.

The Midway unit may be one of the Lake Talquin Forest's most impressive tracts. There is a wide assortment of native communities here and the area is little used outside of hunting season. Central Road leads through some particularly scenic woodlands before reaching the loop near the lake. Though there is no direct lake access from the loop, and the woods along the roadside are dense, it is possible to follow an old road and fishing trail to the water near the loop's eastern end.

A better lake approach is at the end of Landing Road, which is off New Bridge Road. The landing is not suitable for boat trailers, but canoeists will find it an easy access point. The small launch site is located at the narrow headwaters of Lake Talquin, which is somewhat more like a river than a lake at this point. It is possible to paddle upstream into the Ochlockonee River from here, or downstream into the widening lake. The densely vegetated banks are good places to look for songbirds, and the edges are good places to observe large wading birds.

New Bridge Road and the road to the landing are interesting, if somewhat intimidating, thoroughfares. Both are quite passable by most vehicles but are rutted and undulating in places. A small wooden bridge on New Bridge Road passes over Hunter Creek and is an excellent place to stop and explore. There is an assortment of native plants here, including a very healthy population of hazel alder, one of the more shrubby members of the birch family.

The Joe Budd unit is also easily accessible by improved roadways. Like most other locations in the forest, a number of the unit's roads are closed to vehicles and make good walking paths. Rosedale and Pond roads lead to Joe Budd Pond and environmental center. The pond is small and scenic, with a walking path down one side. There is a dilapidated dock and boardwalk near the small parking area. The walking path is actually a levee that perches walkers high above the floor of the adjacent woodlands and is a good place to search for songbirds or scan the lake for turtles.

The Joe Budd Campground and boat launch are located at the end of High Bluff Road, which turns left off the main Joe Budd access road just beyond the end of the pavement. There are no facilities at the campground, just a nice view of the lake and large grassy places to put a tent or camper. The well-maintained landing, which is located about 3 miles west of the Midway unit landing described above, is suitable for powerboats or canoes. It is possible to leave a car at both sites and paddle between these two landings, or make an enjoyable round-trip from one to the other.

The Joe Budd unit is bounded on its western end by the Little River, a shallow, canopied rivulet that drains into the lake. It is possible to put a canoe in at the US 90 or CR 268 bridge and drift downstream along the edges of the forest, then paddle back upstream to the put-in point. Strong paddlers may want to launch at CR 268, journey downstream into the lake, then follow the lake's northern border to the Joe Budd Campground landing.

Best Time of Year

Any time of year outside of hunting season is a good time to visit this forest.

Pets

Allowed on a leash.

OCHLOCKONEE RIVER STATE PARK

The name of this park, as well as the muddy river that borders it, derives from the corruption of two Hitchiti Indian words: *oki*, which means water, and *lagana*, which means yellow. Pronounced "oak-LOCK-knee" by the locals, the river is similar in character to the much larger Apalachicola River that lies farther to the west. It is also one of only a handful of north Florida streams that originate outside the state. In its narrow upper reaches the Ochlockonee is bordered in some places by low

EXPLORING WILD NORTHWEST FLORIDA

bluffs and in other places by fascinating examples of mature floodplain forests. Farther downstream the river widens dramatically; by the time it reaches the park it has become a large, almost lakelike waterway in the first throes of its gradual transition into Ochlockonee Bay.

Location, Mailing Address and Phone

Four miles south of Sopchoppy on US 319, just north of the Ochlockonee River Bridge.

Ochlockonee River State Park, P.O. Box 5, Sopchoppy, FL 32358; (904) 962-2771.

Facilities and Activities

Camping, canoeing, kayaking, birding, picnicking, fishing, boating, nature trails.

This is an outstanding park with a lot to offer. A picnic area with tables as well as a covered pavilion is located on a point that overlooks two rivers. A small but attractive riverside campground is nestled among a grove of pines and sand live oaks and provides a good base camp for exploring the park as well as much of the nearby Apalachicola National Forest and St. Marks National Wildlife Refuge. Wildlife is abundant here and the beautiful pinelands that cover much of the landscape are unparalleled. A nature trail follows along the river and the extensive pine woods are relatively open and offer easy off-trail walking. White-tailed deer, raccoon, bobcat, and gray fox frequent the park and are often seen. A boat landing offers access to the river for powerboats, and both fresh- and saltwater fishing spots are easily accessible by water.

Canoeing and Kayaking

Ochlockonee River State Park is located at the junction of several streams and can serve as the beginning or end for a number of paddling excursions. The small dock at the swimming area juts out into the Dead River, a twisting passageway that empties into the lower Sopchoppy at both ends, but also connects the Sop-

146

choppy with the Ochlockonee adjacent to the park. In addition, a variety of tiny, twisting rivulets turn off the Dead, Sopchoppy, and Ochlockonee Rivers and can offer many hours of exploration and discovery. It should be noted that all the streams in this area are tidally influenced. Strong outgoing tides can add significant velocity to downriver paddling, while strong incoming tides can seemingly reverse the river's natural direction, making the current appear to flow upstream. It is probably wise to consult local tide tables when planning extended paddling trips here.

One of the easiest paddling routes to follow starts at the small beach adjacent to the park's swimming area, then trails along the Dead River more or less northward. A cursory look at the map suggests that the Dead River is actually two rivers, both with the same name. The segment that heads north from the swimming area passes through large expanses of freshwater marsh before joining the Sopchoppy several miles below the US 319 bridge. Turning downriver on the Sopchoppy leads first past the mouth of Buckthorn Creek on the north side of the river (an interesting side excursion), then to the Dead River's lower mouth, near the eastern end of Thoms Island Wilderness (see St. Marks National Wildlife Refuge, p. 104). This is a somewhat long trip; in windy weather or on hot days it can be a tiring adventure. However, the huge mud flats, magnificent marshes, scenic pine islands, and large variety of wading and marsh-loving birds certainly make the trip worth the energy.

The marshy expanse directly across the Dead River from the park is also a good paddling location. Narrow, tightly twisting streams crisscross this area and are outstanding for seeing wildlife. Otters, raccoons, sora, herons, egrets, rails, marsh and sedge wrens, and swamp, seaside, and sharp-tailed sparrows are common. Some of these little waterways pass all the way through this marshy area, connecting one arm of the Dead River with another; others merely dead-end in muddy shallows. The Sopchoppy, Fla. USGS topographic quadrangle map is extremely helpful when exploring this area and should be carried along to help you keep your sense of direction.

Across the Ochlockonee River and upstream from the park,

another small creek turns off the south side of the river in an easterly direction. This is another meandering stream that winds through marshes as well as along upland terrain. There is a boat landing on the creek which is visible from the Ochlockonee and makes a good landmark for finding the stream from the river. The St. Theresa Beach USGS topographic quadrangle map will help you find your way.

Another trip uses the park as the termination point. The Apalachicola National Forest's Wood Lake campground is located about 10 miles upriver from the park. Launching a canoe here offers a relatively long but interesting paddle. There is likely to be powerboat traffic on this part of the river, especially as you near the park, but the adjacent national forest lands are quite scenic and contribute to an enjoyable trip.

Thoms Island is also accessible from the park. Paddling routes through the island are included in the discussion of the St. Marks National Wildlife Refuge (p. 104).

Birding

This park is best known to birders for its populations of red-cockaded woodpecker and Bachman's sparrow. The former is an endangered species that makes its home in the center of old live pines. Populations of this delightful bird typically live in close-knit colonies that may include individuals of several ages. Glistening bands of oozing sap often coat the trunks of cavity trees, making them an easy-to-observe landmark.

The Bachman's sparrow, named in honor of John Bachman, a Lutheran minister, consummate naturalist, and protegé of John James Audubon, is another of the park's special inhabitants. It is a secretive creature that is easiest to find during nesting season when the males begin singing. Though present during the remainder of the year, its hideaway habits make it difficult to locate. So good is this sparrow's ability to decoy intruders that neither Audubon nor Bachman himself were ever able to find one of its nests.

The park is also a good haunt for the brown-headed nuthatch, a tiny bird that is restricted in range to the southern United States. It is the smallest of Florida's three nuthatches and is

Brown-headed Nuthatch

found most commonly in pinelands where it tends to forage toward the ends of branches. It nests in cavities, often high up in old dead pines, and its call has been likened to the squeak of a rubber duck. Its preferred habitat and brown cap make it easy to distinguish from its two, more wide-ranging, cousins.

In addition to the three species above, and the marsh birds that are found along the river, this park can also be good for observing spring and fall migrants. During both times of year, the grove of low oaks around the campground can be a good spot for warblers, as can the picnic area. In addition, swallow-tail and Mississippi kites are also sometimes seen over the river, and several species of hawks and owls frequent the park's pinelands.

Best Time of Year

Summer is a popular season for camping, but winter is better. Paddlers must compete with powerboats on the larger waterways in summer; winter paddling is cooler and less crowded. Birding is best in spring, summer, and fall; however, the Bachman sparrow, red-cockaded woodpecker, and brown-headed nuthatch can be seen any time of year, though the first of these three is easiest to find in summer.

Pets

Allowed on a 6-foot leash; not allowed in the campground or swimming area.

PINE LOG STATE FOREST

Pine Log State Forest is one of the panhandle's lesser known but more outstanding inland parks. It takes its name from Pine Log Creek, a tiny, twisting, tannin-stained rivulet that flows through the forest's northwestern quadrant and serves as part of the dividing line between Bay and Washington Counties. In total, the forest encompasses 6,911 acres, but it is the much smaller environmental education area that lies on the Washington County side of the forest that is of most interest to naturalists. Though much of the forest is included within the Point Washington Wildlife Management Area and is open for hunting, the environmental education area is reserved year-round for birding, botanizing, hiking, camping, and nature study. Like most of Florida's state forests, Pine Log is not well advertised and no informational signs are posted along the highway to lead to its entrance. A single sign on SR 79 marks the entrance to the forest's developed recreation areas.

Location, Mailing Address and Phone

On SR 79 about 1.4 mi. south of SR 20, or about 30 mi. south of I-10.

Division of Forestry, 715 W. 15th St., Panama City, FL 32401; (904) 872-4175.

Activities and Facilities

Camping, picnicking, hiking, backpacking, nature trail, botanizing, birding.

Trails

Pine Log State Forest has an outstanding system of interconnecting nature trails, all of which can be accessed from the campground and environmental center. The main campground loop and midpoint connector trails are relatively short walks of 1.3 miles and 1 mile, respectively. Both pass through a variety of the forest's habitats and provide many opportunities for studying the area's plants and wildlife.

For longer walks, the Edgar "Dutch" Tiemann Trail, marked in blue, is a 4-mile loop that is coterminous with the campground loop for part of its route, and intersects the midpoint trail at the latter's southern extent. The Tiemann Trail is named for the first park ranger at Pine Log. He retired in 1992 after 25 years of service and is credited with laying out many of the forest's existing trails and campsites. The current trail offers outstanding opportunities for exploring the forest's natural areas. It passes alternately through wet pinelands and pine–turkey oak woodlands, as well as along the edges of swamp cyrilla and black titi swamps. One section of the trail follows along the densely vegetated edges of Pine Log Creek for a mile or so, offering glimpses of this enchanting waterway. At another point, it skirts the edge of a nearly pure stand of myrtle-leaved holly, a narrow-leaved evergreen native holly that provides a magnificent show of red and green during the fall fruiting period. In yet another particularly scenic spot, the pathway disappears briefly into the center of a completely canopied wetland where the darkened, twisted trunks of numerous black titi line the trail and suggest how this shrubby tree came by its common name.

In addition to the nature trails, an 8-mile section of the Florida Trail crosses the forest. The FT is easily accessible from several points within the forest, including a marked access on SR 79 just below Pine Log Creek and another marked access at the north end of the cypress-ringed lake at the environmental center.

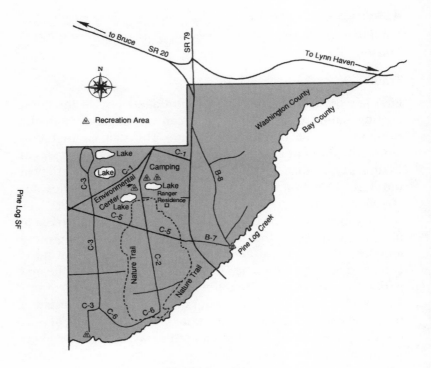

Pine Log State Forest

The part of the trail west of SR 79 follows the Dutch Tiemann trail described above for much of its route but is marked by orange rather than blue paint swabs. In addition, there are about 4.5 miles of the Florida Trail east of 79 that also make good walking. Some of these eastern sections pass through terrain similar to that along the forest's other trails. A scenic savannah lies along the southern edge of the trail less than a mile east of the Highway 79 crossing and is an outstanding place to look for some of the threatened plant species listed below. Backpackers are permitted to use the trail, but campfires are not allowed except in designated areas at the environmental center; the portion of the trail east of SR 79 is also closed during hunting season.

Wildlife

Wildlife is abundant along all of Pine Log's trails and includes an interesting variety of birds, reptiles, amphibians, and mammals. It is not uncommon to hear the banjolike twang of the bronze frog or the deep resonant drone of the common bullfrog when passing adjacent to the wetter areas, or to happen upon literally hordes of newly metamorphosed southern toads as they move away from their hatching grounds. Raccoons, white-tailed deer, eastern cottontail, bobcat, and opossum are also often seen. Bird life ranges from pileated woodpeckers and pine warblers to a variety of sparrows and songbirds. Wild turkeys are common along the ridges, and river otter are sometimes seen in the creeks. Endangered and threatened wildlife include the gopher tortoise, an easily found species in the forest's sandy uplands, as well as the eastern indigo snake and flatwoods salamander.

Plants

In addition to the wildlife, Pine Log Forest's vegetative assemblages encompass the vast majority of the interior central panhandle's indigenous trees, shrubs, vines, and herbaceous flowering plants, including a number of threatened or endangered species. Common wildflowers include yellow-eyed grass, meadow beauty, Barbara's buttons, yellow-fringed orchid, green eyes, St. Johns-wort, red root, black root, colic root, several species of grape vines, and the showy white and red blossoms of pineland hibiscus. Endangered and threatened species include Chapman's crownbeard, Catesby's or pine lily, Chapman's butterwort, giant water dropwort, Apalachicola milkweed, and white-topped pitcher plant, all of which are more likely found in mesic to wet areas.

The trees and shrubs present in the forest encompass dozens of representatives from a variety of plant families. The more common and easily seen species include red maple, black titi, swamp cyrilla, black tupelo, sparkleberry, deer berry, flowering dogwood, black cherry, turkey oak, sand post oak, common persimmon, sweetbay magnolia, witch hazel, bluejack oak, and several species of pines. Cypress is common along the edges of ponds, and some portions of the trails are outstanding for comparing the differences between the two species of highbush blueberry.

Canoeing

There is a canoe trail along Pine Log Creek that begins at SR 79, just south of the entrance to the environmental education area. It is 12 miles from the put-in point to the Choctawhatchee River (which is well outside the confines of the forest), but only about 2 miles to take-out points on Forest Roads C-3 and C-9, both of which are within the forest. The route is narrow and twisting but quite scenic. Black titi and swamp cyrilla line much of its course and the reddish black, tannin-stained water is typical of many north Florida streams. It should be noted that water levels may be too low to paddle this stream during some parts of the year.

Camping and Picnicking

The environmental center features a well-developed picnic area and campground. There are 20 campsites with electricity and water, a restroom with showers, and a dump station. There is also a small lake that allows swimming and a large pavilion available by reservation. Campsites are available on a first-come first-served basis; no reservations are taken and there is a small fee. Maximum stay is 14 days. A group camping area is also available, separate from the regular campsites.

Best Time of Year

Spring, summer, and fall are best for birding and for wildflowers; cool winter days are excellent for hiking. Canoeing is good year-round, provided there is enough water.

Pets

Allowed on a leash; not allowed in the water.

PONCE DE LEON SPRINGS STATE RECREATION AREA

The gurgling pools of crystal clear liquid that mark the headwaters of Florida's numerous springs have always been among the state's most important natural attractions. Tiny Ponce de Leon Spring is no exception. Appropriately named for the well-known Spanish explorer whose search for the fabled fountain of youth probably led him to a number of these refreshing reservoirs, the bubbling boils of Ponce de Leon Spring are forever preserved by the enchanting 443-acre state recreation area that currently bears its name. Even though the area contained within the park may or may not have been on the wily Spaniard's trip list, it is still a favored recreation spot for central panhandle outdoorspeople as well as the few lucky tourists who venture off the interstate highways to visit here.

Location, Mailing Address and Phone

One mi. south of US 90 on CR 181A, just east of the little panhandle town of Ponce de Leon.

Ponce de Leon Springs State Recreation Area, c/o Falling Waters State Recreation Area, Rt. 5, Box 660, Chipley, FL 32428; (904) 836-4281.

Facilities and Activities

Swimming, picnicking, nature trail, fishing.

By most standards, Ponce de Leon Spring is not considered one of the state's largest springs; it is not, for example, listed among the 27 that are considered first magnitude. Nevertheless, its 20-cubic-foot-per-second output results in nearly 14 million gallons of new water per day being added to Sandy Creek, and eventually to the Choctawhatchee River.

At least three openings discharge the 68-degree water. The main vent lies at a depth of about 16 feet in the center of the 100-by-75-foot, kidney-shaped pool. A second, chimney-shaped vent is located near the pool's north bank. This latter opening is a circular orifice about 8 feet in diameter and 19 feet deep. The third vent is smaller and somewhat less impressive.

Much of the spring's perimeter is lined by a cement wall that was installed in the 1930s. A set of steps that lead through the wall into the main part of the pool were added to provide easier access for swimmers as well as for the rural ministers who once used the natural waters to baptize the members of their congregations. The grassy lawn that surrounds the spring includes a picnic area and two large, shrubby mountain laurels that are located just inside the fence near the restroom building. The mountain laurel is an uncommon plant in Florida's panhandle; the planted specimens at this park offer an excellent opportunity to become familiar with its characteristics.

There are two nature trails in the park, one on each side of the 350-foot run that connects the outflow from the spring to Sandy Creek. One trail can be accessed via a footbridge that crosses the creek just below the main spring. The other begins on the east side of the picnic area. Both contain a variety of native flora including haws, ironwood, and cypress, and are well worth the time to explore them.

Best Time of Year

Summer is best for swimming and snorkeling; spring, summer and fall are best for studying the plants; cool winter days are good for hiking the trail.

Pets

Allowed on a 6-foot leash; not allowed in the spring or swimming area.

RIVER BLUFF STATE PICNIC SITE

The directional sign on the highway that proclaims *River Bluff State Picnic Site* seems a rather mundane accolade for this small but enchanting park. It is much more than just a tiny wayside eating station. The rolling hills, streamcut ravines, calcareous bluffs, seepage creeks, mature hardwood forest, and smattering of rare, threatened, and uncommon plants make it a prized remnant of the state's Tallahassee Hills geologic province.

Location, Mailing Address and Phone

On Jack Vause Rd. (a clay thoroughfare) off SR 20 about 11 miles west of SR 263.

Lake Talquin State Recreation Area, 1022 Desoto Park Dr., Tallahassee, FL 32301; (904) 922-6007.

Facilities and Activities

Picnic site, pavilion, nature trail, boardwalk, canoeing, boating, fishing.

River Bluff includes about 400 acres located on the southern shore of Lake Talquin, a humanmade 12,000-acre reservoir that was created in 1927 with the construction of a hydroelectric dam across the Ochlockonee River. Since its inundation the lake has become one of north Florida's favored freshwater fishing sites. It is accessible by motorboat or canoe from several landings on either side of the lake, including one just beyond River Bluff, and provides outstanding angling opportunities for largemouth bass, bream, and speckled perch.

The park is often used for large group cook-outs; special arrangements may be made with park personnel for after-hours use. A large, covered pavilion and cooking area and a number of open-air tables are located just off the parking lot under a canopy of hickories, pines, and sweetgum. Electricity is available and the pavilion is lighted for evening use.

For nature lovers, the rich, deciduous forest that clothes the park's rolling terrain is the major attraction. Behind the cooking area a nature trail skirts the upper rim of a drainage ravine that contains an interesting assortment of uncommon plants. Jack-in-the-pulpits and green dragons grow in the ravine's lower regions, including in the bottoms near the creek, and the beautiful trout lily blooms in abundance in early spring along the

157

upper slope. The diminutive and often overlooked spring coral root, a saprophytic orchid that receives its sustenance from the decaying remains of other plants, pops out in late winter and very early spring, long before most people's attention turns to wildflower watching.

Below the picnic pavilion, a footpath drops off toward the lake, then angles eastward to a rustic stairway. The wooden steps descend to the other end of the same ravine traversed by the nature trail. At their lowest point the stairs exit onto a boardwalk that extends westward along the shoreline. The boardwalk, which is perched over the water, provides an expansive view of the lake as well as a good opportunity for studying the lower reaches of the steep bluff that leads back up to high ground. American beech, oak leaf hydrangea, red maple, southern magnolia, and ironwood line the walk, and turtles are sometimes seen sunning on stumps or logs out in the lake.

At its western terminus the boardwalk climbs back up to high ground and intersects another trail that leads either back to the picnic area or downslope toward the water. The first stop along the latter route is a short, T-shaped dock that pokes out into a small cove and offers an expansive, 180-degree view of the lake. Cypress trees stand in the water near the dock's entrance, and the shallow waters support a variety of aquatic plants.

Past the dock, the trail follows first along the lake edge but quickly turns inland and becomes more narrow and less obvious. The walkway continues along the lower slope adjacent to a fern-filled seepage stream but eventually appears to stop in the middle of an open woodland of hickory, white oak, loblolly pine, eastern hophornbeam, and sourwood. It is possible to keep going here because the ground cover is relatively sparse, and it is rather difficult to become lost. Turning upslope at almost any point will lead to the parking lot or entrance road.

In addition to the trails and boardwalk, the main park road may also be used as a walking path. The 0.5-mile strip of blacktop cuts through upland woods that include sparkleberry, American beauty berry, arrowwood, pines, and ironwood; a number of places along the road are ideal for entering the woodlands. Exploring the edges of the roadway and the woods that border it can be a rewarding experience.

For birdwatchers, the forested ridges at this park can be a good place to search for woodland-dwelling songbirds. Woodpeckers, thrushes, towhees, and thrashers prefer the dense woods, and bald eagles and osprey can be seen over the lake.

About 0.2 mile beyond the entrance to the park, Jack Vause Road terminates at a small landing on the lake. Although not under the auspices of River Bluff, the landing is public and is a good place to launch canoes, sea kayaks, or small motorboats. Paddling west from the landing leads past the park and boardwalk and offers an additional opportunity for studying the edges of the lake.

Best Time of Year

Any time of year is good; spring is best for some of the early flowering plants.

Pets

Allowed on a leash; not allowed in the picnic area.

ROCKY BAYOU STATE RECREATION AREA

As its name suggests, this 357-acre state recreation area is located on the shores of Rocky Bayou, a large, brackish-water lake with open access to Choctawhatchee Bay. The area was once managed by the U.S. Forest Service but was transferred to state control in 1966. Its boat launch and picnic area are heavily used on weekends by nearby residents, but its location on SR 20 places it somewhat out of the way for many trans-state visitors. Nevertheless, it harbors one of the panhandle's best remaining examples of coastal scrub and is an outstanding place for exploring the westernmost Florida version of this important natural community.

Location, Mailing Address and Phone
On SR 20, about 5 miles east of Niceville.

Rocky Bayou State Recreation Area, 4281 Hwy. 20, Niceville, FL 32578; (904) 833-9144.

Facilities and Activities
Camping, nature trails, botanizing, boating, picnicking, fishing.

This park has a large picnic area and a large campground, both of which overlook Rocky Bayou. The picnic area is situated under a canopy of oaks and hickories with a good view of the water. Several stairways lead down to the edge of the lake. Restroom facilities are nearby. The boat ramp is just beyond the picnic area.

The 45-unit campground is set among a scenic hammock of magnolias, hickories, sand pine, and other scrub vegetation. The sites are large, well-separated, have electricity, and are near the restrooms and bathhouse. There is also a covered pavilion for campers and their guests.

Trails

There are three short but very interesting nature trails, all of which pass through varying phases of coastal scrub habitat. Each is circular in design and exits at or near its starting point.

The Red Cedar Trail begins across from the picnic area and leads through an open woodland that includes several species of native trees, shrubs, and herbaceous plants. As suggested by the name of the trail, red cedar is common but there are also healthy populations of hickory, southern magnolia, sparkleberry, high-bush blueberry, myrtle oak, dogwood, eastern hophornbeam, pawpaw, and the attractively flowered red basil. Deer moss covers the ground in many places and there is a particularly good population of woody goldenrod, a low-growing shrub that is most common on coastal dunes and deep sand ridges, chiefly west of the Apalachicola River. According to Ann Johnson, botanist with the Florida Natural Areas Inventory, this plant is one of the first species to replace the pioneer community on developing barrier beaches. As a result, its presence is generally restricted to the more stabilized portions of islands and spits, as well as to the deep sands of old beach ridges.

The other two nature trails both begin near the end of the campground loop at a sandy walkway that crosses the northern extent of Puddin Head Lake. The Rocky Bayou Trail leads off to the left just past the lake; the Sand Pine Trail leads off to the right. Both pass through sand pine–evergreen oak woodlands and are very scenic. The large, mature sand pines that are found along parts of these routes make both walks worthwhile.

One of the most interesting aspects of these trails is the conglomeration of trees and shrubs that occurs here. Though none of these plants are outside of a habitat that might be expected for the species, the diverse assortment of species and sheer number of individuals make this an excellent place for botanizing. Sourwood, the tree known across the southern Appalachians for its smooth-tasting honey and brilliant fall foliage, intermingles with the chinquapin, a close relative of the American chestnut that is well known for its coarsely dentate leaves and spiny, burrlike fruit. The ornately flowered fringe tree blooms in profusion in early spring above a shrub layer that includes the Chapman and myrtle oaks, sparkleberry, highbush blueberry, and Alabama cherry. The small but attractive Arkansas oak, one of Florida's more geographically restricted oak trees, is also common here.

Best Time of Year
Summer is best for water-related activities. Spring is good for flowering plants. The trails are enjoyable year-round.

Pets
Allowed on a leash; not allowed in the campground.

ST. ANDREWS STATE RECREATION AREA

Green Gulf waters, sugar-white sands, and coastal zone woodlands are the defining characteristics of St. Andrews State Recreation Area. One of the most popular outdoor recreation sites in

Florida, this nearly 1,300-acre preserve is an outstanding contribu-
tion to the state's park system and serves as an important outdoor
classroom for first-hand study of the panhandle's coastal strip.

Location, Mailing Address and Phone

*There are actually two parts to St. Andrews State Recreation Area.
To reach the mainland side, turn onto Bay CR 3031 from US 98
between Panama City and the beaches. The other part of the park
consists of the western end of Shell Island, which lies across a
deepwater channel from the mainland. The latter portion of the
park may be reached by boat from the park's Grand Lagoon
landing.*

*St. Andrews State Recreation Area, 4415 Thomas Dr., Panama
City, FL 32408; (904) 233-5140.*

Facilities and Activities

*Camping, swimming, snorkeling, bathhouse, concession, picnic
area, jetty, tidal pool, fishing, nature trails, birding, boating.*

The Mainland

The mainland portion of this park offers nature trails, camping,
sugar-sand beaches, a tidal pool, fishing, and birdwatching. The
campground contains nearly 200 sites and is located on Grand
Lagoon, a large, salty arm of St. Andrew Bay. Some campsites
overlook the water and are relatively exposed; others are separated by native vegetation and offer more privacy. All have water
and electricity.

Several small freshwater depressions dot this otherwise xeric
landscape and offer examples of coastal wetland habitats and
their associated wildlife. The Gator Lake trail, which is located
along the main park road just before reaching the beachside
parking lot, passes along the edge of one of these lakes before
traversing an example of dune scrub vegetation. The nature trail
that leads off the parking lot adjacent to the boat ramp also

passes a small wetland that can be an excellent place for observing wildlife.

Birding is good at this park. An extensive bird list is available at the main gate and includes a surprising number of species. The low woodlands along the nature trails can offer many thrills during spring migration, especially following a strong, late-season cold front, and the beaches are frequented by a variety of gulls and shorebirds. During winter northern gannets can be spotted off the Gulf beaches and large flocks of the delicate Bonaparte's gull sometimes congregate low over the water in the channel or off the jetty. Purple sandpipers have been rarely reported on the jetty in winter, and the only pair of harlequin ducks ever reported from north Florida once spent several weeks in the tidal pool. In summer, least bitterns are regular residents in some of the park's freshwater lakes.

Swimmers can choose between a quiet tidal pool or the open Gulf. The tidal pool is enclosed by a rock jetty that separates it

Piping Plover

163

from the channel. Snorkeling around the rocks that have been in place for many years can mean hours of pleasure. Small, colorful fishes dart in and out of the crevices in the large granite boulders, and the primitive plant life that coats the hardened substrate is fascinating.

For fishing enthusiasts, the boat landing provides access to both St. Andrew Bay and the Gulf of Mexico. A fishing pier adjacent to the boat ramp is a good place to angle for saltwater species. Many fishermen use the jetty that separates the channel from the Gulf; fishing the latter location can be extremely rewarding.

Shell Island

Lying just off Panama City across St. Andrew Bay, Shell Island is one of the panhandle's most magnificent and better preserved barrier beach systems. Originally a spit rather than an island, it was once the eastward extension of the coastal strand that today terminates at the mainland portion of the state recreation area. It was divided from the mainland in the 1930s by the construction of a deepwater channel designed to facilitate easier navigation into the bay. The island is now accessible only by boat and is used extensively for summertime recreation by local residents and personnel from nearby Tyndall Air Force Base. Stretching nearly 7 miles in length, it varies in width from just a few hundred feet in its center to well over a mile on its western end.

Shell Island contains a diversity of natural features. At the island's eastern terminus, which is actually outside the boundaries of the park, Lands End juts into a narrowly twisting natural pass that once served as the only entrance into the bay. Lands End is composed of several acres of shifting sand and is the most unstable part of the island. The area is influenced dramatically by tides, storms, and hurricanes and is dotted with shallow pools of salty water that seemingly change places from year to year. Several acres of additional sand have been added to Lands End since the early 1980s, testimony to its restless nature. Areas that only 20 years ago were under 10 feet of clear Gulf water are now completely emerged and often relatively dry.

Upslope from Lands End the island changes character. Barren sands give way to vegetative communities in the island's interior and beach strips along both of the shorelines.

The eastern half of the island is most notable for its outstanding coastal swale vegetative community. Large patches of saltwort are interspersed with some of the most magnificent populations of sea lavender to be found any place on the Gulf coast. Saltgrass meadows, occasional stands of black needlerush, and several species of marsh pink round out the list of dominant plants.

The Gulf side of the island is lined with wide, white-sand beaches that grade into a near-continuous line of Gulf-front dunes. Overwash fans deposited during previous storms or hurricanes occasionally breach the dunes, offering easy passageway into the island's interior. Consisting of fine white sand pushed up on the beach by waves and wind, the dunes are held in loose cohesion by a sparse vegetation of sea oats, railroad vine, and seaside pennywort. They compose a fragile community unable to withstand the impact of anything but natural processes. Walking across them or walking on them should be avoided.

The western one-fourth of the island, including that portion situated within the park, is different in habitat and ecology from the portions of the island to the east. This part of the island is much wider and supports several different forest communities as well as a freshwater lake. Several systems of inland dune ridges support a community of myrtle oak, chapman oak, and some particularly large specimens of Florida rosemary. Deeper into the island, sand ridge communities give way to hammocks of sand live oak, southern magnolia, and dense wetland thickets characterized by red bay and yaupon.

The bay side of the island is lined with a thin ribbon of beach that is often interspersed with *Juncus* saltmarsh. In some places the inland beach backs up to relatively open pine woodlands composed primarily of longleaf pine. Near the western end of the island, the longleaf is replaced by dense stands of sand pine.

As with most of our barrier islands, Shell Island is visited by a diversity of birds. Large flocks of shorebirds are sometimes seen on the extensive low-tide mud flats of the inland beach as well as

165

on the expanses of sand that compose Lands End. Several species of ducks use the protected coves on the bay side as wintering habitat, and northern gannet are often seen in winter off the Gulf shore. A surprising variety of woodland species also inhabit the island. Participants in the annual Audubon Christmas bird count regularly record between 60 and 80 species of birds in only a single day. Some of the rarer finds over the years have included a varied thrush and several Lapland longspur. More common but no less interesting sightings have included the American woodcock, both snowy and piping plovers, marbled godwit, red knot, and large flocks of black scoter.

Best Time of Year

Birding is good any time of year but winter and spring are probably best. Camping is popular in the summer but is less crowded in winter. Swimming is essentially a summer activity. Fishing the jetty or fishing pier is a year-round activity. Winter is the best time to beachcomb and to explore the backwoods.

Pets

Allowed on a 6-foot leash; not allowed on the beach, near the tidal pool, in the concession area, or in the campground.

ST. GEORGE ISLAND STATE PARK

St. George Island is one of the two most accessible barrier islands along the panhandle coast. Connected to the mainland by a system of bridges and causeways, it is both easy to reach and easy to explore.

St. George is a relatively young landform with a fascinating geological history. Carlton Schade's 1985 master's thesis, completed at Florida State University, outlines one of the most interesting theories of the island's genesis. According to Schade's story, the island began forming about 6,000 years ago when no coastal barriers bounded Franklin County's mainland shore and the Apalachicola River poured its silt-laden waters directly into the open sea. Buffered by the impact with deeper water, the river's velocity diminished significantly as it emptied into the bay, forcing the heavier silts and sands that were suspended in the fast-moving currents to gradually settle to the bottom. Slightly offshore and on either side of the river's mouth, these newly deposited sediments accumulated into two large under-water shoals. About 4,000 years ago the first of these shoals emerged above the waves at what is today the northeastern end of the island. During a drop in sea level about 2,000 years later, Cape St. George Shoal also emerged near what was to become the island's southwestern end. Once above the surface of the ocean the sands stored in these shoals allowed the new land-forms to grow toward each other and to ultimately join together sometime within the last 1,000 years. The narrow aspect of St. George's middle reaches still suggests the point at which these two prograding landforms finally met.

Today, the eastern end of the island is under public ownership and is protected from future development. The western ter-minus is separated from the rest of the island by a passageway between Apalachicola Bay and the Gulf. Named "Sikes Cut" after former Florida congressman Bob Sikes who succeeded in having it constructed, this passageway virtually creates a separate island that is commonly referred to as Little St. George.

The eastern one-fourth of the island is occupied entirely by Dr. Julian G. Bruce St. George Island State Park. Comprising nearly 1,900 acres, this park offers an outstanding opportunity to study barrier island topography and ecology—or to just enjoy the coast. The park contains over 9 miles of undisturbed beaches and dunes, outstanding examples of coastal pine and oak forests, a system of swales and ridges, several expanses of black needlerush saltmarsh, and a luxuriant strand of submerged sea-grass beds that lines its estuarine edge.

Location, Mailing Address and Phone

St. George Island is connected to the mainland by a bridge and causeway; it can be reached by turning south off US 98 at

*Eastpoint. The route is well marked. The state park is located on
the east end of the island.*

   *St. George Island State Park, HCR Box 62, St. George Island, FL
32328; (904) 927-2111.*

Facilities and Activities

Camping, hiking, birding, swimming, boating, picnicking.

Camping

The park supports one family campground that is located in the
center of the island, away from the beach. The sites are sandy,
open, and lightly vegetated. There are modern showers and electric hookups. The road to the campground leads back to the
beach road and to a boardwalk that leads to the beach. Night
walks along the Gulf shore can be breathtaking.

   A short trail also leads from the campground, through the
campfire circle, to the bay side of the island. Wading along the
bayside shallows can reveal a plethora of sea life. However, there
are a number of oysters and other sharp shells here, so be sure to
wear shoes.

Birding

For those interested in birdwatching, St. George Island is unsurpassed. Boasting a species list of over 230, the island is a haven for
both spring and fall migrants. April and May are the best months
for spring migration; September and October are best in fall.
Shorebirds, hawks, warblers and a variety of other songbirds are
likely to be seen. Several species of terns and shorebirds including the American oystercatcher, black skimmer, and least
tern nest on the causeway connecting the island to the mainland.

   There are a number of good locations for birders. Perhaps
the best for spring migration is the patch of open woodlands
that lies behind the restrooms at the youth camp. The youth
camp area is reached by turning left at the first paved road in
the park, then continuing to the end of the pavement. The area
behind the restrooms is sparsely forested with small oaks and
some pines. Warblers can be abundant here, especially fol-

lowing a spring cold front. Birders who spend an entire day in this area often report that both the types and numbers of species change dramatically throughout day. Making only a single stop here will almost certainly insure that you miss some good sightings.

Beyond the pavement and restrooms, a single-lane dirt road leads to a boat landing. Beyond the boat landing an even smaller road leads to the tip of a tiny point of land. This road can yield a variety of birds, including both ospreys and owls. The oyster bars off the boat landing are good for shorebirds and gulls.

The thin woods near and beyond the campground can also be good for migrants. There is a parking lot near the end of the

Osprey

campground that provides parking for those who hike the trail; it can also be used by birders.

Hiking

There are two walking trails. The first is a short nature walk which begins across the park road from the first of two large, beachside pavilions. The path follows a boardwalk through pine woods and terminates at a large platform overlooking East Cove. It is a pleasant, though short, stroll and gives walkers a good overview of the non-beach side of the park.

The other trail is longer and begins at the back end of the campground. There is a parking lot for trail users. This trail is a 2.5-mile, one-way path that terminates at a primitive camping area at Gap Point, one of the oldest parts of the island. The trail passes through sandy beach scrub and sparse pine woods for most of its route and provides interesting birding opportunities. The primitive camp is located on the bayside beach, has no drinking water available, and requires registration with the park office for overnight stays.

The main park road ends at a circular parking lot. Near the end of the parking lot a sandy road (sometimes used by fishermen who have requested permits) leads to a desolate stretch of beach. On weekdays this beach can be deserted and provides outstanding shelling opportunities. Not many people make the complete journey down this beach to East Pass. Those who do are treated to one of the Florida Gulf coast's finest unspoiled beaches.

Swimming and Picnicking

Many people visit St. George Island solely for swimming and sunning. Several large pavilions are located along the main road. Each has restrooms, outdoor showers, a large parking lot, and boardwalks to the beaches. In addition, there are a number of other spots where parking is allowed and beach access possible. In winter these areas are often deserted and are good places to see American oystercatchers. In summer they are good places to see least terns.

Best Time of Year

Spring and fall are best for birding, particularly for migrants. Summer is best for saltwater recreation activities. Winter is good for hiking, camping, and exploring the beaches for shells and other evidence of sea life.

Pets

Not allowed on beaches, in the campground, or in concessions (other restrictions may be applied as needed; check with the ranger station for current policies). Where allowed, pets must be kept on a 6-foot, hand-held leash at all times.

ST. JOSEPH PENINSULA STATE PARK

The hawk migration through St. Joe Spit can be a spectacular event. When conditions are right, large numbers of sharp-shinned, Cooper's, broad-winged, and marsh hawks glide buoy-antly across the mountainous dunes and sand pine woodlands, along with smaller numbers of migrating merlins and peregrine falcons. During the fall, in particular, the birds use this narrow strip of coastal scrub as a kind of staging area before completing their southern exodus. They enter the peninsula from the north, across St. Joseph Bay, then continue southward toward Cape San Blas. If the weather is discouraging, they may congregate in the area for several days before embarking on the challenging voyage across the Gulf. On their return trip in spring, the area is one of the first places they touch down on the mainland.

St. Joseph Peninsula is a narrow finger of land separating St. Joseph Bay from the Gulf of Mexico. Jutting northward from Cape San Blas for nearly 20 miles, this hook-shaped landform probably originated as a barrier island during the last retreat of the sea. Today it is connected to the mainland by a natural land bridge and is protected from further development by virtue of being part of T. H. Stone Memorial St. Joseph Peninsula State Park and its associated wilderness preserve. The more than

2,500 acres that constitute this park encompass one of the state's most outstanding examples of a barrier spit ecosystem.

Location, Mailing Address and Phone

Reached by taking SR 30 and SR 30E south from US 98 just west of Apalachicola.
St. Joseph Peninsula State Park, Star Route 1, Box 200, Port St. Joe, FL 32456; (904) 227-1327.

Facilities and Activities

Camping, cabins, swimming, picnicking, birding, hiking, backpacking, nature trail, sea kayaking, botanizing, boat ramp, marina, boating, saltwater fishing, wildlife observation.

St. Joseph Peninsula State Park offers two campgrounds, a vast area of dune scrub habitat, large coastal sand dunes, and several miles of unspoiled beaches. One campground is located just off the beach near a large platform that overlooks the Gulf. The other is in a flatwoods forest with well-separated sites. Both provide easy access to the park's pristine shoreline.

In addition to the camping opportunities, there are two day-use picnic areas as well as three nature trails. The trail that begins at camping area #1 follows along behind the massive dunes for its entire length, but offers several places to cross over to the beach. Other trails are described below. The waters of St. Joe Bay and Eagle Harbor are often used for scalloping and snorkeling.

Birding

St. Joe Peninsula is an outstanding birding spot for more than hawkwatchers. The nature trails that lead through the area can be outstanding for seeing migrant and resident species alike. Six swallows, all of north Florida's thrushes, nine flycatchers, at least 22 different kinds of warblers, and a large conglomeration of plovers, gulls, terns, and sandpipers have been reported within the park. In addition to migrating raptors, other specialties that occur include the least tern, sandwich tern, black tern, Caspian tern, marbled godwit, both the piping and snowy plovers, and the reddish egret.

The nature trail just inside the main gate is one of the best places for finding migrating songbirds, as are the oak woodlands beyond the picnic area. The bayside nature trail, the beaches along Eagle Harbor, and the Gulf shore are good for shorebirds, gulls, and terns; the Gulf side is also good for northern gannet in winter.

Backpacking and Kayaking

The northern end of the peninsula consists of a 1,650-acre wilderness preserve with a 9 mile, one-way trail that is excellent for backpacking. There are no facilities and no source of fresh water in the preserve; all provisions must be carried in. A road-like firelane bisects the peninsula for most of its extent and provides an oft-used path for hikers. For most of its way the firelane is bordered by the panhandle's version of coastal sand pine woodlands. This outstanding example of coastal zone vegetation is an important addition to state-owned lands and is a perfect place for becoming acquainted with this habitat.

For hikers who wish to stay close to the water, the bayside beach also provides good passage to the tip of the spit. There is no trail here and you will sometimes be walking in the water's edge or along mounds of washed-up seaweed, but the experience is well worth it. The grasslands that spread across the spit as it narrows toward the end support a population of white-tailed deer so large that you are likely to see dozens within the last 2 miles of your walk. The tip itself is an unspoiled expanse of sugar-white sands that provides an unobstructed view from bay to Gulf. Some hikers camp on the end of the spit, braving the blowing sands in deference to the refreshing sea breezes and wide open spaces that characterize the area.

The area adjacent to land's end is not the only place to pitch a tent. Much of the bayside beach is backed by a natural sandy berm of vegetated dunes. Behind this ridge are sparse forests of low oaks and scrubby pines that make superb camping spots. On clear winter nights, when the moon is full, the entire area is clothed in a soft, misty light that imparts an artistic appearance to the darkened landscape.

For those who prefer the serenity of crashing surf and green ocean waters, the Gulf side of the spit is also walkable. Deep sands often make the going here more difficult than on the bay side, but every hiker who visits this preserve should give at least some time to the Gulf. In daytime it is possible to see northern gannets swooping and diving well offshore and brown pelicans gliding along the breakers. At night, ghost crabs scamper across the sands but will sometimes become motionless in the beam of a bright flashlight, allowing close inspection.

Sea kayaking is another good way to make the journey to the tip of the spit. The shallow waters of St. Joe Bay make excellent paddling, and the narrow peninsula helps keep wind to a minimum. However, it is important to check tides carefully and plan accordingly. Huge areas of exposed bottom are not uncommon, especially during extreme winter tides. Such conditions can force paddlers far out into the bay and make landfall a difficult chore.

Best Time of Year

Spring and fall are best for birding; swimming is best in summer; kayaking is good year-round; backpacking is best in the cooler months; camping is popular year-round but is less crowded in winter. Walking this park's unspoiled beaches on a clear winter's night can be unforgettable.

Pets

Allowed on a 6-foot leash. Not allowed in the campground or on the beaches.

SUWANNEE RIVER STATE PARK

Flowing at an average rate of two to four miles per hour, the swift-moving Suwannee River is one of Florida's most famous waterways. Beginning as a meager rivulet near the southern drainage of Georgia's Okefenokee Swamp, it drops into Florida as a full-fledged river, fueled by the crystal clear waters of numerous freshwater springs. At Suwannee River State Park it meets the Withlacoochee River, another of Florida's watercourses that finds its start outside the state. Together, the lively waters of these two captivating streams tumble for another 130 miles before finally emptying into the Gulf of Mexico.

Although Suwannee River State Park is located directly adjacent to its namesake stream, it offers much more than just the river's bounty. Originally established in 1936, it was one of the first installments in Florida's fledgling state park system and has grown from about 300 acres when first dedicated to more than 1,800 acres today. Several natural communities are found in the park that include a variety of plants and wildlife. At least one tree—the cedar elm—occurs in and near the park and is limited in Florida only to the banks of the upper Suwannee. Several nature trails make the park's natural beauty easily accessible.

Location, Mailing Address and Phone

Just north of US 90 at the confluence of the Withlacoochee and Suwannee Rivers, 13 miles west of Live Oak.

Suwannee River State Park, Rt. 8, Box 297, Live Oak, FL 32060; (904) 362-2746.

Facilities and Activities

Canoeing, birding, botanizing, nature trails, picnicking, camping, boating, fishing.

Suwannee River State Park is another of those preserves that is more often used by nearby residents than far-away visitors. Its relaxing picnic area, complete with two pavilions, tables, and grills, is a perfect location for family outings, and its boat landing and superb fishing insure the regular return of resolute anglers. Five species of bass are caught in the Suwannee and

Withlacoochee, including the Suwannee, shoal, redeye, striped, and largemouth. A pleasant, shaded, family campground offers 31 sites, each with electricity, water, grill, and table. A large wooden overlook hangs out over the water just below a train overpass and offers a good view of the river.

The park is also steeped in Florida history; several significant remains are found within its confines. The trail and boardwalk that lead to the overlook pass over a series of Confederate earthworks that were constructed near the now-defunct village of Columbus. About 500 people lived in this little riverside town, which supported a sawmill and provided service to the numerous paddlewheelers that plied the Suwannee and Withlacoochee Rivers. Confederate troops were charged with defending the town's ferry crossing and railroad bridge from Union troops; the old wagon road to the ferry landing is still discernible near the end of the boardwalk.

Canoeing

Three canoe trails claim the park as a termination point. The upper Suwannee and Withlacoochee River trails both begin in

Overlooking the Suwannee River

Georgia and end at the park; the lower Suwannee River Canoe Trail begins at the park and ends near the Gulf of Mexico. All three are rather long paddles but can be divided into day-long outings if desired.

For example, putting into the Withlacoochee at SR 6, 10 miles east of Madison, makes for an easy and scenic 12-mile down-river paddle to the park. Blue Spring flows into the river just below the put-in point and a number of small shoals dot the watercourse along the way. After reaching the confluence with the Suwannee, canoeists must turn north and paddle upstream for a short distance to the park's boat landing.

It is also possible to put into the Suwannee near its confluence with the Alapaha River for an 8-mile run downriver to the park. There are intermittent houses along the banks, which somewhat mitigates the wilderness scenery, but the trip is still an enjoyable paddle.

The trip south from the park is along a large, fully mature river. Springs and creeks are common, especially in the section within a few miles of the park. Even though the distance from the park to the Gulf exceeds 100 miles, there are numerous state, federal, and county roads that provide termination points along the way. Planning shorter trips that begin at the park poses little difficulty.

Canoeists should be reminded that the park closes at sundown. Cars left in the park cannot be retrieved until the next day if a trip extends past closing time, unless the car has been registered or prior arrangements have been made with park staff.

Nature Trails

Several short nature trails interconnect throughout the park to offer nearly 3 miles of hiking and nature exploration. The Suwannee River and Lime Sink Run trails lead through an outstanding hammock as well as along the banks of the river. Two boardwalk bridges provide easy passage across Lime Sink Run, and the section along the river offers several scenic vistas. Several cedar elms, some of considerable size, are easily found along the Lime Sink Run trail. Larger specimens of this elm may be easily mistaken for eastern red cedar if you don't raise your head to inspect the crown branches; the trunks of the two trees are remarkably similar. The leaves of the cedar elm are similar in shape to most other elms, though they are much smaller than all but the cork elm. Their upper surfaces are also rough to the touch with a feel similar to fine sandpaper. There are also a variety of other plants along the trail. The overstory and understory includes Carolina silverbell, ironwood, parsley haw, cypress, wafer ash, and hickory; a variety of herbaceous annuals and perennials round out the ground cover.

The Lime Sink Run trail can also be outstanding for birding. A variety of warblers, vireos, and other songbirds move through these woodlands on their way south.

The Sandhills Trail leads through a typical stretch of sandy pinelands and is much different in aspect than the hammock trails. Lush woodlands give way to a sparser forest of longleaf pine and turkey and sand-post oak, and the ground cover includes such species as the dainty and attractive sensitive briar, the pale blue climbing butterfly pea, and the low-growing pawpaw. The Sandhills Trail follows a circular route that passes along the edge of the old Columbus Cemetery, one of the oldest cemeteries in the state. Located just off the remains of an old stagecoach road, the cemetery is another reminder of the 1800s town; the ages etched into many of the still-standing tombstones suggest how harsh life must have been in the early Florida frontier.

The Big Oak Trail is a scenic, 11.2-mile trail that uses part of the Florida Trail system to access the park property on the north side of the Suwannee River. The trailhead is located in the park's parking lot and follows the banks of the Withlacoochee to a primitive campsite, then returns along both the Suwannee and Withlacoochee.

Best Time of Year

Late fall, winter, and spring are best for camping; spring, summer, and fall are best for botanizing and general interest birding; fall is probably best for migrating birds.

Pets

Allowed on a 6-foot leash; not allowed in the campground.

THREE RIVERS STATE RECREATION AREA

Three Rivers State Recreation Area takes its name from the convergence of three southern streams. Both the Flint and Chattahoochee tumble out of Georgia to give birth to the roiling Apalachicola, one of the Sunshine State's most impressive waterways. In earlier days the Flint and Chattahoochee converged naturally near the town of Chattahoochee. Today, they come together at Lake Seminole, a huge, humanmade reservoir that was created in 1956 with the construction of the Jim Woodruff Dam.

The theory of the Apalachicola's origin is an interesting story. Geological evidence suggests that there were once only two rivers here; the Chattahoochee was the larger of the two and the Flint flowed into it from the east as a primary tributary. Sometime in the early Pleistocene a steephead (see Chapter 3, p. 41) formed in the eastern bank of the Chattahoochee, somewhat south of the two rivers' confluence. Through natural erosion, this steephead grew northward, eventually intersecting the Flint and capturing most of its flow. As the newly formed channel deepened and widened, the Chattahoochee, too, began to follow this altered path, changing direction from its former route and cutting off some of its historical streambed. This combination of events gave rise to the Apalachicola and left the Chattahoochee's old valley as a series of well-defined lowlands that are particularly evident at Jackson County's Ocheesee Pond.

Location, Mailing Address and Phone

Turn north off US 90 onto SR 271 in Sneads. The park is located 2 miles north of the intersection.

Three Rivers State Recreation Area, 7908 Three Rivers Rd., Sneads, FL 32460; (904) 482-9006.

179

Facilities and Activities

Camping, boating, fishing, picnicking, nature trails.

Three Rivers is an out-of-the-way and little-used park that is situated in an outstanding location for studying the unique and fascinating natural systems of the northern panhandle. Much of the park is covered with beautiful hardwood hammock woodlands or high pinelands, both of which support an array of wildlife and offer an outstanding show of flowering herbs, shrubs, and trees in spring and summer.

Two nature trails offer the most direct access. The Half-dry Creek Trail is the shorter of the two and begins at the woods on the eastern edge of the picnic area. The trail follows a sloping route and winds through a parklike natural woodland of oaks, hickories, dogwood, plums, and haws.

The Lakeside Nature Trail, which begins on the eastern boundary of Wayside Camping Area, is considerably longer. It passes through woodlands that are similar in aspect to those along the Dry Creek Trail, but also runs along the lakeside for much of its route. Both of these trails are outstanding places to look for northern Florida's more uncommon plants.

Wildlife is also abundant along these trails. The beautiful fox squirrel is found here, as are the grey fox, white-tailed deer, raccoon, and a variety of diminutive songbirds. The lake supports a population of the American alligator as well as a number of very large alligator snapping turtles.

Three Rivers State Recreation Area's 682 acres supports two family campgrounds as well as a youth group camp. Wayside Camping Area, which is located on the lake and offers lakeside fishing, is the more popular of the two. It contains about 25 sites, all of which have electric hookups and picnic tables. Highlands Camping Area is more wooded and offers about 35 sites. Though Highlands Camping Area is not located directly adjacent to the lake, the latter is only a short walk away.

The large picnic area overlooks a sloping, shaded yard that is characterized by oaks and large hickories and drops down to the lake and a fishing dock. The expansive lake offers a restful vista from any of the several large pavilions that dot the hilltop.

Lake Seminole is well known for its fishing opportunities. Large- and smallmouth bass, bluegill, bream, catfish, and speckled perch are commonly taken here. A well-maintained boat ramp at the park allows access to the lake for many types of watercraft including motorized fishing boats as well as canoes. It should be noted, however, that this lake is very large and subject to strong breezes which can make canoeing a challenging adventure unless paddlers stay close to the shore.

Best Time of Year

Camping is best in the cooler seasons, though summer camping is possible. Fishing is a year-round activity. Botanizing is best in spring, summer, and fall.

Pets

Allowed on a 6-foot leash; not allowed in the campground.

TORREYA STATE PARK

Few of Florida's natural areas rival the unique attributes of Torreya State Park. Located along the western edge of the Tallahassee Hills geologic province, its terrain is characterized by high rolling hills, magnificent bluffs, and deeply cut ravines. Elevations in the park range from as little as 50 to more than 250 feet above sea level, and the distances between the highs and lows are sometimes extremely short. The inclines here are certainly not typical of a state that is generally known for its flatland terrain.

Many of the plants that carpet Torreya's hills and intervening ravines are equally unique. A number have very limited ranges within the state and are generally typical of a more northern flora. Such species as baneberry, bladdernut, honewort, hound's tongue, and leatherwood are remnant species that were pushed southward by the ice age glaciers described in Chapter 2. Others, such as the Florida yew, are endemic to the region and are found nowhere else in the world.

The park takes its name from the torreya tree or stinking cedar, one of Florida's rarest plants. Technically a member of the yew rather than the cedar family, the torreya was once widespread along the eastern banks of the Apalachicola River from Chattahoochee southward to Bristol. Oldtimers report that the tree was one of the region's most common plants during the 20s and 30s and that it once found regular use as a Christmas tree because of its attractive, shiny, dark green foliage. Today, the species is in grave danger due to its susceptibility to a fungus that has all but wiped out the population. There are likely no full-grown trees now standing in the wild; the few remaining speci-

Torreya Tree

182

mens are only suckers that have sprung up from the roots of previously diseased trees. Most of these latter individuals are only one or two meters tall and, though they often appear healthy and vital, are likely to meet the same demise as their forerunners.

The torreya is also sometimes referred to as the gopherwood, an appellation that has led to an interesting, but largely unsubstantiated, local folk tale. One story holds that the area in and around the park was the site of the Biblical story of Noah and the Ark. Since the ark was purportedly made from an ancient tree referred to as gopherwood, and since the countryside near the park is one of the only known locations of the species, it seemed logical that the ark must have been built here. E. E. Callaway, a former resident of Bristol who is now deceased, developed an elaborate theory that the region was the site of the Garden of Eden, and that Adam and Eve were buried nearby. At least part of Callaway's theory rests on the wide number of plants that can be found here.

Location, Mailing Address and Phone

On CR C-1641 off SR 12 about halfway between Bristol and Greensboro.

Torreya State Park, HC 2, Box 70, Bristol, FL 32321; (904) 643-2674.

Facilities and Activities

Hiking, backpacking, camping, botanizing, birding, picnicking, museum.

Carside Camping

Torreya State Park offers a popular but generally uncrowded camping area that is used mainly by weekend campers who are less than 200 miles from home. Its peaceful, natural setting attracts a variety of interesting people, nearly all of whom are nature lovers. The campground has 35 sites as well as a restroom and shower facility. The towering pines that provide shade to the area make good perches for barred owls which can often be heard issuing their cackling hoots throughout the night.

Hiking and Backpacking

Two trails traverse Torreya's terrain. The Weeping Ridge Trail leaves the campground near the restrooms and leads off through a mature woodland toward a trickling waterfall that can be a beautiful site following periods of heavy rainfall. The trail is short, generally follows the ridge, and has a minimum of ups and downs, making it an easy walk.

The other of Torreya's trails is an 8-mile circular route that dips and climbs through some of the park's most magnificent scenery. Walking the entire path can be a day-long activity if you move slowly and take the time to explore the surrounding woodlands; it is by far the best way to experience the park's captivating charm.

The longer trail is also excellent for backpacking. Two primitive campsites are located along the route, one on a high bluff overlooking the Apalachicola River, the other on a low bluff overlooking Rock Creek. Both are located off spur trails. Each has a deep-pit latrine and established fire circles, but no running water. Each is also large enough to accommodate more than one party; both are seldom crowded.

Compared to other Florida hiking trails, the trail at Torreya is somewhat rugged and demanding. It includes numerous ascents and descents, some with angles approaching 45 degrees. Although small in comparison to the more mountainous regions of the country, the hills and slopes along the trail at Torreya are, nevertheless, quite high for Florida. Inexperienced or out-of-shape hikers should be forewarned: some of the hills along the trail are extremely steep and may require a significant output of energy.

The Torreya hiking trail may be accessed from several places. The first access point is off the parking lot just inside the park's main gate. The trail crosses the road at this point and can be followed in either direction. Taking the western route from here leads directly to the red rock vista, an interesting outcropping of

Primitive campsite at Torreya State Park

sandstone. Two other access points are located adjacent to the parking lot at the picnic area. One of these leads through the group camp; the other is directly across the main park road. Both of these latter routes are actually spur routes off the main trail and are marked with blue, rectangular blazes. Single blazes mark the footpath's main route and double blazes advise hikers of a change in direction. The main trail is marked in white.

The last trail access is from the bluffs trail found on the river side of the Gregory House Museum at the termination of the main park road. Due to limited parking at the museum, you should leave your car at the picnic area and walk the short distance to the Gregory House. This last access winds its way down the bluffs and connects to the loop trail near the river's edge. A map of the trail is available at the self-service pay station on the main park road and will be useful in your exploration of the area.

Botanizing

Few regions of Florida offer a more varied flora or larger number of rare or endemic plants than the eastern edge of the upper Apalachicola River (see also Apalachicola Bluffs and Ravines

Preserve, p. 196 and Chattahoochee Nature Park, p. 204). Situated in a strategic location at the juxtaposition of several overlapping biotic systems, this extraordinary sector of the state shares the floral and faunal attributes of regions to its north, south, east, and west.

Walking the trail is the best way to explore the park's plant life. Though space does not permit a complete treatment of all the plants one might find here, there are at least a few specialties that should not be missed. Dropping down the sloping trail toward the east just inside the main gate leads quickly to two of the park's better known and more showy species: the Ashe magnolia and Florida flame azalea.

The huge, nearly 2-foot long leaves of the Ashe magnolia make this shrubby tree almost impossible to overlook along the edges of the trail during the summer, and its equally large, creamy white flowers with deep purple centers add special charm to late spring woodlands.

In some places, these big-leaved magnolias are set against an understory of the equally beautiful Florida flame azalea. This thickly vegetated shrub blends into the background during much of the year; during its March-April flowering season, however, its bright orange, honeysucklelike blossoms are difficult to miss.

The spur trail into the Rock Creek primitive camping area just downslope from the picnic area is one of the better places to see the Florida yew. Another good place is along Rock Creek at the old stone bridge constructed by the Civilian Conservation Corps. Several particularly impressive specimens are situated in these areas, as well as beyond the Rock Creek campsites. Several small torreya trees are also scattered along the trail throughout the park and offer ample opportunity to distinguish it from the yew.

Green dragons, jack-in-the-pulpits, wake robins, and lizard's tails are also scattered along the trail, as are some especially large specimens of needle palm. On the western side of the road, the trail passes directly through a large patch of leatherwood and white baneberry or doll's eyes. The latter is known in Florida only from the park and its surrounding area (the Florida

Natural Areas Inventory has reported several locations north of the park).

Gregory House

The Gregory House is an 1840s plantation home that was originally built across the river from its current location. In the 1930s the house was disassembled, then floated and then trucked to its current location on the majestic bluff overlooking the roiling Apalachicola River. The house has since been restored and is open for guided public tours periodically throughout the week. Tours are given once a day on weekdays, and three times a day each weekend or state holiday. Inquire about the current schedule either at the house or in the office at the center of the campground.

Best Time of Year

Spring, summer, and fall are best for studying the plants; camping and hiking are good year-round but may be warm in the middle of summer.

Pets

Allowed on 6-foot leash; not allowed in the camping area or in any structures.

WAKULLA SPRINGS STATE PARK

In the early days of Florida tourism, the Sunshine State's major enticements weren't dominated by high-gloss amusement centers, fabricated attractions, or imaginary fairytale kingdoms. The outstanding natural bounty was reward enough to those who chose to travel the state's narrow, picturesque highways. Sun-drenched beaches, green ocean waters, huge flocks of large wading birds, swaying palms, junglelike hammocks, expansive vistas of undisturbed marshlands, and the crystal clear waters of numerous springs constituted the standard fare for most of the state's vacationing public.

The magnificent first-magnitude spring that now serves as the centerpiece of Wakulla Springs State Park was one of these special places. Owned most recently by the late Ed Ball, a well-known Florida businessman, nature lover, and philanthropist, the spring was for many years a popular north Florida landmark that catered to the recreational interests of some of the state's earliest tourists. Today, it serves as a well-preserved remnant of a more pristine Florida landscape.

The Wakulla Springs complex constitutes Florida's largest spring system and ranks among the deepest freshwater springs in the world. Its flow averages 400,000 gallons per minute and its crystal clear waters form one of the state's most beautiful rivers. In 1973 its record outflow reached nearly 1.2 billion gallons per day, a staggering figure that taxes the imagination. Though it seldom reaches such proportions today, its average output is still impressive.

This spring has long been regarded as both a paleontological and geological treasure. It has been of continuing interest to a variety of scientists who have spent countless hours exploring its depths and piecing together its ancient story. It is one of the best-known and most easily accessible components of the Woodville Karst Plain geologic province described in Chapter 2 (see pp. 21) and displays many characteristics of these limestone-based subterranean systems.

Intensive study has uncovered a massive labyrinth of underground waterways that have helped confirm the generally accepted theory about the subsurface character of karst terrain. Divers from the U.S. Deep Cave Diving Team and the Woodville Karst Plain Project have followed the underground channelways to 360 feet below the surface and mapped a system of at least six major passageways that extend over 6,000 feet from the spring's major vent.

In addition to its karst geology, the spring is also known for its paleontological and archaeological discoveries. In the 1930s, for example, the near-perfect skeleton of an American mastodon was found in the spring's sandy floor. Removed with the assistance of professionals from the Florida Geological Survey, the fully restored fossil now stands as a major exhibit in the Museum of Florida History located in Tallahassee. Later expeditions uncovered a variety of Pleistocene bones as well an assorted collection of spear points manufactured by early Florida Indians.

Location, Mailing Address and Phone

Drive south on US 319 from Tallahassee to SR 61, then south on 61 to Florida 267. The entrance to the park is just east of the SR 61 and 267 intersection. Florida state park road signs mark the route along the way.

Edward Ball Wakulla Springs State Park, 1 Spring Drive, Wakulla Springs, FL 32305; (904) 922-3633.

Activities and Facilities

Nature trails, picnicking, swimming, glass bottom boats, river cruise, birding, botanizing, lodge, restaurant, gift shop, snack bar.

Concessions and Swimming Area

When the Florida Park Service acquired this park it decided to leave the boat tour concessions and swimming area intact. The small beach, multilevel diving platform, and cool waters are favored places for many nearby residents and school groups, and the long history of the boat tours has made them a cultural legacy worth preserving.

Boat tours require a fee in addition to the park entrance fee and leave periodically from the dock below the lodge. The river cruise leads downriver for a 2-mile round-trip and a good look at the otherwise inaccessible river. Bird life can be abundant along the route and often includes purple gallinules, limpkins, ospreys, pileated woodpeckers, anhingas, and a variety of ducks and long-legged waders. Common animal life can include turtles, alligators, snakes, and white-tailed deer.

The glass-bottom boat takes visitors out over the spring and allows an unobstructed view of the abundant fish that find refuge in the water's relatively constant temperature. Mastodon bones are visible on the sandy bottom, and the spring's gaping vent is clearly visible even at 120 feet below the water's surface.

The swimming area and beach are located adjacent to the boat tour concession; the former is marked with a boundary rope. It is important to stay within the designated swimming area at this park. The river is well populated with alligators; straying too far from the confines of regularly used recreation areas can be dangerous.

Nature Trail

There is an outstanding system of nature trails at this park. Though the entire route is probably less than 3 miles long, it can take the better part of a day to explore it thoroughly and even at this speed you are likely to miss something. The Sally Ward Spring Trail leaves the parking lot adjacent to the lodge. There is a trail guide for this part of the trail. Ask for it at the entrance station, waterfront office, or in the lodge. The guide highlights some of the park's special trees and shrubs, all of which are keyed to a series of trail markers. Some of the more prominent plants that are not marked include the passion flower, southern crabapple, Walter viburnum, red maple, red mulberry, and Carolina laurel cherry.

The Sally Ward trail eventually intersects the main park road just outside the entrance station. You can cross the road here, angle slightly to the left, then enter the woods again, this time in a mature and extremely attractive hammock. A large number of plants can be found here including cork elm, ironwood, sweetgum, green dragon, ruellia, yaupon, American holly, swamp chestnut oak, parsley haw, horse sugar, witch hazel, wild olive, American basswood, American beech, cane, and hickory, to name only a few. The limestone outcrops along the trail are natural, and at one point the path passes adjacent to a cypress swamp. The first part of the trail eventually intersects the main road, then turns back into the woods on the same side of the road less than 100 yards from where it emerged. The next time the trail intersects the main road it continues across the pavement, then terminates at the starting point, making a complete circle.

In addition to plants, the trail can be good for birds during varying times of the year. It is one of the locations visited on the St. Marks Christmas Bird Count and can be quite good for songbirds during spring migration. A variety of hawks, including the Mississippi Kite, can be seen in the more open areas, and barred owls are commonly heard but difficult to see.

Lodge and Conference Center, Restaurant, Snack Bar, Gift Shop

In addition to its natural endowments, the park also supports a lodge, restaurant, snack bar, and gift shop, making it an excellent daytime or evening retreat during extended explorations of sites in the Florida Big Bend. The lodge is available for conferences as well as for individual patrons. The lodge was constructed in 1937 and is worth a visit even for day users. It is an authentic Florida structure with marbled floors and high ceilings. A stuffed alligator, affectionately known as "Old Joe," graces a huge glass case at one end of the lobby. A resident of the springs before his demise, "Old Joe" is listed as 11' 2" long and is said to have weighed about 650 pounds. Estimates are that he was over 200 years old when he died.

Reservations at the park's lodge are accepted by phone at (904) 224-5950. Further information about the lodge may be obtained by writing the park.

Best Time of Year

Summer is best for swimming; spring is best for birding; spring, summer, and fall are good for botanizing; glass-bottom boat and jungle cruise rides are good anytime; winter is a wonderful time to spend a weekend at the lodge.

Pets

Allowed on a 6-foot leash; not allowed on the beach, in the swimming area, in any facilities, in the concession area, or in the park overnight.

VII
NATURAL AREAS: PRIVATE LANDS

AUCILLA RIVER AND SINKHOLES

Images of prehistoric Indians fill your head. Ancient Timucuans line the eastern bank; warriors of the Apalachee tribe line the west. You can almost imagine small bands of hunters moving stealthily through the woods in search of the deer, turkeys, and abundance of small game that inhabit the area. Your mind's eye can see the dying embers of overnight campfires, their thin columns of bluish smoke wisping through the trees in the cool first light of a clear fall morning.

The Aucilla River has the power to conjure up powerful visions of a more primitive Florida lifestyle. In many ways it still seems as free and untamed today as it must have been several thousand years ago when its only human inhabitants were the aboriginal Florida residents.

The more one learns about this remarkable river the more one senses that it has long been an important part of the Florida landscape. Prehistoric mastodons have gathered at its waters to drink. Ancient Indian battles as well as a minor Civil War skirmish have been fought along its banks. Trading vessels have plied its waters, transporting products from deep within early Florida to the waiting ships at the river's mouth in Apalachee Bay. During its history it has defined the limits of Indian nations, served as the dividing line between Spanish possessions, demarcated territorial governments, and bounded the outer edges of the Apalachee mission province. Even today it marks the borders between three of Florida's counties.

Some maps show the Aucilla arising just across the state line in southern Georgia, though this headwater is difficult to find. For most of its 69 miles, however, it is strictly a Florida stream, draining some of the most fascinating terrain in the state.

Location, Mailing Address and Phone

For canoeing, the bridges that cross the river at US 27 just east of Lamont and CR 257 several miles south of Lamont are the easiest-to-find access points. Continuing down CR 257 beyond this second bridge, then bearing right where the road divides, then right again as the road divides for the second time, will lead to a third put-in spot that also makes a good termination point for trips begun farther upstream.

For hiking, the Florida Trail turns off CR 257 to the west 1.4 mi. beyond the bridge. Continuing south on CR 257 from this point, then bearing right where the road divides, then left where it divides again will lead to Goose Pasture Road (less than 2 mi. farther on). The latter is seldom marked but is the only place along the route where you can turn both left and right. Turning right (west) onto Goose Pasture Road leads to a cattle gap (a series of railroad tracks crossing the road that deter the movement of cattle) and a small parking area. The Florida Trail leaves the road in both directions here and is marked by signs.

The Aucilla flows largely through private, but open, paper and lumber company lands. There is no address or phone.

Facilities and Activities

Canoeing, hiking, birding, plant study, fishing.

Canoeing

The best way to learn about the Aucilla is to spend time traversing its corridor. Although many avenues are open for exploring this outstanding waterway, canoeing is probably still the most popular. Dropping a canoe into the water at either the US 27 or SR 14 bridge will offer a day's canoeing replete with magnificent scenery and abundant opportunity to study nature.

Canoeing the Aucilla can be a challenging adventure, especially for the novice. More than a few uninitiated paddlers have dumped the entire contents of their boats into the fast-flowing waters. The river's contorted course often twists and turns. Large limestone boulders and stumps from fallen trees jut out of the dark black water, requiring presence of mind and at least a moderate degree of canoeing skill. The portion south of CR 257 even includes a small stretch of rapids—one of the few in Florida. By and large, however, the obstacles are few, not particularly dangerous, and can usually be easily avoided by the attentive paddler.

Hiking

Canoeing isn't the only way to explore the Aucilla; nor is it even always the best way. Some of the finest mileage of the Florida Trail lies adjacent to the middle reaches of this distinctive stream. A walk along the river's limestone-studded banks is sure to bring tranquility, peace of mind, and a greater appreciation of north Florida's outstanding natural beauty.

One of the most interesting sections of the river lies a short distance above the US 98 bridge, several miles east of Newport. After cutting its way for several miles through a narrow crevice in the multimillion-year-old limestone, the river appears to come to an abrupt end. It is seemingly swallowed up by the earth, leaving no trace of its existence.

In actuality, the river vanishes for only a short distance before reappearing as a series of steep-sided limestone sinkholes with magnificently sculptured walls. Some of these sinks are only a few yards wide; at least one is up to 2 miles long. Water flows in one end and out the other, playing peek-a-boo with the land. It is peculiar, indeed, to find a small hole in the ground, the breadth of which might be measured only in feet, but the water of which moves with the currents of a river as if controlled by some mysterious underground force.

The first access point for hikers is the one that lies about 1.4 miles south of the bridge on CR 257. This crossing is at an obvious intersection and is marked with a Florida Trail sign and orange blazes. The trail itself follows a series of these brightly colored swabs painted at eye level on some of the larger trees.

The footpath reaches the Aucilla in less than 2 miles, then follows the streambed for nearly 11 miles before finally turning easterly and away from the river.

The Goose Pasture Road access is the fastest route to the sinkholes section of the trail. The road itself is a sandy but hard-surfaced byway that eventually leads to the Goose Pasture Recreation Area on the banks of the Wacissa River. This latter location is a nice place to relax following a hike.

To reach the point at which the river first goes underground, follow the trail northward off Goose Pasture Road. In just a few yards the trail will begin to pass along several sinkholes. In less than a mile it reaches a fence. Crossing under the fence leads immediately to the river's termination. You may continue upstream along the river from here. Alternatively, you may return to Goose Pasture Road by retracing your steps or by following the primitive road that turns right just beyond the fence crossing.

South of Goose Pasture Road the trail passes at least 16 sinkholes in less than 4 miles, allowing an outstanding view of this unique portion of the river. This latter section of trail offers one of Florida's best opportunities for studying the state's karst topography (see p. 20).

Best Time of Year

Fall, winter, and spring are best for hiking, though early mornings in summer are also nice. Spring, summer, and fall are best for canoeing.

Pets
Allowed.

APALACHICOLA
BLUFFS AND RAVINES PRESERVE

There is no other place like it in Florida. Majestic bluffs overlook unparalleled vistas. Mature woodlands of stately trees, densely vegetated shrubs, and diminutive ground-hugging herbs carpet the rolling hillsides, shaded valleys, and steep-sided slopes. At least a dozen plants that are found here occur no other place in the world; many others occur no other place in the state. It is truly a Florida paradise. Thanks to Florida's chapter of The Nature Conservancy (TNC), it is also a paradise preserved.

The Apalachicola Bluffs and Ravines Preserve, located south of Torreya State Park along the eastern bank of the Apalachicola River, is a prime example of The Nature Conservancy's work and is one of its few publicly accessible holdings. Committed to the preservation of biological diversity through the purchase and protection of important natural areas, TNC seeks out and acquires properties that provide native habitat to the most critically endangered of our plants and wildlife. The 6,267 acres of pine and sandhill uplands, river bluffs, seepage streams, steep-sided ravines, and magnificent steepheads that make up this important natural area certainly meet this definition.

The eastern bank of the Apalachicola River, including the land within the Bluffs and Ravines Preserve, has been referred to by Florida naturalist Bruce Means as a *paleorefugia*. Writing for *The Nature Conservancy News*, Means defined this term as a "site where ancient species, long gone from the surrounding landscape, continue to survive." This is certainly an appropriate accolade for this outstanding natural area. Many of the plants that grow here are remnant species that were left over by retreating Miocene seas. A significant number of these plants are unique to Florida; many others are geographic isolates that are well separated from the remainder of their populations.

Location, Mailing Address and Phone
Turn west onto Garden of Eden Rd. off SR 12, about 1.5 mi. north of Bristol.

Northwest Florida Steward, Apalachicola Bluffs, c/o Tallahassee Field Office, 625 N. Adams St., Tallahassee, FL 32301; (904) 222-0199.

Facilities and Activities
Hiking, birding, wildlife observation, botanizing.

The Apalachicola Bluffs and Ravines' designated hiking trail is an outstanding walkway that passes through or adjacent to virtually all of the preserve's major habitats. Accessed off Garden of Eden Road (a sandy but driveable thoroughfare), the trail begins by traversing the preserve's upland woods, then continues to Alum Bluff, one of the preserve's best-known landmarks. A map of the trail is usually available at the trailhead.

Alum Bluff is a 180-foot precipice that overlooks the middle reaches of the Apalachicola River, one of Florida's largest and most impressive waterways. Standing atop this majestic promontory offers a scenic panorama that spreads to the horizon and leaves one with the feeling of having been transported out of Florida and into some of the southeast's more mountainous regions. Geologists have long been interested in Alum Bluff. Its nearly vertical face is one of Florida's most important fossil sites, and its dramatic relief makes it the state's most outstanding topographic feature. Climbing on the bluff, and collecting or disturbing plants, animals, fossils, or historical and archaeological artifacts are prohibited.

From Alum Bluff the trail follows first along the edge of the river, dipping in and out of a series of shallow valleys, before eventually turning away from the water and dropping into the bottom of a steephead ravine. The vegetation at these lower elevations is luxuriant, varied, and as unique as any place in the state. The torreya tree and Florida yew, both of which are Florida endemics, are found here as well as a variety of less-obvious species. Several trillium, including the threatened lance-leaved wake-robin, flower in early spring, as does the endangered croomia, a small, glabrous herb that forms a conspicuous colony on some of the shaded lower slopes. Other distinctive plants in the ravine floor include lizard tail, bladdernut, mountain laurel, green dragon, and jack-in-the-pulpit.

After leaving the lowlands, the trail climbs steeply up the ravine slope, passing through several levels of changing vegetation. In addition to massive southern magnolia, white oak, spruce pine, tulip poplar, and tall, straight hickories, slope vegetation also includes dog banana, pyramid magnolia, eastern hophornbeam, ruellia, spiderwort, wild ginger, red bay, sweetleaf, sourwood, oak-leaf hydrangea, sassafras, sweetgum, Sebastian bush, Florida flame azalea, sparkleberry, and the rare trailing arbutus. These plants constitute only a small part of the expansive flora represented at the bluffs. A complete accounting of the plants to be found here could fill many pages; exploring them thoroughly can fill a lifetime.

Wildlife is also abundant at Apalachicola Bluffs and Ravines. Both the Mississippi and swallow-tailed kites, as well as the American bald eagle, are commonly seen soaring in the wide open spaces above the river, and a number of songbirds are found in the woodlands. Several species of kinglets, warblers, thrushes, vireos, wrens, and woodpeckers can be abundant during various parts of the year, and wild turkey are commonly seen in the sparse, sandy woodlands east of the river. The ubiquitous six-lined racerunner, a fast-moving, bluish-tinted lizard that thrives in dry sandy habitats throughout the state, is a common sight, as is the gopher tortoise. Other reptiles found here include the eastern indigo snake, one-toed amphiuma, and Apalachicola dusky salamander. The more conspicuous mammals include the eastern cottontail rabbit, white-tailed deer, and river otter.

Best Time of Year

Any time of year offers something at this preserve. Spring, summer, and fall are best for flowering plants, but many of the shrubs here are evergreen and can be studied in winter as well as summer. Hiking the area on a clear, cold winter's day is invigorating and refreshing; the air on such days can be crystal clear and the view from the bluff extraordinary.

Pets

Not allowed.

VIII
ADDITIONAL SITES
AND INFORMATION

ANNOTATED LIST OF
ADDITIONAL NATURAL AREAS

There are a number of other natural places within northwest Florida that are excellent for exploration. While a few of these sites have well-developed facilities or offer interpretive trails or exhibits, most do not. However, for those who wish to get away from developed parks and embark on personally defined explorations, these latter sites often provide outstanding opportunities. To make this guide as complete as possible, the better of these sites are described below. Please note that state forests, wildlife management areas, and state reserves (as opposed to preserves) allow hunting as well as nonconsumptive use; care should be taken when visiting such areas during hunting season.

For information and maps of those sites listed as wildlife management areas (WMA), contact the Florida Game and Fresh Water Fish Commission, 620 S. Meridian St., Tallahassee, FL 32399-1600; (904) 488-3831.

For information about state forests, contact the Florida Department of Agriculture and Consumer Services, Division of Forestry, Forest Management Bureau, 3125 Conner Blvd., Tallahassee, FL 32399-1650.

Apalachee Wildlife Management Area

Size: 7,952 acres
Location: Jackson County
Ownership: Public

Apalachee WMA is a narrow strip of federally owned property that borders the western edge of Lake Seminole, north of US 90. It is accessed by SR 271 north from Sneads. Apalachee contains a combination of upland hardwood forest, pine plantation, turkey oak uplands, open fields, minor agricultural plots, freshwater marsh, and open freshwater lakes and ponds. The area is used primarily for hunting and freshwater fishing but is also outstanding for nature study. The plethora of interconnecting freshwater lakes, nearly all of which were created with the construction of Jim Woodruff Dam, offer many miles of paddling and also provide access to some of the management area's more remote locations. Butler Road, which turns west off 271, is a good access to a number of these ponds. Several landings on the east side of 271 provide direct paddling or powerboat access to Lake Seminole. Neal's Landing, located off SR 2 just east of its intersection with 271, features a well-developed U.S. Army Corps of Engineers campground.

Apalachicola River Wildlife and Environmental Area

Size: 46,992 acres
Location: Franklin and Gulf Counties
Ownership: Public

This area encompasses large tracts of river-bottom swamp and hydric hammock on both sides of the Apalachicola River (see the description of the Apalachicola River in the Apalachicola National Forest section, p. 78). Motorized boats, canoes, or sea kayaks provide the only means of exploration in the area. One of the best access points on the east side of the river is from Gardner Landing (which is described on p. 85). The best western access is at Howard Creek. This latter landing is reached by turning west onto CR 387 off SR 71 just north of the little town of White City.

Aucilla Wildlife Management Area

Size: 75,110 acres
Location: Jefferson, Taylor, and Wakulla Counties

Ownership: Public and private

The Aucilla WMA is located south of US 98 between the St. Marks and Econfina Rivers. It consists largely of pine flatwoods with large tracts of clearcut forests. The area lies along the northern boundary of the St. Marks National Wildlife Refuge and supports an abundance of white-tailed deer and wild turkey. Bald eagles as well as swallow-tailed and Mississippi kites are also frequently seen. The barely visible remains of the old city of Port Leon are accessible from the WMA's western end (ask for directions at the visitor center in nearby St. Marks National Wildlife Refuge). Aucilla WMA is accessible off SR 59 (the access road to the St. Marks National Wildlife Refuge) as well as from SR 14. A marked road that turns south off US 98 just east of the Aucilla River bridge leads to a boat landing on the Aucilla. This landing provides easy and interesting access to the lower river, Apalachee Bay, and the associated saltmarshes.

Big Bend Wildlife Management Area

Size: 46,784
Location: Taylor and Levy Counties
Ownership: Public

The Big Bend Wildlife Management Area is located along the Gulf Coast between CR 14 and CR 351. This entire region is characterized by a seaward fringe of pristine saltmarshes bordered along their inland edges by a nearly continuous line of wet coastal hammocks. Four main units define this WMA: Hickory Mound Impoundment (14,221 acres, see p. 134), Spring Creek (14,899 acres), Tide Swamp (20,285 acres), and Jena (8,772 acres). Spring Creek is accessible off CR 356 and CR 361A. The Tide Swamp and Jena Units are accessible off county roads 361 and 351. A number of boat landings allow access to the Gulf as well as to numerous tidewater creeks. An intricate system of roadways is also available for driving, biking, or walking. Those roads that are closed to vehicles are the best routes for walking and wildlife observation.

Big Shoals State Forest and Wildlife Management Area

Size: 3,459 acres
Location: Hamilton County
Ownership: Public

This state forest takes its name from the Suwannee River's Big Shoals Rapids, Florida's most dangerous stretch of whitewater. The forest supports a variety of wildlife, including white-tailed deer, wild turkey, gopher tortoise, Florida black bear, Florida pine snake, eastern indigo snake, and a variety of upland bird species. There are a number of native habitats, including pine flatwoods, beech–magnolia forests, floodplain forests, and small sections of cypress swamp. There are also 6 miles of frontage on the Suwannee River. The area is accessible off Hamilton CR 135 and is crossed by improved roads open to vehicles and a number of other roadways that serve as trails. The Nature Conservancy purchased the property in 1986 and later transferred it to the state.

Champion International Wildlife Management Area

Size: 21,078 acres
Location: Escambia County
Ownership: Private

This is the westernmost WMA in Florida and is somewhat similar in terrain to the Blackwater State Forest (see p. 114). Several creeks pass through the area and a variety of hiking trails provide walking access. Access is off US 29, a few miles north of its intersection with US 97. A single graded road passes through the area from east to west.

Chattahoochee Nature Park

Size: 21 acres
Location: Gadsden County
Ownership: Public

This little park is managed by the City of Chattahoochee and is a credit to small-town interest in preservation and conservation.

The area was first acquired by the city in the 1930s and was used as a community swimming pool. In the 1940s it became a Boy Scout reservation. In the early 1970s, the entire 21-acre site was designated the Chattahoochee Nature Park. What it lacks in size, it more than makes up for in the number and kinds of native plants it preserves. The park's plant list contains over 100 native species, including several that are rare or endangered. A short trail leads off into a ravine and is bordered on one side by inordinately tall specimens of the Florida flame azalea, a panhandle specialty, and on the other side by a unique array of native species. Both varieties of southern sugar maple grow side by side here as do such plants as chinquapin oak, solomon's-seal, hearts-a-bustin'-with-love, several species of fern, fringed campion, red buckeye, southern crab apple, both species of north Florida's herbaceous smilaxes, and at least one very small specimen of the rare and endangered torreya tree. Bring your tree and wildflower identification books if you visit in spring or summer. The park may be accessed in Chattahoochee by turning south on Bolivar Street, then continuing several blocks before traveling down and back up a steep ravine to a stop sign. The entrance to the park is straight ahead beyond the stop sign. For information, contact the Recreation Director, City Hall, P.O. Box 188, Chattahoochee, FL 32324; (904) 663-2123.

Cypress Creek Wildlife Management Area

Size: 18,451
Location: Hamilton County
Ownership: Private and public

This is another holding on the upper Suwannee River. There are several miles of river frontage, a boat ramp, several improved roads suitable for vehicles, and a number of unimproved roads suitable for hiking. The area near the river is characterized by floodplain woodlands; other parts of the WMA support upland forests. The best access is along Woodpecker Route which turns north at the intersection of SR 6 and Hamilton CR 135.

Dead Lakes State Recreation Area

Size: 83 acres (including 17.5 submerged acres)
Location: Gulf County
Ownership: Public

This enchanting state recreation area is located near the Dead Lakes, a natural lake that was first formed from overflow waters of the Apalachicola and Chipola Rivers. It was, for some time, stabilized by a dam that has since been removed. The park has a nice nature trail through an upland pine woods as well as along a marshy lake. There are also campsites and a boat ramp. The park is located 1 mile north of Wewahitchka off SR 71.

Econfina River State Park

Size: 3,400 acres
Location: Taylor County
Ownership: Public

The facilities at Econfina River State Park are dominated mostly by independent concessionaires that operate under an agreement with the state. The area has been the site of a private fishing resort for many years and still contains a privately run restaurant, small store, campground, and lodge. The state park operates a boat ramp on the scenic Econfina River, as well as a small campground and picnic area. The river is by far this park's most popular attraction. Saltwater fishermen come here because of the easy access to Apalachee Bay, and freshwater fishermen try their luck upstream from the landing. Paddlers also use the park as a put-in or take-out point for a variety of Econfina River explorations. The park also offers a system of hiking trails that run along the remains of old roadways. Certain of the roads are now kept mowed as walking paths. Some of these trails pass through attractive hardwood hammock woodlands. A map of the trails and information about accessing them can be requested from the park store. The park is accessed off US 98; a highway marker points the way.

Edward Ball Wildlife Management Area

Size: 66,945
Location: Gulf and Franklin Counties
Ownership: Private

Ed Ball WMA is bisected by Lake Wimico and the Intracoastal Waterway. Depot Creek, which leads into Lake Wimico from the south off US 98, is a particularly scenic area that runs through marshes before intersecting the lake. The area is accessed off US 98 or SR 71. A boat landing on Cypress Creek, which leads southward to Lake Wimico, is accessible south of CR 387 on the north side of the WMA.

Eglin Air Force Base

Size: 464,000 acres
Location: Okaloosa and Walton Counties
Ownership: Public

Special permits are required to visit this area. They can be obtained by visiting the Natural Resources Branch on SR 85 North in Niceville. Permits may be purchased by mail by contacting Eglin Natural Resources Branch, 107 Highway 85 North, Niceville, FL 32578. This is an active air force base and certain areas are closed, or may be closed without warning. However, there are a variety of outdoor exploration opportunities here, including birding, hiking, botanizing, and canoeing. It is wise to write to the address above and request the outdoor recreation, hunting, and freshwater fishing regulations before visiting.

Escambia River Wildlife Management Area

Size: 73,977 acres
Location: Santa Rosa County
Ownership: Private and public

This WMA is located along the eastern side of the Escambia River, northwest of Milton. There are several camping areas along the river and an assortment of improved and unimproved roads. It is most easily accessed off Santa Rosa CR 197, north of its intersection with CR 184.

Henderson Beach State Recreation Area

Size: 209
Location: Okaloosa County
Ownership: Public

Henderson Beach is primarily a swimming and fishing area located on the panhandle Gulf coast. Boardwalks lead across the dunes and provide access to the saltwater. Though this park is situated on a nonbarrier island beach, its ecology is similar in many respects to many of the panhandle's coastal parks. See St. Andrews State Recreation Area (p. 161), Grayton Beach State Recreation Area (p. 131), and the Santa Rosa Area of the Gulf Islands National Seashore (p. 89) for general discussions of the habitats, plants, and animals that are likely to be found here. For further information, contact Henderson Beach State Recreation Area, 17000 Emerald Coast Parkway, Destin, FL 32541; (904) 837-7550.

Holmes Creek and Choctawhatchee River Water Management Areas

Size: 41,990
Location: Holmes, Walton, and Washington Counties
Ownership: Public

The land included in this tract constitutes one of northwest Florida's most wildlife-rich areas. There are a variety of birds, mammals, reptiles, amphibians, and a number of interesting plant species. The area is open to hunting but is also excellent for nature study. The floodplain of the Choctawhatchee River is a well-preserved and highly productive ecosystem with vast acreage to wander and explore. Holmes Creek joins the Choctawhatchee near the southern part of this area, just north of Ebro. See the description of Holmes Creek Canoe Trail, p. 214.

Point Washington State Forest and Wildlife Management Area

Size: 141,592 acres
Location: Bay, Walton, and Washington Counties
Ownership: Private and Public

This huge tract is best known as a hunting area. The area is crisscrossed by driveable roads and is accessible from SR 77, SR 79, SR 388, US 98, and US 331. The area lies close to both the Gulf of Mexico and West Bay and supports pine flatwoods and coastal swamps. The Intracoastal Waterway bisects the westernmost part of the area. Pine Log Forest occupies the northernmost arm of this vast acreage. The description of this latter location (see p. 150) offers insight to the kind of terrain included within Point Washington.

Robert Brent Wildlife Management Area

Size: 89,184 acres
Location: Gadsden and Liberty Counties
Ownership: Private

Robert Brent WMA is located north of SR 20 between SR 12 and SR 267. It is easily accessed from SR 65 north of Hosford, as well as from SR 20 east of Hosford. Numerous roads traverse this area, which includes sandy upland woods and creek swamps.

Steinhatchee Wildlife Management Area

Size: 32,700 acres
Location: Dixie County
Ownership: Private

This large-acreage tract is located just north of Cross City and is bordered on its southern edge by Dixie CR 351 (turn north on 351, or Cedar Street, in the middle of Cross City). The area is forested with moist to wet pinelands that are dotted with willow-edged marshes, patches of upland hammock, and hardwood swamps. There is an elaborate and well-maintained system of sand and clay roadways that allow extensive access. There are no developed recreation areas except for a single hunt camp, and no developed walking trails. However, there are a number of woods roads that are used primarily by four-wheel-drive vehicles during hunting season. These roads make excellent walking paths for exploring some of this WMA's more remote locations.

Tate's Hell State Forest

Size: 215,252 acres
Location: Franklin and Liberty Counties
Ownership: Public

This area was an outstanding purchase by the state. It is rich in wildlife and is known to harbor at least 18 species of rare plants, all of which are part of the herbaceous ground cover. The area has been under private control for many years and has been managed without concern for natural preservation. The Division of Forestry's management plan sets its primary objective as restoring, maintaining, and preserving the natural ecosystems contained within the forest. Tate's Hell lies along the southern border of the Apalachicola National Forest, east of SR 65.

Twin Rivers Wildlife Management Area

Size: 9,340
Location: Hamilton, Madison, and Suwannee Counties
Ownership: Public

This WMA takes its name from the confluence of the Withlacoochee and Suwannee Rivers. The five management units border various portions of each of these fascinating waterways and preserve important remnants of north Florida's hardwood hammock and river swamp communities. The area is owned by the Suwannee River Water Management District and is managed in conjunction with the Florida Game and Fresh Water Fish Commission. Much of the area is open to hunting as well as to nature study. There are few facilities, but lots of beautiful scenery. All five units provide either walking or driving access to one of the rivers. Both the Ellaville and Mill Creek North Units have designated picnic areas on the Withlacoochee and Suwannee Rivers, respectively. The Ellaville picnic area can be reached from the extension of CR 141 by turning south onto the first graded road west of the Withlacoochee River bridge, then continuing south for about 0.8 mile before turning east toward the river. The Mill Creek picnic area is located at the terminus of the unit's main entrance road. Both of these sites provide good places to leave a vehicle while exploring the adjacent woodlands.

Tyndall Air Force Base Wildlife Management Area

Size: 29,000 acres
Location: Tyndall Air Force Base, near Panama City
Ownership: Public

This is an active air force base. Visitors must obtain a permit from the visitor center to enter. A nature trail and short board-walk offer opportunity to study pine flatwoods, pitcher plant bogs, and sand pine scrub. Birding is good here, especially for shorebirds along the beaches. However, springtime also brings many migrant warblers. There is an active wading bird rookery that is visible from the boardwalk.

DESIGNATED NORTHWEST FLORIDA CANOE TRAILS

Florida has 36 officially designated canoe trails; 18 are within the area covered by this book. The Florida Recreational Canoe Trails System is managed by the Florida Department of Environmental Protection in conjunction with several other agencies. A brochure is available for each trail, as well as a map that shows the location of each stream. These items are available by writing the Division of Recreation and Parks, Florida Department of Environmental Protection, 3900 Commonwealth Blvd, Tallahassee, FL 32399-3000; (904) 488-2850.

Perdido River

Mileage: 24
Location: Escambia County

Difficulty: Easy
Access Points: Old Water Ferry Landing; Barrineau Bridge, SR 99; Muscogee Bridge, SR 184.

The Perdido River is a remote and scenic stream that forms the dividing line between Florida and Alabama in the westernmost panhandle. Wildlife is abundant along much of the river due to the undeveloped woodlands that border much of the river's course. The sand bottom, relatively clear water, and forested banks make this an outstanding paddling excursion.

Coldwater Creek

Mileage: 18
Location: Santa Rosa County
Difficulty: Easy to moderate
Access Points: SR 4; Coldwater Creek Recreation Area; Berrydale Bridge; Tomahawk Landing; Old Steel Bridge; SR 191.

This is a fairly swift-moving, clearwater creek that runs over white-sand bottoms. Like many western panhandle streams, there are many scenic sandbars along the river that make outstanding picnicking and camping areas. (See the Blackwater River State Forest section, p. 120, for further information.)

Sweetwater/Juniper Creeks

Mileage: 13
Location: Santa Rosa County
Difficulty: Easy to moderate
Access Points: SR 4; Munson School Bridge; Red Rock Bridge; Indian Ford Bridge.

This is another clearwater route that flows relatively swiftly within scenic, narrow banks. The upper part of the creek is twisting and requires a bit of canoeing skill to navigate successfully. (See the Blackwater River State Forest section, p. 120, for further information.)

Blackwater River

Mileage: 31
Location: Okaloosa and Santa Rosa Counties
Difficulty: Easy
Access Points: Kennedy Bridge, Forest Rd. 24; Peadon Bridge, Forest Rd. 50; Cotton Bridge, SR 4; Bryant Bridge, Forest Rd. 21; Blackwater State Park.

The magnificent stands of Atlantic white cedar, dark water, white sand banks, and peaceful setting make this one of the panhandle's most outstanding paddling trips. (See the Blackwater River State Forest section, p. 119, for further information.)

Yellow River

Mileage: 56
Location: Okaloosa and Santa Rosa Counties
Difficulty: Moderate
Access Points: SR 2; US 90; SR 189; SR 87.

The hardwood hammocks and sandy banks that line this river make it particularly attractive. It is relatively fast flowing, particularly in its upper reaches, and can be challenging to novice canoeists. Part of the river flows through the Eglin Air Force Base (see p. 207); an Eglin recreational permit is required to paddle this portion of the stream.

Shoal River

Mileage: 27
Location: Okaloosa and Walton Counties
Difficulty: Easy
Access Points: SR 285; SR 393; US 90; SR 85.

The Shoal is a narrow, shallow, sandy-bottomed river that is one of the panhandle's best wilderness waterways. There are high banks, many small rivulets, scenic woodlands, and little development. It drains some of Florida's highest lands and is one of the major tributaries of the Yellow River, described above.

Holmes Creek

Mileage: 16
Location: Washington County
Difficulty: Easy
Access Points: SR 79; Brunson Landing; Hightower Springs
Landing; Live Oak Landing off SR 284.

This is a twisting, slow moving creek that flows through
cypress and blackgum swamps. High banks at the beginning of
the trail quickly give way to a system of backwaters and sloughs
that make delightful paddling. Several springs, including
Cypress and Becton Springs, feed clear water into the creek.
Watch out for submerged stumps and overhanging limbs.

Econfina Creek

Mileage: 22
Location: Bay and Washington Counties
Difficulty: Moderate to strenuous
Access Points: Scott's Bridge; Walsingham Bridge; Econfina Out-
fitters; SR 20; SR 388.

This creek is a challenging adventure that should be
attempted only by experienced canoeists. It is a twisting course
that slices its way between high banks and through scenic woodlands. Deadfalls are common obstacles, and paddlers are often
required to portage, or pull their craft over logjams. However,
wild azalea blooms abundantly in the spring and offers a beautiful contrast to the river's dark, reddish black water, and a
variety of plants and wildlife are easily observed along the banks.

Chipola River

Mileage: 52
Location: Calhoun and Jackson Counties
Difficulty: Easy to moderate
Access Points: Florida Caverns State Park; SR 167; SR 280-A; SR
278; SR 274; SR 20; SR 71.

In its upper reaches the Chipola River is a clearwater, spring-fed stream that flows between limestone studded banks and is overshadowed by majestic beech–magnolia forests. Though it becomes wider farther downstream, it still retains its beauty and, at least in low water, remains relatively clear. There are a number of places where the limestone is visible along the river bottom and several places where small springs enter the currents. This is one of two panhandle streams that pass over small, whitewater rapids. The Look and Tremble Falls (their name sounds more menacing than their appearance) are located just below the SR 274 bridge and are accessible by the sandy road on the west side of the river.

Ochlockonee River (Upper)

Mileage: 25
Location: Gadsden and Leon Counties
Difficulty: Easy to moderate
Access Points: SR 12; SR 157; Tower Rd.; US 90.

This part of the Ochlockonee is more narrow and twisting than its counterpart below Lake Talquin. Its rich brown waters tumble out of Georgia and flow through upland woods as well as through corridors of cypress. There is the potential for many portages and obstructions, hence the moderate rating.

Ochlockonee River (Lower)

Mileage: 67
Location: Franklin, Leon, Liberty, and Wakulla Counties
Difficulty: moderate
Access Points: SR 20; Pine Creek Landing; Ochlockonee River State Park.

This alluvial stream offers many miles of wooded banks, good fishing, and plenty of opportunity to view wildlife. See the Apalachicola National Forest section, p. 75, and the Ochlockonee River State Park section, p. 145, for more information about this river.

Sopchoppy River

Mileage: 15
Location: Wakulla County
Difficulty: Easy to moderate
Access Points: Oak Park Cemetery, National Forest Rd. 365; Mt. Beeser, National Forest Rd. 343; SR 375; US 319.

The Sopchoppy is the Apalachicola National Forest's most enchanting waterway. See p. 72 for a description of this stream.

Wakulla River

Mileage: 4
Location: Wakulla County
Difficulty: Easy
Access Points: SR 365; US 98

This is a clearwater, spring-fed stream with lush underwater vegetation and swampy edges. It is well known for its large frog, bird, and mammal populations. At least part of the river is under increasing development pressure and a number of houses are visible along the banks in some places. Though not part of the official trail, the section of the river that extends south of US 98 is a good location for seeing manatees. A large cypress tree on the east side of the river less than a mile below the bridge marks the location for many sightings. Most sightings in this part of the state occur in summer, particularly August and September.

Wacissa River

Mileage: 14
Location: Jefferson County
Difficulty: Easy
Access Points: Wacissa Springs, SR 59; Goose Pasture Rec Area (see directions for Aucilla River Sinks, p. 193); Nutall Rise Landing, off US 98.

This is a beautiful spring-fed river that passes mostly through junglelike woodlands with swampy banks. A number of small to medium-sized springs pour into the upper river, some of which are accessible through navigable spring runs. The water is extremely clear and the basin is filled with a variety of aquatic vegetation and freshwater fishes, both of which are clearly visible from the surface at almost any depth. Wildlife, especially wading birds, turtles, and snakes, are abundant and easily seen during most times of the year. The Wacissa is one of the last known locations for the ivory-billed woodpecker, a huge woodpecker that once inhabited the deepest of Florida's swamps. Unfortunately, this magnificent bird is now considered extirpated in the United States.

Aucilla River

Mileage: 19
Location: Jefferson, Madison, and Taylor Counties
Difficulty: Moderate to strenuous
Access Points: US 27; SR 257; old logging rd.
   Some maps show the Aucilla arising just across the state line in southern Georgia. For most of its length, however, it is strictly a Florida stream. See the section on the Aucilla sinks, p. 193, for more information about this stream.

Withlacoochee River (North)

Mileage: 32
Location: Hamilton and Madison Counties
Difficulty: easy
Access Points: SR 145; SR 150; SR 6; Suwannee River State Park.
   One of the best places to put in on the Withlacoochee is at the bridge on SR 6. It is an easy 12-mile paddle from here to Suwannee River State Park. Two of the most fascinating attributes along this stretch are the numerous clearwater springs that empty into the river's currents and the high, limestone bluffs that line portions of its banks. The Withlacoochee joins the Suwannee just below the Suwannee River State Park, one of two potential take-out points. The state park take-out requires paddling up the Suwannee from the confluence; alternatively, it is

possible to continue down the Suwannee for a short distance to a picnic area at the DeSoto Trail Site located at the terminus of an abandoned portion of old US 90 on the western side of the river.

Suwannee River (Upper)

Mileage: 64
Location: Columbia, Hamilton, Suwannee Counties
Difficulty: Easy to strenuous
Access Points: SR 6; Cone Bridge Rd.; US 41; SR 136; US 129; SR 249; Suwannee River State Park.

See the section on Suwannee River State Park for information about canoeing the Suwannee.

Suwannee River (Lower)

Mileage: 62
Location: Hamilton, Lafayette, and Madison Counties
Difficulty: Easy
Access Points: Suwannee River State Park; US 90; SR 250; SR 51; US 27.

See the section on Suwannee River State Park for information about canoeing the Suwannee.

WILDLIFE CHECKLISTS

The following checklists were compiled from *Checklist of Florida's Birds, A Checklist of Florida's Mammals,* and *A Checklist of Florida's Amphibians and Reptiles* distributed by the Nongame Wildlife Program of the Florida Game and Fresh Water Fish Commission. They are intended to include the known native and some of the more common naturalized species found in north Florida.

Population status is given in relative terms as follows:
abundant—likely to be seen in the right habitat
common—often seen in the right habitat
occasional—sometimes seen
uncommon—infrequently seen

rare—not likely to be seen

resident (bird checklist only)—present year-round

migrant (bird checklist only)—passes through on way to wintering/summering grounds

visitor (bird checklist only)—north Florida is the final migration destination

+ (bird checklist only)—known breeder in Florida

E—endangered species

Bird Checklist

Loons

☐ **Red-throated loon** (*Gavia stellata*)–uncommon winter visitor; offshore

☐ **Arctic loon** (*Gavia arctica*)–occasional in winter in coastal waters

☐ **Common loon** (*Gavia immer*)–fall to spring; common offshore and in saltwater bays along the coast, occasionally on inland lakes

Grebes

☐ **+Pied-billed grebe** (*Podilymbus podiceps*)–resident; freshwater ponds and saltwater bays along the coast

☐ **Horned grebe** (*Podiceps auritus*)–winter visitor; typically in saltwater

☐ **Red-necked grebe** (*Podiceps grisegena*)–winter; occasional offshore and in coastal waters

☐ **Eared grebe** (*Podiceps migricollis*)–rare winter visitor in Gulf coastal waters

☐ ' **Western grebe** (*Aechmophorus occidentalis*)–occasional along the Gulf coast in winter

Storm-petrels

☐ **Wilson's storm-petrel** (*Oceanites oceanicus*)–occasional spring through winter offshore

☐ **Band-rumped storm-petrel** (*Oceanodroma castro*)–rare off Gulf coast in August and December

Tropicbirds

☐ **White-tailed tropicbird** (*Phaethon lepturus*)–occasional in spring and summer off the Gulf coast

Boobies and Gannets

☐ **Masked booby** (*Sula dactylatra*)–fairly common in summer in offshore Gulf waters

☐ **Brown booby** (*Sula leucogaster*)–occasional year-round in offshore Gulf waters

☐ **Northern gannet** (*Sula bassanus*)–commonly seen along the coast from early fall to summer

Pelicans

☐ **American white pelican** (*Pelecanus erythrorhynchos*)–variably common year-round in near-coastal and inland waters

☐ **+Brown pelican** (*Pelecanus occidentalis*)–Common resident along the coast

Cormorants

☐ **+Double-crested cormorant** (*Phalacrocorax auritus*)–common to abundant resident, chiefly along the coast

Darters

☐ **Anhinga** (*Anhinga anhinga*)–common resident in freshwater habitats

Frigatebirds

☐ **Magnificent frigatebird** (*Fregata magnificens*)–uncommon in offshore waters; spring through early winter

Bitterns and Herons

☐ **+American bittern** (*Botaurus lentiginosus*)–fairly common in dense marshlands but seldom seen due to secretive habits; fall to spring

☐ **+Least bittern** (*Ixobrychus exilis*)–fairly common in marshlands; spring to fall

☐ **+Great blue heron** (*Ardea herodias*)–common resident in many fresh- and saltwater habitats

☐ **+Great egret** (*Casmerodius albus*)–common resident in many fresh- and saltwater habitats

☐ **+Snowy egret** (*Egretta thula*)–common resident in many fresh- and saltwater habitats

☐ **+Little blue heron** (*Egretta caerulea*)–common resident in many fresh- and saltwater habitats

☐ **+Tricolored heron** (*Egretta tricolor*)–common resident in many fresh- and saltwater habitats

☐ **+Reddish egret** (*Egretta rufescens*)–variously common resident in shallow saltwater

☐ +**Cattle egret** (*Bubulcus ibis*)–common to abundant resident in a variety of habitats

☐ +**Green-backed heron** (*Butorides striatus*)–fairly common in fresh- and saltwater habitats; spring to fall

☐ +**Black-crowned night-heron** (*Nycticorax nycticorax*)–fairly common resident in fresh- and saltwater habitats

☐ +**Yellow-crowned night-heron** (*Nycticorax violaceus*)–occasional in fresh- and saltwater habitats; spring to fall

Ibis and Spoonbills

☐ +**White ibis** (*Eudocimus albus*)–common resident in fresh- and saltwater habitats

☐ +**Glossy ibis** (*Plegadis falcinellus*)–variously occasional to abundant resident in fresh- and saltwater marshes

☐ **White-faced ibis** (*Plegadis chihi*)–occasional in spring in western panhandle

☐ **Roseate spoonbill** (*Ajaia ajaja*)–rare to occasional from spring to fall along the Gulf coast

Storks

☐ +**Wood stork** (*Mycteria americana*)–locally common in fresh- and saltwater wetlands; spring to early winter **E**

Flamingos

☐ **Greater flamingo** (*Phoenicopterus ruber*)–rare along the coast; spring to fall

Swans, Geese, and Ducks

☐ **Fulvous whistling-duck** (*Dendrocygna bicolor*)–occasional winter visitor in freshwater marshes

☐ **Tundra swan** (*Cygnus columbianus*)–estuaries and lakes; winter to early spring

☐ **Greater white-fronted goose** (*Anser albifrons*)–casual winter visitor

☐ **Snow goose** (*Chen caerulescens*)–occasional winter visitor to coastal marshes

☐ **Brant** (*Branta bernicla*)–rare winter visitor in bays and estuaries

☐ +**Canada goose** (*Branta canadensis*)–common winter visitor in fields and coastal marshes

☐ +**Wood duck** (*Aix sponsa*)–fairly common resident in woodlands bordering ponds, sloughs, and rivers

- [ ] **Green-winged teal** (*Anas crecca*)–common winter visitor in brackish and freshwater ponds
- [ ] **American black duck** (*Anas rubripes*)–occasional winter visitor along the coast
- [ ] **+Mottled duck** (*Anas fulvigula*)–fairly common local resident in coastal marshes
- [ ] **+Mallard** (*Anas platyrhynchos*)–fairly common winter visitor in coastal and inland marshes
- [ ] **White-cheeked pintail** (*Anas bahamensis*)–rare winter visitor in coastal marshes
- [ ] **Northern pintail** (*Anas acuta*)–common winter visitor in open fresh- and saltwater ponds
- [ ] **+Blue-winged teal** (*Anas discors*)–common winter visitor on ponds and bays
- [ ] **Cinnamon teal** (*Anas cyanoptera*)–uncommon winter visitor in Gulf coast ponds and marshes
- [ ] **Northern shoveler** (*Anas clypeata*)–fairly common winter visitor in marshes, ponds, and bays
- [ ] **Gadwall** (*Anas strepera*)–fairly common winter visitor on ponds and bays
- [ ] **Eurasian wigeon** (*Anas penelope*)–very occasional winter visitor along the coast
- [ ] **American wigeon** (*Anas americana*)–common in winter on ponds and bays
- [ ] **Canvasback** (*Aythya valisineria*)–fairly common winter visitor in lakes and marshes
- [ ] **Redhead** (*Aythya americana*)–abundant winter visitor along the coasts, particularly offshore in shallow bays
- [ ] **+Ring-necked duck** (*Aythya collaris*)–common winter resident in marshes, ponds, and lakes
- [ ] **Greater scaup** (*Aythya marila*)–common winter resident, chiefly offshore along the coasts
- [ ] **+Lesser scaup** (*Aythya affinis*)–common to abundant winter visitor in ponds, marshes, and bays
- [ ] **Harlequin duck** (*Histrionicus histrionicus*)–rare winter visitor along the coasts
- [ ] **Oldsquaw** (*Clangula hyemalis*)–occasional winter visitor along the coasts
- [ ] **Black scoter** (*Melanitta nigra*)–uncommon (to common in some years) along the coasts

☐ **Surf scoter** (*Melanitta perspicillata*)–rare to occasional along the coasts, winter to about midsummer

☐ **White-winged scoter** (*Melanitta fusca*)–occasional in winter along the coast

☐ **Common goldeneye** (*Bucephala islandica*)–fairly common in winter in bays and offshore

☐ **Bufflehead** (*Bucephala albeola*)–abundant winter visitor in bays and coastal lakes

☐ **+Hooded merganser** (*Lophodytes cucullatus*)–fairly common to common winter visitor in ponds, marshes, and rivers

☐ **Common merganser** (*Mergus merganser*)–occasional in winter near the coast, especially in brackish waters

☐ **Red-breasted merganser** (*Mergus serrator*)–fairly common to common year-round in coastal waters

☐ **+Ruddy duck** (*Oxyura jamaicensis*)–occasional to common year-round in lakes and shallow, saltwater bays

☐ **Masked duck** (*Oxyura dominica*)–rare along the Gulf coast in December

Vultures

☐ **+Black vulture** (*Coragyps atratus*)–common resident throughout the state

☐ **+Turkey vulture** (*Cathartes aura*)–common resident throughout the state

Kites, Eagles and Hawks

☐ **+Osprey** (*Pandion haliaetus*)–fairly common to common resident, primarily coastal areas

☐ **+American swallow-tailed kite** (*Elanoides forficatus*)–uncommon to common summer visitor in a variety of habitats

☐ **Snail kite** (*Rostrhamus sociabilis*)–rare winter visitor E

☐ **+Mississippi kite** (*Ictinis mississippiensis*)–fairly common summer visitor in a variety of habitats

☐ **+Bald eagle** (*Haliaeetus leucocephalus*)–fairly common, nearly year-round

☐ **+Northern harrier** (*Circus cyaneus*)–fairly common winter visitor in fields and wetland marshes

☐ **+Sharp-shinned hawk** (*Accipiter striatus*)–fairly common to common from about August to May

☐ **+Cooper's hawk** (*Accipiter cooperii*)–uncommon resident in woodland edges

- [ ] **Northern goshawk** (*Accipiter gentilis*)–rare in winter
- [ ] **+Red-shouldered hawk** (*Buteo lineatus*)–fairly common to common resident in a variety of habitats including fields, marshes, and woodlands
- [ ] **+Broad-winged hawk** (*Buteo platypterus*)–fairly common summer visitor in woodlands
- [ ] **Short-tailed hawk** (*Buteo brachyurus*)–rare summer visitor
- [ ] **Swainson's hawk** (*Buteo swainsoni*)–rare winter visitor
- [ ] **+Red-tailed hawk** (*Buteo jamaicensis*)–fairly common resident in woodlands
- [ ] **Ferruginous hawk** (*Buteo regalis*)–very rare winter visitor
- [ ] **Golden eagle** (*Aquila chrysaetos*)–rare winter visitor

Caracaras and Falcons

- [ ] **+American kestrel** (*Falco sparverius*)–common resident in fields, along roadsides, and in woodland edges
- [ ] **Merlin** (*Falco columbarius*)–uncommon but regular in winter, most often along the coast
- [ ] **Peregrine falcon** (*Falco peregrinus*)–uncommon but regular winter visitor, mostly along the coast **E**

Pheasants, Turkeys, and Quail

- [ ] **+Wild turkey** (*Meleagris gallopavo*)–common resident in upland woods and turkey oak–pineland ridges
- [ ] **+Northern bobwhite** (*Colinus virginianus*)–fairly common resident in open woods

Rails, Gallinules, and Coots

- [ ] **Yellow rail** (*Coturnicops noveboracensis*)–rare winter visitor in fresh and brackish marshes
- [ ] **+Black rail** (*Laterallus jamaicensis*)–rare and secretive resident in brackish marshes and saltmarshes
- [ ] **+Clapper rail** (*Rallus longirostris*)–common resident in salt- and tidal marshes
- [ ] **+King rail** (*Rallus elegans*)–uncommon resident, chiefly in freshwater marshes
- [ ] **+Virginia rail** (*Rallus limicola*)–uncommon winter visitor in salt- and brackish marshes
- [ ] **Sora** (*Porzana carolina*)–uncommon winter resident in freshwater and brackish marshes
- [ ] **+Purple gallinule** (*Porphyrula martinica*)–fairly common spring to fall visitor, chiefly in freshwater marshes

☐ **+Common moorhen** (*Gallinula chloropus*)–common resident in marshes

☐ **+American coot** (*Fulica americana*)–common to abundant resident in fresh and saltwater marshes

Limpkins

☐ **+Limpkin** (*Aramus guarauna*)–fairly common resident in clear water rivers

Cranes

☐ **+Sandhill crane** (*Grus canadensis*)–uncommon to common resident in fields

Plovers and Lapwings

☐ **Black-bellied plover** (*Pluvialis squatarola*)–common resident along coastal shores

☐ **Lesser golden-plover** (*Pluvialis dominica*)–rare winter visitor in fields

☐ **+Snowy plover** (*Charadrius alexandrinus*)–uncommon resident of sand beaches

☐ **+Wilson's plover** (*Charadrius wilsonia*)–fairly common summer visitor to beaches and shores

☐ **Semipalmated plover** (*Charadrius semipalmatus*)–common to abundant resident of beaches and shores

☐ **Piping plover** (*Charadrius melodus*)–uncommon nearly year-round on beaches

☐ **+Killdeer** (*Charadrius vociferus*)–common resident in fields, near coasts, on golf courses, large grassy areas

☐ **Mountain plover** (*Charadrius montanus*)–rare winter visitor

Oystercatchers

☐ **+American oystercatcher** (*Haematopus palliatus*)–fairly common resident along coasts

Stilts and Avocets

☐ **+Black-necked stilt** (*Himantopus mexicanus*)–uncommon to locally common in summer, chiefly along the coast

☐ **American avocet** (*Recurvirostra americana*)–fairly common in fall, winter, and spring in shallow ponds and marshes near the coast

Sandpipers

☐ **Greater yellowlegs** (*Tringa melanoleuca*)–fairly common nearly throughout the year in coastal marhses and mud flats

☐ **Lesser yellowlegs** (*Tringa flavipes*)–fairly common nearly year-round in coastal marshes and mud flats

☐ **Solitary sandpiper** (*Tringa solitaria*)–uncommon summer visitor in brackish waters along the coast

☐ **+Willet** (*Catoptrophorus semipalmatus*)–common resident along the coast

☐ **Spotted sandpiper** (*Actitis macularia*)–fairly common nearly year-round on shores of freshwater ponds, marshes, and streams

☐ **Upland sandpiper** (*Bartramia longicauda*)–rare summer visitor

☐ **Whimbrel** (*Numenius phaeopus*)–fairly common winter visitor, chiefly along the coast

☐ **Long-billed curlew** (*Numenius americanus*)–rare summer visitor, inland

☐ **Hudsonian godwit** (*Limosa haemastica*)–rare in spring and fall along the east coast

☐ **Marbled godwit** (*Limosa fedoa*)–uncommon but regular winter visitor along the coast

☐ **Ruddy turnstone** (*Arenaria interpres*)–common resident on coastal shores

☐ **Red knot** (*Calidris canutus*)–fairly common nearly year-round on beaches

☐ **Sanderling** (*Calidris alba*)–common resident along sandy beaches

☐ **Semipalmated sandpiper** (*Calidris pusilla*)–common migrant along the coast

☐ **Western sandpiper** (*Calidris mauri*)–common to abundant winter visitor along the coast

☐ **Least sandpiper** (*Calidris minutilla*)–common winter visitor to mud flats and coastal wetlands

☐ **White-rumped sandpiper** (*Calidris fusciollis*)–rare to uncommon visitor along the coast during migration

☐ **Baird's sandpiper** (*Calidris bairdii*)–rare visitor during migration

☐ **Pectoral sandpiper** (*Calidris melanotos*)–fairly common visitor during migration, fields and marshes

☐ **Purple sandpiper** (*Calidris maritima*)–uncommon to rare winter visitor

☐ **Dunlin** (*Calidris alpina*)–abundant winter visitor along the coast

☐ **Curlew sandpiper** (*Calidris ferruginea*)–very rare in migration

☐ **Stilt sandpiper** (*Calidris himantopus*)–rare during migration

☐ **Buff-breasted sandpiper** (*Tryngites subruficollis*)–rare during spring and fall migration

☐ **Ruff** (*Philomachus pugnax*)–rare during spring migration

☐ **Short-billed dowitcher** (*Limnodromus griseus*)–common to abundant resident along coastal mud flats

☐ **Long-billed dowitcher** (*Limnodromus scolopaceus*)–uncommon winter visitor along coastal mud flats

☐ **Common snipe** (*Gallinago gallinago*)–fairly common to common in marshes

☐ **+American woodcock** (*Scolopax minor*)–uncommon but regular winter visitor in thickets and moist woodlands

☐ **Wilson's phalarope** (*Phalaropus tricolor*)–rare spring and fall migrant

☐ **Red-necked phalarope** (*Phalaropus lobatus*)–rare spring and fall migrant

☐ **Red phalarope** (*Phalaropus fulicaria*)–rare spring and fall migrant

Jaegers, Gulls, Terns, and Skimmers

☐ **Parasitic jaeger** (*Stercorarius parasiticus*)–possible year-round in pelagic waters

☐ **Long-tailed jaeger** (*Stercorarius longicaudus*)–rare during winter in pelagic waters

☐ **+Laughing gull** (*Latrus atricilla*)–common to abundant resident in coastal areas

☐ **`Franklin's gull** (*Larus pipixcan*)–rare winter visitor along coast

☐ **Little gull** (*Larus minutus*)–rare winter visitor along the east coast

☐ **Bonaparte's gull** (*Larus philadelphia*)–common to abundant winter visitor along the coast

☐ **Ring-billed gull** (*Larus delawarensis*)–abundant resident along coasts and inland

☐ **Herring gull** (*Larus argentatus*)–common resident along the coast

☐ **Black-legged kittiwake** (*Risa tridactyla*)–rare in midwinter, chiefly offshore

☐ **+Gull-billed tern** (*Sterna nilotica*)–uncommon to common in summer along beaches and coastal marshes

☐ **+Caspian tern** (*Sterna caspia*)–uncommon resident along the coast

☐ **+Royal tern** (*Sterna maxima*)–common to abundant resident along the coast

☐ **Sandwich tern** (*Sterna sandvicensis*)–uncommon winter visitor along the coast

☐ **Roseate tern** (*Sterna dougallii*)–rare in spring and fall, offshore

☐ **Common tern** (*Sterna hirundo*)–rare to uncommon in winter

☐ **Forster's tern** (*Sterna forsteri*)–common in fall, winter, and spring, chiefly coastal

- [ ] **+Least tern** (*Sterna antillarum*)–common to abundant summer visitor along the coast and inland
- [ ] **Bridled tern** (*Sterna anaethetus*)–rare in summer off the east coast
- [ ] **Sooty tern** (*Sterna fuscata*)–rare in summer off east coast
- [ ] **Black tern** (*Chlidonias niger*)–common to abundant in summer along the coast
- [ ] **Brown noddy** (*Anous stolidus*)–rare in summer and fall off the coast
- [ ] **+Black skimmer** (*Rynchops niger*)–uncommon to abundant resident along the coast

Pigeons and Doves

- [ ] **+Rock dove** (*Columba livia*)–abundant resident, cosmopolitan
- [ ] **White-winged dove** (*Zenaida asiatica*)–rare in winter
- [ ] **Zenaida dove** (*Zenaida aurita*)–rare in winter
- [ ] **+Mourning dove** (*Zenaida macroura*)–common resident in fields
- [ ] **Inca dove** (*Columbina inca*)–very rare in spring or early summer
- [ ] **+Common ground-dove** (*Columbina talpacoti*)–common resident of open woods, often along the coast

Cuckoos, Anis, and Allies

- [ ] **Black-billed cuckoo** (*Coccyzus erythropthalmus*)–rare in woodlands during migration
- [ ] **+Yellow-billed cuckoo** (*Coccyzus americanus*)–fairly common but secretive summer visitor in woodlands
- [ ] **Groove-billed ani** (*Crotophaga sulcirostris*)–rare in winter in marsh edges

Barn-Owls

- [ ] **+Common barn-owl** (*Tyto alba*)–occasional resident, chiefly in old buildings and barns

Typical Owls

- [ ] **+Eastern screech-owl** (*Otus asio*)–fairly common resident in woodlands
- [ ] **+Great horned owl** (*Bubo virginianus*)–fairly common resident in rich upland woods
- [ ] **+Barred owl** (*Strix varia*)–fairly common resident in floodplain and lowland woods

☐ **Short-eared owl** (*Asio flammeus*)–rare winter visitor over fields and open marshes

☐ **Northern saw-whet owl** (*Aegolius acadicus*)–very rare winter visitor

Nightjars

☐ **+Common nighthawk** (*Chordeiles minor*)–common in spring, summer, and fall in a variety of habitats

☐ **+Chuck-will's-widow** (*Caprimulgus carolinensis*)–fairly common summer visitor in open, pine–oak woods

☐ **Whip-poor-will** (*Caprimulgus vociferus*)–uncommon in winter, most often heard and seen during spring migration

Swifts

☐ **+Chimney swift** (*Chaetura pelagica*)–common summer visitor near cities and dwellings

☐ **Vaux's swift** (*Chaetura vauxi*)–very rare winter visitor

Hummingbirds

☐ **Broad-billed hummingbird** (*Cynanthus latirostris*)–very rare in winter

☐ **+Ruby-throated hummingbird** (*Archilochus colubris*)–com-mon summer visitor inland and along coast

☐ **Rufous hummingbird** (*Selasphorus rufus*)–rare in winter

Kingfishers

☐ **+Belted kingfisher** (*Ceryle alcyon*)–common resident near wetlands

Woodpeckers

☐ **+Red-headed woodpecker** (*Melanerpes erythrocephalus*)– fairly common resident of upland woods

☐ **+Red-bellied woodpecker** (*Melanerpes carolinus*)–common resident in a variety of woodland habitats

☐ **Yellow-bellied woodpecker** (*Sphyrapicus varius*)–uncommon winter visitor in woodlands

☐ +**Downy woodpecker** (*Picoides pubescens*)–fairly common resident in woodlands

☐ +**Hairy woodpecker** (*Picoides villosus*)–uncommon resident in woodlands

☐ +**Red-cockaded woodpecker** (*Picoides borealis*)–uncommon to locally common resident of mature longleaf pine woodlands and adjacent habitats

☐ +**Northern flicker** (*Colaptes auratus*)–common resident in woodlands

☐ +**Pileated woodpecker** (*Dryocopus pileatus*)–common resident in wetlands, swamps, and floodplains

Tyrant Flycatchers

☐ **Olive-sided flycatcher** (*Contopus borealis*)–occasional spring and fall migrant in woodlands

☐ +**Eastern wood-pewee** (*Contopus virens*)–fairly common summer visitor in woodlands

☐ +**Acadian flycatcher** (*Empidonax virescens*)–fairly common summer visitor in woodlands

☐ **Alder flycatcher** (*Empidonax alnorum*)–rare fall migrant in woodlands

☐ **Willow flycatcher** (*Empidonax traillii*)–rare fall migrant in woodlands

☐ **Least flycatcher** (*Empidonax minimus*)–rare spring and fall migrant in woodlands

☐ **Eastern phoebe** (*Sayornis phoebe*)–fairly common winter visitor near wetlands

☐ **Vermillion flycatcher** (*Pyrocephalus rubinus*)–rare but regular winter visitor on west coast

☐ **Ash-throated flycatcher** (*Myiarchus cinerascens*)–rare winter visitor in woodlands

☐ +**Great crested flycatcher** (*Myiarchus crinitus*)–common summer visitor in a variety of woodland habitats

☐ **Brown-crested flycatcher** (*Myiarchus tyrannulus*)–very rare in midwinter

☐ **Western kingbird** (*Tyrannus verticalis*)–occasional winter visitor in open areas and along the coast

☐ +**Eastern kingbird** (*Tyrannus tyrannus*)–common summer visitor in woodlands and fields

☐ +**Gray kingbird** (*Tyrannus dominicensis*)–fairly common along the coast

☐ **Scissor-tailed flycatcher** (*Tyrannus forficatus*)–rare winter visitor along the coast

Larks

☐ **Horned lark** (*Eremophila alpestris*)–rare winter visitor in open areas along the coast

Swallows

☐ **+Purple martin** (*Progne subis*)–common to abundant spring and summer visitor

☐ **Tree swallow** (*Tachycineta bicolor*)–nearly year-round, chiefly near large bodies of water

☐ **+Northern rough-winged swallow** (*Stelgidopteryx serripennis*)–uncommon to fairly common summer visitor

☐ **Bank swallow** (*Riparia riparia*)–fairly common spring and fall migrant

☐ **Cliff swallow** (*Hirundo pyrrhonota*)–rare during spring and fall migration

☐ **Cave swallow** (*Hirundo fulva*)–very rare during spring migration and other times of the year

☐ **+Barn swallow** (*Hirundo rustica*)–common to abundant summer visitor, often near bridges but also in other places

Jays, Magpies, and Crows

☐ **+Blue jay** (*Cyanocitta cristata*)–abundant resident in a variety of habitats

☐ **+American crow** (*Corvus brachyrhynchos*)–abundant and often-seen resident

☐ **+Fish crow** (*Corvus ossifragus*)–abundant and often-seen resident

Titmice

☐ **+Carolina chickadee** (*Parus carolinensis*)–common woodland resident

☐ **+Tufted titmouse** (*Parus bicolor*)–common woodland resident

Nuthatches

☐ **Red-breasted nuthatch** (*Sitta canadensis*)–occasional winter visitor in woodlands

☐ **+White-breasted nuthatch** (*Sitta carolinensis*)–fairly common resident in woodlands

☐ **+Brown-headed nuthatch** (*Sitta pusilla*)–fairly common resident in pinelands

Creepers

☐ **Brown creeper** (*Certhia americana*)–occasional winter visitor in woodlands

Wrens

☐ **+Carolina wren** (*Thryothorus ludovicianus*)–abundant resident in many habitats

☐ **Bewick's wren** (*Thryomanes bewickii*)–rare winter visitor

☐ **House wren** (*Troglodytes aedon*)–fairly common winter visitor in shrubby and brushy areas

☐ **Winter wren** (*Troglodytes troglodytes*)–rare winter visitor, chiefly near streams and wet areas

☐ **Sedge wren** (*Cistothorus platensis*)–uncommon but regular winter visitor in marshes and grassy meadows

☐ **+Marsh wren** (*Cistothorus palustris*)–fairly common resident in marshes

Old World Warblers, Kinglets, etc.

☐ **Golden-crowned kinglet** (*Regulus satrapa*)–uncommon winter visitor in woodlands

☐ **Ruby-crowned kinglet** (*Regulus calendula*)–common winter visitor in woodlands

☐ **+Blue-gray gnatcatcher** (*Polioptila caerulea*)–fairly common resident in woodlands

☐ **+Eastern bluebird** (*Sialia sialis*)–common resident in open woodlands

☐ **Veery** (*Catharus fuscescens*)–uncommon spring and fall migrant, woodlands

☐ **Gray-checked thrush** (*Catharus minimus*)–uncommon spring and fall migrant, woodlands

☐ **Swainson's thrush** (*Catharus ustulatus*)–uncommon spring and fall migrant, woodlands

☐ **Hermit thrush** (*Catharus guttatus*)–uncommon to common winter visitor in woodlands

☐ **+Wood thrush** (*Hylocichla mustelina*)–fairly common summer visitor in woodlands

☐ **+American robin** (*Turdus migratorius*)–abundant winter resident in woodlands, fields, yards

Mimic Thrushes

- [ ] **+Gray catbird** (*Dumetella carolinensis*)–fairly common to common winter resident in woodlands
- [ ] **+Northern mockingbird** (*Mimus polyglottos*)–common resident in a variety of habitats
- [ ] **Sage thrasher** (*Oreoscoptes montanus*)–rare in winter and early spring
- [ ] **+Brown thrasher** (*Toxostoma rufum*)–common resident in woodlands

Wagtails and Pipits

- [ ] **Water pipit** (*Anthus spinoletta*)–fairly common to common winter visitor, fields
- [ ] **Sprague's pipit** (*Anthus spragueii*)–occasional winter visitor, fields

Waxwings

- [ ] **Cedar waxwing** (*Bombycilla cedrorum*)–fairly common winter visitor in neighborhoods and woodlands

Shrikes

- [ ] **+Loggerhead shrike** (*Lanius ludovicianus*)–fairly common resident in open areas near woodlands

Starlings

- [ ] **+European starling** (*Sturnus vulgaris*)–abundant resident in many habitats

Vireos

- [ ] **+White-eyed vireo** (*Vireo griseus*)–fairly common resident in dense moist woodlands
- [ ] **Bell's vireo** (*Vireo bellii*)–rare in spring and fall migration
- [ ] **Solitary vireo** (*Vireo solitarius*)–uncommon but regular winter visitor, woodlands
- [ ] **+Yellow-throated vireo** (*Vireo flavifrons*)–fairly common summer visitor in rich woodlands
- [ ] **Warbling vireo** (*Vireo gilvus*)–rare spring and fall migrant in woodlands
- [ ] **Philadelphia vireo** (*Vireo philadelphicus*)–rare spring and fall migrant in woodlands
- [ ] **+Red-eyed vireo** (*Vireo olivaceus*)–common summer visitor in woodlands
- [ ] **Black-whiskered vireo** (*Vireo altiloquus*)–rare spring and early summer visitor, chiefly along the coast

Wood Warblers

☐ **Blue-winged warbler** (*Vermivora pinus*)–occasional spring and fall migrant

☐ **Golden-winged warbler** (*Vermivora chrysoptera*)–occasional spring and fall migrant

☐ **Tennessee warbler** (*Vermivora peregrina*)–uncommon spring and fall migrant

☐ **Orange-crowned warbler** (*Vermivora celata*)–uncommon to fairly common winter resident in woodlands

☐ **Nashville warbler** (*Vermivora ruficapilla*)–rare spring and fall migrant

☐ **+Northern parula** (*Parula americana*)–common summer resident in rich woodlands and hammocks

☐ **+Yellow warbler** (*Dendroica petechia*)–uncommon spring and fall migrant

☐ **Chestnut-sided warbler** (*Dendroica pensylvanica*)–uncommon spring and fall migrant

☐ **Magnolia warbler** (*Dendroica magnolia*)–uncommon spring and fall migrant

☐ **Cape May warbler** (*Dendroica tigrina*)–uncommon spring and fall migrant

☐ **Black-throated blue warbler** (*Dendroica caereulescens*)–uncommon spring and fall migrant

☐ **Yellow-rumped warbler** (*Dendroica coronata*)–abundant winter visitor in a variety of habitats

☐ **Black-throated gray warbler** (*Dendroica nigrescens*)–occasional spring and fall migrant

☐ **Townsend's warbler** (*Dendroica townsendi*)–rare winter visitor

☐ **Black-throated green warbler** (*Dendroica virens*)–uncommon spring and fall migrant

☐ **Blackburnian warbler** (*Dendroica fusca*)–uncommon spring and fall migrant

☐ **+Yellow-throated warbler** (*Dendroica dominica*)–fairly common resident in open woodlands

☐ **+Pine warbler** (*Dendroica pinus*)–common resident in pinelands and woodlands

☐ **Kirtland's warbler** (*Dendroica kirtlandii*)–rare spring and fall migrant **E**

☐ **+Prairie warbler** (*Dendroica discolor*)–common summer visitor in woodlands

☐ **Palm warbler** (*Dendroica palmarum*)–common winter visitor in a variety of habitats

- [ ] **Bay-breasted warbler** (*Dendroica castanea*)–uncommon during spring and fall migration
- [ ] **Blackpoll warbler** (*Dendroica striata*)–occasional but regular spring and fall migrant in woodlands
- [ ] **Cerulean warbler** (*Dendroica cerulea*)–occasional spring and fall migrant, chiefly in the tops of trees
- [ ] **Black-and-white warbler** (*Mniotilta varia*)–uncommon to fairly common in fall, winter, and spring, woodlands
- [ ] **+American redstart** (*Setophaga ruticilla*)–fairly common spring and fall migrant, woodlands
- [ ] **+Prothonotary warbler** (*Protonotaria citrea*)–common summer visitor, wet areas, never far from water
- [ ] **+Worm-eating warbler** (*Helmitheros vermivorus*)–uncommon to fairly common spring and fall migrant
- [ ] **+Swainson's warbler** (*Limnothlypis swainsonii*)–uncommon summer visitor, low woods
- [ ] **Ovenbird** (*Seiurus aurocapillus*)–uncommon to fairly common in open woodlands
- [ ] **Northern waterthrush** (*Seiurus noveboracensis*)–uncommon spring and fall migrant
- [ ] **+Louisiana waterthrush** (*Seiurus motacilla*)–uncommon to fairly common summer visitor
- [ ] **+Kentucky warbler** (*Oporornis formosus*)–uncommon summer visitor in thickets
- [ ] **Connecticut warbler** (*Oporornis agilis*)–rare spring and fall migrant
- [ ] **Mourning warbler** (*Oporornis philadelphia*)–rare spring and fall migrant
- [ ] **+Common yellowthroat** (*Geothlypis trichas*)–common resident, low, wet to moist woodlands
- [ ] **+Hooded warbler** (*Wilsonia citrina*)–fairly common summer resident, rich woodlands and several other habitats
- [ ] **Wilson's warbler** (*Wilsonia pusilla*)–rare spring and fall migrant
- [ ] **Canada warbler** (*Wilsonia canadensis*)–rare spring and fall migrant
- [ ] **+Yellow-breasted chat** (*Icteria virens*)–fairly common summer visitor, a variety of woodland habitats

Tanagers
- [ ] **+Summer tanager** (*Piranga rubra*)–common summer visitor in woodlands and neighborhoods
- [ ] **Scarlet tanager** (*Piranga olivacea*)–uncommon spring and fall migrant, woodlands
- [ ] **Western tanager** (*Piranga ludoviciana*)–occasional in winter

Cardinals and Allies

- ☐ **+Northern cardinal** (*Cardinalis cardinalis*)–abundant resident in woodlands and neighborhoods
- ☐ **Rose-breasted grosbeak** (*Pheucticus lucovicianus*)–uncommon spring and fall migrant, rich woodlands
- ☐ **Black-headed grosbeak** (*Pheucticus melanocephalus*)–rare spring migrant
- ☐ **+Blue grosbeak** (*Guiraca caerulea*)–common summer visitor in thin woods, as well as shrubby and bushy areas
- ☐ **+Indigo bunting** (*Passerina cyanea*)–common summer visitor in shrubby and bushy woodland edges
- ☐ **+Painted bunting** (*Passerina amoena*)–locally common summer visitor
- ☐ **Dickcissel** (*Spiza americana*)–occasional spring and fall migrant

Towhees, Sparrows, and Allies

- ☐ **+Rufous-sided towhee** (*Pipilo erythrophthalmus*)–abundant resident in woodlands and thickets
- ☐ **+Bachman's sparrow** (*Aimophila aestivalis*)–fairly common but secretive, pine woodlands
- ☐ **+Chipping sparrow** (*Spizella passerina*)–common winter visitor, often seen at feeders
- ☐ **Clay-colored sparrow** (*Spizella pallida*)–occasional spring and fall migrant
- ☐ **+Field sparrow** (*Spizella pusilla*)–fairly common resident along the edges of thin woodlands and in fields
- ☐ **Vesper sparrow** (*Pooecetes gramineus*)–fairly common winter visitor in grasslands
- ☐ **Lark sparrow** (*Chondestes grammacus*)–occasional spring and fall migrant
- ☐ **Savannah sparrow** (*Passerculus sandwichensis*)–common winter visitor in grasslands and edges
- ☐ **Grasshopper sparrow** (*Ammodramus savannarum*)–rare winter visitor, pastures and fields E
- ☐ **Henslow's sparrow** (*Ammodramus henslowii*)–rare winter visitor, shrubby fields and edges
- ☐ **Le Conte's sparrow** (*Ammodramus leconteii*)–occasional winter visitor in wet grassy areas
- ☐ **Sharp-tailed sparrow** (*Ammodramus caudacutus*)–fairly common winter visitor in tidal and saltwater marshes
- ☐ **+Seaside sparrow** (*Ammodramus maritimus*)–fairly common resident, tidal marshes

- [ ] **Fox sparrow** (*Passerella iliaca*)–rare in midwinter
- [ ] **Song sparrow** (*Melospiza melodia*)–common winter visitor, brushy areas, low thickets, and grassy areas with shrubs
- [ ] **Lincoln's sparrow** (*Melospiza lincolnii*)–occasional in winter
- [ ] **Swamp sparrow** (*Melospiza georgiana*)–fairly common to common winter visitor, generally in wet, grassy, or shrubby areas
- [ ] **White-throated sparrow** (*Zonotrichia albicollis*)–common to abundant winter visitor in a variety of habitats
- [ ] **White-crowned sparrow** (*Zonotrichia leucophrys*)–rare winter visitor
- [ ] **Dark-eyed junco** (*Junco hyemalis*)–uncommon to common winter resident in edges and woodlands
- [ ] **Lapland longspur** (*Calcarius lapponicus*)–rare in winter, chiefly along grassy coastal beaches
- [ ] **Snow bunting** (*Plectrophenax nivalis*)–very rare in winter, beaches and open areas

Blackbirds, Orioles, and Allies
- [ ] **Bobolink** (*Dolichonyx oryzivorus*)–fairly common to common spring and fall migrant in open, grassy areas
- [ ] **+Red-winged blackbird** (*Agelaius phoeniceus*)–abundant resident in wet grasslands and marshes
- [ ] **+Eastern meadowlark** (*Sturnella magna*)–fairly common to common resident, grasslands and fields
- [ ] **Western meadowlark** (*Sturnella neglecta*)–rare winter visitor
- [ ] **Yellow-headed blackbird** (*Xanthocephalus xanthocephalus*)–rare spring and fall migrant, often near freshwater marshes
- [ ] **Rusty blackbird** (*Euphagus carolinus*)–fairly common to common winter visitor, wet woodlands
- [ ] **Brewer's blackbird** (*Euphagus cyanocephalus*)–fairly common to common winter visitor in a variety of habitats
- [ ] **+Boat-tailed grackle** (*Quiscalus major*)–abundant resident, chiefly coastal
- [ ] **+Common grackle** (*Quiscalus quiscula*)–abundant resident in a variety of habitats
- [ ] **+Brown-headed cowbird** (*Molothrus ater*)–abundant resident in a variety of habitats
- [ ] **+Orchard oriole** (*Icterus spurius*)–fairly common to common summer visitor in open woods
- [ ] **+Northern oriole** (*Icterus galbula*)–occasional winter visitor, suburbs and open woods

Northern Finches

☐ **Purple finch** (*Carpodacus purpureus*)–irregular but sometimes common winter visitor in a variety of habitats

☐ **Pine siskin** (*Carduelis pinus*)–uncommon to fairly common winter visitor

☐ **American goldfinch** (*Carduelis tristis*)–common to abundant winter visitor in woodlands and at feeders

☐ **Evening grosbeak** (*Coccothraustes vespertinus*)–rare winter visitor

Old-World Sparrows

☐ **+House sparrow** (*Passer domesticus*)–abundant resident near cities and in suburban neighborhoods

Mammal Checklist

☐ **Virginia opossum** (*Didelphis virginiana*)–abundant in most habitats, statewide

☐ **Southeastern shrew** (*Sorex longirostris*)–rare in wet forests, northern two-thirds of the state

☐ **Southern short-tailed shrew** (*Blarina carolinensis*)–common in forests, statewide

☐ **Least shrew** (*Cryptotis parva*)–common in fields, statewide

☐ **Eastern mole** (*Scalopus aquaticus*)–abundant in most habitats, statewide

☐ **Little brown bat** (*Myotis lucifugus*)–rare in caves and buildings, northern border of the state

☐ **Gray bat** (*Myotis grisecens*) rare in caves of the northern panhandle E

☐ **Silver-haired bat** (*Lasionycteris noctivagans*)–rare in trees, panhandle

☐ **Eastern pipistrelle** (*Pipistrellus subflavus*)–common in caves and trees, statewide

☐ **Rafinesque's big-eared bat** (*Plecotus rafinesquii*)–uncommon in trees and cabins, northern two-thirds of the state

☐ **Big brown bat** (*Eptesicus fuscus*)–rare in caves and trees, statewide

☐ **Hoary bat** (*Lasiurus cinereus*)–common in trees, northern one-third of the state

☐ **Red bat** (*Lasiurus borealis*)–common in trees, northern two-thirds of the state

☐ **Seminole bat** (*Lasiurus seminolus*)–common in trees, statewide

☐ **Yellow bat** (*Lasiurus intermedius*)–abundant in trees, statewide

☐ **Evening bat** (*Nycticeius humeralis*)–common in trees and buildings, statewide

☐ **Brazilian free-tailed bat** (*Tadarida brasiliensis*)–common in trees and buildings, statewide

☐ **Nine-banded armadillo** (*Dasypus novemcinctus*)–abundant in most habitats, statewide

☐ **Eastern cottontail** (*Sylvilagus floridanus*)–abundant in fields, statewide

☐ **Marsh rabbit** (*Sylvilagus palustris*)–abundant in marshes, statewide

☐ **Eastern chipmunk** (*Tamias striatus*)–rare in mesic forests, Okaloosa County

☐ **Gray squirrel** (*Sciurus carolinensis*)–abundant in most forests, statewide

☐ **Fox squirrel** (*Sciurus niger*)–locally common in open pine and cypress woodlands, statewide

☐ **Southern flying squirrel** (*Glaucomys volans*)–abundant in oak forests, statewide

☐ **Southeastern pocket gopher** (*Geomys pinetis*)–abundant in upland areas, northern two-thirds of the state

☐ **Beaver** (*Castor canadensis*)–common in streams and lakes, northern one-third of the state

☐ **Eastern woodrat** (*Neottoma floridana*)–common in northern two-thirds of the state

☐ **Hispid cotton rat** (*Sigmodon hispidus*) abundant in fields, statewide

☐ **Eastern harvest mouse** (*Reithrodontomys humulis*)–uncommon in fields, northern two-thirds of the state

☐ **Marsh rice rat** (*Oryzomys palustris*)–common in marshes, statewide

☐ **Oldfield or beach mouse** (*Peromyscus polionotus*)–common in fields and coastal dunes, northern two-thirds of the state

☐ **Cotton mouse** (*Peromyscus gossypinus*) abundant in forests statewide

☐ **Golden mouse** (*Ochrotomys nuttalli*)–common in forests, northern two-thirds of the state

☐ **Pine vole** (*Microtus pinetorum*)–common in upland forests, northern one-third of the state

☐ **Meadow vole** (*Microtus pennsylvanicus*)–rare in saltmarshes along the coast of Levy County E

☐ **Round-tailed muskrat** (*Neofiber alleni*)–common in marshes and along lakeshores, peninsula and eastern panhandle

☐ **House mouse** (*Mus musculus*)–common in buildings, on farms and coastal dunes, statewide

239

☐ **Black or roof rat** (*Rattus rattus*)–abundant in buildings and on farms, statewide

☐ **Norway rat** (*Rattus norvegicus*)–common in buildings and on wharves, statewide

☐ **Nutria** (*Myocastor coypus*)–common in marshes, lakes, and streams, statewide

☐ **Florida black bear** (*Ursus americanus floridanus*)–rare in most habitats, statewide

☐ **Raccoon** (*Procyon lotor*)–abundant in most habitats, statewide

☐ **Mink** (*Mustela vison*)–rare in marshes, along the coast

☐ **Long-tailed weasel** (*Mustela frenata*)–rare in most habitats, statewide

☐ **Striped skunk** (*Mephitis mephitis*)–common in most habitats, statewide

☐ **Eastern spotted skunk** (*Spilogale putorius*)–common in fields and open forests, statewide

☐ **River otter** (*Lutra canadensis*)–common in streams and lakes, statewide

☐ **Gray fox** (*Urocyon cinereoargenteus*)–common in most habitats, statewide

☐ **Red fox** (*Vulpes vulpes*)–common in uplands, statewide

☐ **Coyote** (*Canis latrans*)–rare in fields, northern two-thirds of the state

☐ **Bobcat** (*Felis rufus*)–common in most habitats, statewide

☐ **Rough-toothed dolphin** (*Steno bredanensis*)–rare in the Gulf of Mexico

☐ **Long-snouted spinner dolphin** (*Steno longirostris*)–rare in the Gulf of Mexico

☐ **Short-snouted spinner dolphin** (*Stenella clymene*)–rare in the Gulf of Mexico

☐ **Striped dolphin** (*Stenella coeruleoalba*)–rare in the Gulf of Mexico

☐ **Atlantic spotted dolphin** (*Stenella frontalis*)–common in the Gulf of Mexico

☐ **Pantropical spotted dolphin** (*Stenella attenuata*)–rare in the Gulf of Mexico

☐ **Saddle-backed dolphin** (*Delphinus delphis*)–common in the Gulf of Mexico

☐ **Fraser's dolphin** (*Lagenodelphis hosei*)–rare in the Gulf of Mexico

☐ **Bottle-nosed dolphin** (*Tursiops truncatus*)–abundant in the Gulf of Mexico

☐ **False killer whale** (*Pseudorca crassidens*)–rare in the Gulf of Mexico

☐ **Killer whale** (*Orcinus orca*)–rare in the Gulf of Mexico

- [ ] **Pygmy killer whale** (*Feressa attenuata*)–rare in the Gulf of Mexico
- [ ] **Risso's dolphin or grampus** (*Grampus griseus*)–rare in the Gulf of Mexico
- [ ] **Short-finned pilot whale** (*Globicephala macrorhynchus*)– abundant in the Gulf of Mexico
- [ ] **Harbor porpoise** (*Phocoena phocoena*)–rare in the Gulf of Mexico
- [ ] **Pygmy sperm whale** (*Kogia breviceps*)–rare in the Gulf of Mexico
- [ ] **Dwarf sperm whale** (*Kogia simus*)–rare in the Gulf of Mexico
- [ ] **Sperm whale** (*Physeter macrocephalus*)–rare in the Gulf of Mexico E
- [ ] **Goose-beaked whale** (*Ziphius cavirostris*)–rare in the Gulf of Mexico
- [ ] **Dense-beaked whale** (*Mesoplodon densirostris*)–rare in the Gulf of Mexico
- [ ] **Antillean beaked whale** (*Mesoplodon europaeus*)–rare in the Gulf of Mexico
- [ ] **True's beaked whale** (*Mesoplodon mirus*)–rare in the Gulf of Mexico
- [ ] **Fin whale** (*Balaenoptera physalus*)–rare in the Gulf of Mexico
- [ ] **Minke whale** (*Balaenoptera acutorostrata*)–rare in the Gulf of Mexico
- [ ] **Sei whale** (*Balaenoptera borealis*)–rare in the Gulf of Mexico
- [ ] **Bryde's whale** (*Balaenoptera edeni*)–rare in the Gulf of Mexico
- [ ] **Humpback whale** (*Megaptera novaeangliae*)–rare in the Gulf of Mexico E
- [ ] **Right whale** (*Balaena glacialis*)–rare in the Gulf of Mexico E
- [ ] **Manatee** (*Trichechus manatus*)–rare in rivers and coastal marine environments, statewide E
- [ ] **Wild boar** (*Sus scrofa*)–abundant in most habitats, statewide
- [ ] **White-tailed deer** (*Odocoileus virginianus*)–abundant in most habitats, statewide
- [ ] **Sambar deer** (*Cervus unicolor*)–common in wetland borders, St. Vincent Island

Amphibian And Reptile Checklists

Frogs and Toads

- [ ] **Oak toad** (*Bufo quercicus*)–throughout north Florida, common in pine flatwoods, dry hammocks, and scrub
- [ ] **Southern toad** (*Bufo terrestris*)–throughout north Florida, abundant in neighborhoods, hammocks, pine flatwoods, freshwater marshes
- [ ] **Fowler's toad** (*Bufo woodhousii fowleri*)–panhandle, uncommon and local in sandy habitats and agricultural areas

241

- [ ] **Northern cricket frog** (*Acris crepitans crepitans*)–panhandle, locally common in freshwater habitats
- [ ] **Southern cricket frog** (*Acris gryllus gryllus*)–panhandle, common in all freshwater habitats
- [ ] **Florida cricket frog** (*Acris gryllus dorsalis*)–throughout north Florida, common in freshwater wetlands
- [ ] **Pine barrens treefrog** (*Hyla andersonii*)–panhandle, uncommon and local in titi swamps
- [ ] **Bird-voice treefrog** (*Hyla avivoca*)–panhandle, common in river swamps and freshwater wetlands
- [ ] **Cope's gray treefrog** (*Hyla chrysoscelis*)–throughout north Florida, common in damp woods, farmlands, parks
- [ ] **Green treefrog** (*Hyla cinerea*)–throughout north Florida, common in pinelands, freshwater marshes and ponds, neighborhoods
- [ ] **Southern spring peeper** (*Hyla crucifer bartramiana*)–north Florida, common in woodlands near ponds, roadside ditches, shallow ponds
- [ ] **Northern spring peeper** (*Hyla crucifer crucifer*)–panhandle, common in woodlands near ponds, roadside ditches, shallow ponds
- [ ] **Pinewoods treefrog** (*Hyla femoralis*)–throughout north Florida, common in pinelands and a variety of other habitats, including neighborhoods
- [ ] **Barking treefrog** (*Hyla gratiosa*)–throughout north Florida, common in pinelands and pineland depressions
- [ ] **Squirrel treefrog** (*Hyla squirella*)–throughout north Florida, common in freshwater marshes, ponds, and neighborhoods
- [ ] **Little grass frog** (*Limnaoedus ocularis*)–throughout north Florida, common in shallow ponds, marshes, savannas, wet prairies
- [ ] **Southern chorus frog** (*Pseudacris nigrita nigrita*)–throughout north Florida, common in freshwater ponds, marshes, ditches
- [ ] **Florida chorus frog** (*Pseudacris nigrita verrocosa*)–throughout north Florida, common in freshwater ponds, marshes, ditches
- [ ] **Ornate chorus frog** (*Pseudacris ornata*)–throughout north Florida, common in freshwater ponds, marshes, and pinelands
- [ ] **Upland chorus frog** (*Pseudacris triserita feriarum*)–panhandle, locally common in pinelands and uplands
- [ ] **Eastern narrowmouth toad** (*Gastrophryne carolinensis*)–throughout north Florida, common burrower found under leaf litter in hammocks

242

☐ **Eastern spadefoot toad** (*Scaphiopus holbrookii holbrookii*)–throughout north Florida, common in dry, sandy areas

☐ **Florida gopher frog** (*Rana areolata aesopus*)–throughout north Florida, uncommon in gopher tortoise burrows in sandy pinelands

☐ **Dusky gopher frog** (*Rana areolata sevosa*)–panhandle, uncommon in habitats similar to the gopher frog, above

☐ **Bullfrog** (*Rana catesbeiana*)–throughout north Florida, common in freshwater ponds

☐ **Bronze frog** (*Rana clamitans clamitans*)–throughout north Florida, common in freshwater marshes, swamps, and ponds

☐ **Pig frog** (*Rana grylio*)–throughout north Florida, common in shallow lakes, ponds, wet marshes

☐ **River frog** (*Rana heckscheri*)–throughout north Florida, uncommon in river swamps and freshwater marshes

☐ **Florida bog frog** (*Rana okaloosae*)–rare and local in steephead seepage streams in the central panhandle

☐ **Southern leopard frog** (*Rana utricularia*)–throughout north Florida, common in both freshwater and brackish habitats

Salamanders

☐ **Flatwoods salamander** (*Ambystoma cingulatum*)–throughout north Florida, rare in wet areas of pine flatwoods

☐ **Marbled salamander** (*Ambystoma opacum*)–throughout north Florida, locally common under debris and logs in hydric and mesic hammocks

☐ **Mole salamander** (*Ambystoma talpoideum*)–throughout north Florida, common under logs and debris in wet places

☐ **Eastern tiger salamander** (*Ambystoma tigrinum tigrinum*)–throughout north Florida, rare in mixed woodlands and temporary ponds

☐ **Two-toed amphiuma** (*Amphiuma means*)–throughout north Florida, common in freshwater sloughs and marshes

☐ **One-toed amphiuma** (*Amphiuma pholeter*)–throughout north Florida, rare and local in freshwater sloughs and seepage streams

☐ **Alabama waterdog** (*Necturus alabamensis*)–western panhandle, common in muddy-bottomed, moderately-sized streams

☐ **Southern dusky salamander** (*Desmognathus auriculatus*)–throughout north Florida, common in ponds, bogs, and streams

- ☐ **Spotted dusky salamander** (*Desmognathus fuscus conanti*)–panhandle, uncommon and local under logs in ravines and small streams
- ☐ **Seal salamander** (*Desmognathus monticola monticola*)–westernmost panhandle, rare and local in seepage areas of deep ravines
- ☐ **Southern two-lined salamander** (*Eurycea cirrigera*)–throughout north Florida, common underground as well as under rocks, logs, and leaf litter
- ☐ **Three-lined salamander** (*Eurycea longicauda guttolineata*)–panhandle, common under rocks and debris along small streams
- ☐ **Dwarf salamander** (*Eurycea quadridigitata*)–throughout north Florida, common in a variety of wetlands
- ☐ **Georgia blind salamander** (*Haideotriton wallacei*)–panhandle, rare and local, water-filled caves
- ☐ **Four-toed salamander** (*Hemidactylium scutatum*)–panhandle, rare and local in boggy areas of hammocks
- ☐ **Slimy salamander** (*Plethodon glutinosus glutinosus*)–throughout north Florida, common in moist, rotting logs and under leaf litter in damp places
- ☐ **Gulf coast mud salamander** (*Pseudotriton montanus flavissimus*)–panhandle, uncommon in streams
- ☐ **Rusty mud salamander** (*Pseudotriton montanus floridanus*)–throughout north Florida, uncommon under logs in sandy spring runs
- ☐ **Southern red salamander** (*Pseudotriton ruber vioscai*)–throughout north Florida, common in clear streams of ravines
- ☐ **Many-lined salamander** (*Stereochilus marginatus*)–throughout north Florida, uncommon and local in blackwater streams, ponds, ditches
- ☐ **Central newt** (*Notophthalmus viridescens louisianensis*)–throughout north Florida, common in shallow ponds and heavily vegetated, slow-moving streams
- ☐ **Peninsula newt** (*Notophthalmus viridescens piaropicola*)–north Florida, common in the root system of water hyacinths
- ☐ **Striped newt** (*Notophthalmus perstriatus*)–north Florida, rare in a variety of freshwater ponds
- ☐ **Narrow-striped dwarf siren** (*Pseudobranchus striatus axanthus*)–north Florida, common in aquatic vegetation, especially in the roots of water hyacinth

☐ **Gulf hammock dwarf siren** (*Pseudobranchus striatus lustricolus*)–north Florida, rare in aquatic vegetation

☐ **Slender dwarf siren** (*Pseudobranchus striatus spheniscus*)–throughout north Florida, common in aquatic vegetation

☐ **Broad-striped siren** (*Pseudobranchus striatus striatus*)–north Florida, common in aquatic vegetation

☐ **Eastern lesser siren** (*Siren intermedia intermedia*)–throughout north Florida, common in aquatic vegetation in ditches, ponds, and cypress heads

☐ **Greater siren** (*Siren lacertina*)–throughout north Florida, common in aquatic vegetation in shallow ponds

Alligators and Crocodiles

☐ **American alligator** (*Alligator mississipiensis*)–throughout north Florida, common in marshes, ponds, lakes, rivers, and a variety of other wetland habitats

Turtles

☐ **Loggerhead** (*Caretta caretta caretta*)–Atlantic and Gulf, common

☐ **Atlantic green turtle** (*Chelonia mydas mydas*)–Atlantic and Gulf, uncommon, E

☐ **Atlantic hawksbill** (*Eretmochelys imbricata imbricata*)–Atlantic and Gulf, rare, E

☐ **Atlantic ridley** (*Lepidochelys kempi*)–Atlantic and Gulf, rare, E

☐ **Florida snapping turtle** (*Chelydra serpentina osceola*)–north Florida, common in nearly all freshwater bodies

☐ **Common snapping turtle** (*Chelydra serpentina serpentina*)–throughout north Florida, common in freshwater habitats

☐ **Alligator snapping turtle** (*Macroclemys temminckii*)– throughout north Florida, uncommon in slow-moving streams and lakes

☐ **Leatherback sea turtle** (*Dermochelys coriacea coriacea*)– Atlantic and Gulf, rare, E

☐ **Spotted turtle** (*Clemmys guttata*)–north Florida, rare in sphagnum and slow-moving waters, possibly exotic

☐ **Florida chicken turtle** (*Deirochelys reticularia chrysea*)– north Florida, common in ponds, marshes, sloughs

☐ **Eastern chicken turtle** (*Deirochelys reticularia reticularia*)– throughout north Florida, common in ponds, marshes, sloughs

☐ **Barbour's map turtle** (*Graptemys barbouri*)–panhandle, uncommon and local in the Chipola and Apalachicola Rivers

- [ ] **Alabama map turtle** (*Graptemys pulchra*)–panhandle, common but local in ponds of the western panhandle
- [ ] **Diamondback terrapin** (*Malaclemys terrapin*)–north Florida, locally common in coastal marshes and estuaries
- [ ] **Ornate diamondback terrapin** (*Malaclemys terrapin macrospilota*)–north Florida, locally common in coastal marshes and estuaries
- [ ] **Mississippi diamondback terrapin** (*Malaclemys terrapin pileata*)–panhandle, locally common in coastal marshes and estuaries
- [ ] **Eastern river cooter** (*Pseudemys concinna concinna*)–panhandle, common in rivers and slow-moving streams
- [ ] **Suwannee cooter** (*Pseudemys concinna suwanniensis*)– north Florida, common in rivers and slow-moving streams
- [ ] **Florida cooter** (*Pseudemys floridana floridana*)–throughout north Florida in rivers and slow-moving streams
- [ ] **Peninsula cooter** (*Pseudemys floridana peninsularis*)– north Florida, common in rivers and slow-moving streams
- [ ] **Florida redbelly turtle** (*Pseudemys nelsoni*)–throughout north Florida, common in rivers and slow-moving streams
- [ ] **Florida box turtle** (*Terrapene carolina bauri*)– throughout north Florida in mesic hammocks and pine flatwoods
- [ ] **Eastern box turtle** (*Terrapene carolina carolina*)–north Florida, common in mesic hammocks and pine flatwoods
- [ ] **Gulf coast box turtle** (*Terrapene carolina major*)– throughout north Florida, common in upland hammocks and flatwoods
- [ ] **Three-toed box turtle** (*Terrapene carolina triunguis*)–panhandle, common in mesic hammocks and flatwoods
- [ ] **Yellowbelly slider** (*Trachemys scripta scripta*)–throughout north Florida, common in rivers
- [ ] **Striped mud turtle** (*Kinosternon baurii*)–north Florida, common, shallow marshes ponds, **E**
- [ ] **Florida mud turtle** (*Kinosternon subrubrum steindachneri*)–north Florida, common in swamps, ponds, lake edges, saltmarshes
- [ ] **Eastern mud turtle** (*Kinosternon subrubrum subrubrum*)–throughout north Florida, common in swamps and marshes
- [ ] **Loggerhead musk turtle** (*Sternotherus minor minor*)–throughout north Florida, common in shallow ponds, streams, spring runs
- [ ] **Stripneck musk turtle** (*Sternotherus minor peltifer*)–panhandle, common in shallow ponds, streams, spring runs

☐ **Stinkpot** (*Sternotherus odoratus*)–throughout north Florida in lakes, ponds, and streams

☐ **Gopher tortoise** (*Gopherus polyphemus*)–throughout north Florida, dry, sandy, well-drained habitats

☐ **Florida softshell** (*Apalone ferox*)–throughout north Florida, common in lakes, marshes, and ditches

☐ **Gulf coast smooth softshell** (*Apalone mutica calvata*)– western panhandle, rare and local in the Escambia River and its tributaries

☐ **Gulf coast spiny softshell** (*Apalone spinifera aspera*)– throughout north Florida, common in slow-moving rivers and streams

Worm Lizards

☐ **Florida worm lizard** (*Rhineura floridana*)–north Florida, common in dry, sandy habitats

Lizards

☐ **Eastern slender glass lizard** (*Ophisaurus attenuatus longicaudus*)–throughout north Florida, common in grasslands

☐ **Island glass lizard** (*Ophisaurus compressus*)–north Florida, uncommon in marshes and pinelands

☐ **Mimic glass lizard** (*Ophisaurus mimicus*)–throughout north Florida, uncommon in hammocks and pinelands

☐ **Eastern glass lizard** (*Ophisaurus ventralis*)–throughout north Florida, common in hammocks and pinelands

☐ **Mediterranean gecko** (*Hemidactylus turcicus*)–north Florida, uncommon in urban areas

☐ **Green anole** (*Anolis carolinensis*)–throughout north Florida, common in many habitats, including yards and gardens

☐ **Texas horned lizard** (*Phrynosoma cornutum*)–throughout north Florida, uncommon, exotic, found in open, sandy areas

☐ **Southern fence lizard** (*Sceloporus undulatus undulatus*)–throughout north Florida in pine flatwoods, turkey oak hammocks, and dry woodlands

☐ **Southern coal skink** (*Eumeces anthracinus pluvialis*)–panhandle, rare under rocks and logs in pine flatwoods

☐ **Cedar Key mole skink** (*Eumeces egregius insularis*)–north Florida, uncommon

☐ **Northern mole skink** (*Eumeces egregius similis*)–throughout north Florida, common

☐ **Five-lined skink** (*Eumeces fasciatus*)–throughout north Florida, rare around hydric hammocks in rotting logs and trash piles

247

- [ ] **Southeastern five-line skink** (*Eumeces inexpectatus*)–throughout north Florida, common in dry and pineland habitats as well as around suburban homes
- [ ] **Broadhead skink** (*Eumeces laticeps*)–throughout north Florida, common in mesic hammocks and moist habitats
- [ ] **Sand skink** (*Neoseps reynoldsi*)–north Florida, uncommon in sand pine scrub, turkey oak woods, and other dry habitats
- [ ] **Ground skink** (*Scincella lateralis*)–throughout north Florida, common under leaves in almost any habitat
- [ ] **Six-lined racerunner** (*Cnemidophorus sexlineatus sexlineatus*)–throughout north Florida, common in dry areas, including beach areas

Nonpoisonous Snakes
- [ ] **Florida scarlet snake** (*Cemophora coccinea coccinea*)– north Florida, common in pine flatwoods and sandy uplands
- [ ] **Northern scarlet snake** (*Cemophora coccinea copei*)– throughout north Florida, common in pine flatwoods and sandy uplands
- [ ] **Brownchin racer** (*Coluber constrictor helvigularis*)–panhandle, common locally near the Apalachicola River
- [ ] **Southern black racer** (*Coluber constrictor priapus*)– throughout north Florida, common in nearly all habitats
- [ ] **Southern ringneck snake** (*Diadophis punctatus punctatus*)–throughout north Florida, common in pine flatwoods and other moist, open areas
- [ ] **Eastern indigo snake** (*Drymarchon corasis couperi*)– throughout north Florida, uncommon in gopher tortoise burrows
- [ ] **Corn snake** (*Elaphe guttata guttata*)–throughout north Florida, common in nearly all habitats
- [ ] **Yellow rat snake** (*Elaphe obsoleta quadrivittata*)–north Florida, common along woodland edges as well as near building and trash piles
- [ ] **Gray rat snake** (*Elaphe obsoleta spiloides*)–throughout north Florida, common in woods and near swamps, also in suburban neighborhoods
- [ ] **Eastern mud snake** (*Farancia abacura abacura*)–throughout north Florida, common in marshes, swamps, bogs, savannas, prairies
- [ ] **Rainbow snake** (*Farancia erytrogramma*)–north Florida, common in swamps, bogs, marshes, spring runs, rivers, clear streams
- [ ] **Eastern hognose snake** (*Heterodon platyrhinos*)–throughout north Florida, common in dry pinelands and turkey oak woodlands

☐ **Southern hognose snake** (*Heterodon simus*)–throughout north Florida, common in same areas as eastern hognose snake

☐ **Mole kingsnake** (*Lampropeltis calligaster rhombomaculata*)–throughout north Florida, rare, little is known about its habitat

☐ **Eastern kingsnake** (*Lampropeltis getulus getulus*)–throughout north Florida, common near wetlands, along canals, and in trash piles

☐ **Scarlet kingsnake** (*Lampropeltis triangulum elapsoides*)–throughout north Florida, uncommon

☐ **Eastern coachwhip** (*Masticophis flagellum flagellum*)–throughout north Florida, common in dry, sandy areas

☐ **Gulf saltmarsh snake** (*Nerodia clarkii clarkii*)–throughout north Florida, locally common in saltmarshes

☐ **Green water snake** (*Nerodia cyclopion*)–panhandle, uncommon in ponds, marshes, roadside ditches

☐ **Redbelly water snake** (*Nerodia erythrogaster erythrogaster*)–throughout north Florida, common along large rivers

☐ **Yellowbelly water snake** (*Nerodia erythrogaster flavigaster*)–panhandle, common in many aquatic habitats

☐ **Banded water snake** (*Nerodia fasciata fasciata*)–throughout north Florida, common in many aquatic habitats

☐ **Florida banded water snake** (*Nerodia fasciata pictiventris*)–north Florida, common in many aquatic habitats

☐ **Florida green water snake** (*Nerodia floridana*)–throughout north Florida, common in ponds, marshes, roadside ditches

☐ **Midland water snake** (*Nerodia sipedon pleuralis*)–panhandle, uncommon and local in the Yellow, Escambia, and Choctawhatchee Rivers

☐ **Brown water snake** (*Nerodia taxispilota*)–throughout north Florida, common in rivers and lakes

☐ **Rough green snake** (*Opheodrys aestivus aestivus*)–throughout north Florida, common in shrubs along the edges of rivers, lakes, and ponds

☐ **Florida pine snake** (*Pituophis melanoleucus mugitus*)–throughout north Florida, uncommon in longleaf-turkey oak woods

☐ **Striped crayfish snake** (*Regina alleni*)–north Florida, common in swamps, ponds, and lakes

☐ **Glossy crayfish snake** (*Regina rigida rigida*)–throughout north Florida, uncommon, not much is known about its habitat

- ☐ **Gulf crayfish snake** (*Regina rigida sinicola*)–throughout north Florida, uncommon
- ☐ **Queen snake** (*Regina septemvittata*)–panhandle, uncommon in small to medium streams
- ☐ **Pine woods snake** (*Rhadinaea flavilata*)–throughout north Florida, rare in flatwoods and cypress heads
- ☐ **North Florida swamp snake** (*Seminatrix pygaea pygaea*)–throughout north Florida, common in aquatic vegetation of lakes and ponds
- ☐ **Marsh brown snake** (*Storeria dekayi limnetes*)–panhandle, rare and local in coastal marshes of Pensacola Bay
- ☐ **Florida brown snake** (*Storeria dekayi victa*)–north Florida, common in many aquatic habitats
- ☐ **Midland brown snake** (*Storeria dekayi wrightorum*)–throughout north Florida, uncommon
- ☐ **Florida redbelly snake** (*Storeria occipitomaculata obscura*)–north Florida, uncommon in mesic hammocks and moist woods
- ☐ **Northern redbelly snake** (*Storeria occipitomaculata occipitomaculata*)–panhandle, uncommon
- ☐ **Southeastern crowned snake** (*Tantilla coronata*)–panhandle, uncommon in dry, sandy habitats
- ☐ **Bluestripe ribbon snake** (*Thamnophis sauritus nitae*)–northwest Florida, locally common in aquatic habitats of the Big Bend
- ☐ **Peninsula ribbon snake** (*Thamnophis sauritus sackenii*)–north Florida, common in aquatic habitats
- ☐ **Eastern ribbon snake** (*Thamnophis sauritus sauritus*)–panhandle, common in aquatic habitats
- ☐ **Bluestrip garter snake** (*Thamnophis sirtalis similis*)–north Florida, locally common in a number of habitats
- ☐ **Eastern garter snake** (*Thamnophis sirtalis sirtalis*)–throughout north Florida, common in many habitats
- ☐ **Rough earth snake** (*Virginia striatula*)–throughout north Florida, uncommon in pine flatwoods and dry hammocks
- ☐ **Smooth earth snake** (*Virginia valeriae valeriae*)–throughout north Florida, uncommon in mesic hammocks and moist woods

Poisonous Snakes
- ☐ **Coral snake** (*Micrurus fulvius fulvius*)–throughout north Florida, common in many habitats

☐ **Southern copperhead** (*Agkistrodon contortrix contortrix*)–panhandle, rare and local along the bluffs and ravines of the Apalachicola River

☐ **Florida cottonmouth** (*Agkistrodon piscivorus conanti*)–throughout north Florida, common in many aquatic habitats

☐ **Eastern cottonmouth** (*Agkistrodon piscivorus piscivorus*)–panhandle, common in many aquatic habitats

☐ **Eastern diamondback rattlesnake** (*Crotalus adamanteus*)–throughout north Florida, common in pine-palmetto flatwoods and dry woodlands

☐ **Dusky pigmy rattlesnake** (*Sistrurus miliarius barbouri*)–throughout north Florida, common in many habitats including pinelands and scrub

COMMON, SCIENTIFIC, AND BOTANICAL FAMILY NAMES OF PLANTS MENTIONED IN THE TEXT

Agalinis (*Agalinis* sp.) Scrophulariaceae
Alabama cherry (*Prunus alabamensis*) Rosaceae
American basswood (*Tilia americana*) Tiliaceae
American beautyberry (*Callicarpa americana*) Verbenaceae
American beech (*Fagus grandifolia*) Fagaceae
American chestnut (*Castanea dentata*) Fagaceae
American holly (*Ilex opaca*) Aquifoliaceae
American sycamore (*Platanus occidentalis*) Platanaceae
Angelica (*Angelica* sp.) Umbelliferae
Apalachicola milkweed (*Asclepias viridula*) Asclepiadaceae
Arkansas oak (*Quercus arkansana*) Fagaceae
Arrowhead (*Saggitaria* sp.) Alismataceae
Arrowwood (*Viburnum dentatum*) Caprifoliaceae
Ash (*Fraxinus* sp.) Oleaceae
Ashe magnolia (*Magnolia macrophylla* subsp. *ashei*) Magnoliaceae
Atamasco lily (*Zephyranthes atamasco*) Amaryllidaceae
Atlantic white cedar (*Chamaecyparis thyoides*) Cupressaceae
Bachelor's buttons (*Polygala nana, P. lutea, P. balduinii*) Polygalaceae
Bald-cypress (*Taxodium distichum*) Taxodiaceae
Bandana daisy (*Gaillardia* sp.) Compositae
Baneberry (*Actaea pacypoda*) Ranunculaceae
Barbara's buttons (*Marshallia* sp.) Compositae

Beach elder (*Iva imbricata*) Compositae
Beakrush (*Rhynchospora* sp.) Cyperaceae
Beggar-tick (*Bidens* sp.) Compositae
Black cherry (*Prunus serotina*) Rosaceae
Blackgum (*Nyssa biflora*) Nyssaceae
Blackjack oak (*Quercus marilandica*) Fagaceae
Black needlerush (*Juncus roemerianus*) Juncaceae
Black root (*Pterocaulon pycnostachyum*) Compositae
Black titi (*Cliftonia monophylla*) Cyrillaceae
Black tupelo (*Nyssa sylvatica*) Nyssaceae
Bladdernut (*Staphylea trifolia*) Staphyleaceae
Bladderwort (*Utricularia* sp.) Lentibulariaceae
Blazing star (*Liatris* sp.) Compositae
Bloodroot (*Sanguinaria canadensis*) Papaveraceae
Blue curls (*Trichostema* sp.) Labiatae
Blue flag iris (*Iris virginica*) Iridaceae
Bluejack oak (*Quercus incana*) Fagaceae
Bog buttons (*Lachnocaulon* sp.) Eriocaulaceae
Butterwort (*Pinguicula* sp.) Lentibulariaceae
Cabbage palm (*Sabal palmetto*) Palmae
Cane (*Arundinaria gigantea*) Gramineae
Canna lily (*Canna flaccida*) Commelinaceae
Carolina laurel cherry (*Prunus caroliniana*) Rosaceae
Carolina silverbell (*Halesia carolina*) Styracaceae
Catesby's lily (see pine lily)
Cattail (*Typha* sp.) Typhaceae
Cedar elm (*Ulmus crassifolia*) Ulmaceae
Chapman oak (*Quercus chapmanii*) Fagaceae
Chapman's butterwort (*Pinguicula planifolia*) Lentibulariaceae
Chapman's crownbeard (*Vebersina chapmanii*) Compositae
Chickasaw plum (*Prunus angustifolia*) Rosaceae
Chinquapin oak (*Quercus muehlenbergii*) Fagaceae
Climbing butterfly pea (*Centrosema virginianum*) Leguminosae
Colic root (*Aletris* sp.) Liliaceae
Common persimmon (*Diospyros virginiana*) Ebenaceae
Cordgrass (*Spartina alterniflora*) Gramineae
Cork elm (*Ulmus alata*) Ulmaceae
Croomia (*Croomia pauciflora*) Stemonaceae
Cypress (*Taxodium* sp.) Taxodiaceae
Cypress vine (*Ipomoea quamoclit*) Convolvulaceae
Deer berry (*Vaccinium stamineum*) Ericaceae
Diamond leaf oak (*Quercus laurifolia*) Fagaceae

Dog banana (*Asimina triloba*) Annonaceae
Dogwood (*Cornus* sp.) Cornaceae
Doll's eyes (see Baneberry)
Duck potato (*Sagittaria* sp.) Alismataceae
Eastern hophornbeam (*Ostrya virginiana*) Betulaceae
Elm (*Ulmus* sp.) Ulmaceae
Fetterbush (*Lyonia* sp.) Ericaceae
Florida anise (*Illicium floridanum*) Illiciaceae
Florida flame azalea (*Rhododendron austrinum*) Ericaceae
Florida rosemary (*Ceratiola ericoides*) Empetraceae
Florida yew (*Taxus floridana*) Taxaceae
Flowering dogwood (*Cornus floridana*) Cornaceae
Fringed campion (*Silene polypetala*) Caryophyllaceae
Gallberry (*Ilex glabra*) Aquifoliaceae
Giant water dropwort (*Oxypolis greenmanii*) Umbelliferae
Glasswort (*Salicornia* sp.) Chenopodiaceae
Goldenrod (*Solidago* sp.) Compositae
Gopherwood (see Torreya tree)
Grass-pink (*Calopogon* sp.) Orchidaceae
Green dragon (*Arisaema dracontium*) Araceae
Green eyes (*Berlandiera* sp.) Compositae
Green haw (*Crateagus viridis*) Rosaceae
Hat pins (*Eriocaulon* sp.) Eriocaulaceae
Haw (*Crataegus* sp.) Rosaceae
Hazel alder (*Alnus serrulata*) Betulaceae
Hearts-a-bustin'-with-love (*Euonymous americanus*) Celastraceae
Hickory (*Carya* sp.) Juglandaceae
Highbush blueberry (*Vaccinium corymbosum*) Ericaceae
Honewort (*Cryptotaenia canadensis*) Umbelliferae
Horse sugar (*Symplocos tinctoria*) Symplocaceae
Hound's tongue (*Cynoglossum virginianum*) Boraginaceae
Indian pink (*Spigelia marilandica*) Loganiaceae
Ironweed (*Vernonia* sp.) Convolvulaceae
Ironwood (*Carpinus caroliniana*) Betulaceae
Jack-in-the-pulpit (*Arisaema triphyllum*) Araceae
Lance-leaved wake-robin (*Trillium lancifolium*) Trilliaceae
Lantana (*Lantana camara*) Verbenaceae
Leatherwood (*Dirca palustris*) Thymelaeaceae
Liatris (*Liatris* sp.) Compositae
Live oak (*Quercus virginiana*) Fagaceae
Lizard tail (*Saururus cernuus*) Saururaceae
Lobelia (*Lobelia* sp.) Campanulaceae

253

Loblolly pine (*Pinus taeda*) Pinaceae
Locust (*Gleditsia* sp.) Leguminosae
Longleaf pine (*Pinus palustris*) Pinaceae
Lowbush blueberry (*Vaccinium darrowii, V. myrsinites*) Ericaceae
Manatee grass (*Syringodium filiforme*) Zannichelliaceae
Marsh pink (*Sabatia* sp.) Gentianaceae
Meadow beauty (*Rhexia* sp.) Melastomataceae
Milkweed (*Asclepias* sp.) Asclepiadaceae
Minty rosemary (*Conradina canescens*) Labiatae
Mist flower (*Conoclinium coelestinum*) Compositae
Morning glory (*Ipomoea* sp.) Convolvulaceae
Mountain laurel (*Kalmia latifolia*) Ericaceae
Myrtle oak (*Quercus myrtifolia*) Fagaceae
Myrtle-leaved holly (*Ilex myrtifolia*) Aquifoliaceae
Needle palm (*Rhapidophyllum histrix*) Palmae
Needlerush (see black needlerush)
Oak (*Quercus* sp.) Fagaceae
Oak leaf hydrangea (*Hydrangea quercifolia*) Saxifragaceae
Ogeechee tupelo (*Nyssa ogeche*) Nyssaceae
Overcup oak (*Quercus lyrata*) Fagaceae
Panhandle lily (*Lilium iridollae*) Liliaceae
Parsley haw (*Crataegus marshallii*) Rosaceae
Partridge berry (*Mitchella repens*) Rubiaceae
Passion flower (*Passiflora incarnata*) Passifloraceae
Pawpaw (*Asimina* sp.) Annonaceae
Persimmon (*Diospyros virginiana*) Ebenaceae
Pignut hickory (*Carya glabra*) Juglandaceae
Pine (*Pinus* sp.) Pinaceae
Pine lily (*Lilium catesbaei*) Liliaceae
Pineland hibiscus (*Hibiscus aculeatus*) Malvaceae
Pitcher plant (*Sarracenia* sp.) Sarraceniaceae
Plum (*Prunus* sp.) Rosaceae
Poison ivy (*Toxicodendron radicans*) Anacardiaceae
Poison oak (*Toxicodendron toxicarium*) Anacardiaceae
Poison sumac (*Toxicodendron vernix*) Anacardiaceae
Pond pine (*Pinus serotina*) Pinaceae
Possum haw holly (*Ilex decidua*) Aquifoliaceae
Purple pitcher plant (*Sarracenia purpurea*) Sarraceniaceae
Pyramid magnolia (*Magnolia pyramidata*) Magnoliaceae
Railroad vine (*Ipomoea pes-carprae*) Convolvulaceae
Rattlebox (*Crotolaria* sp.) Leguminosae

Rayless sunflower (*Helianthus debilis*) Compositae
Red basil (*Calamintha coccinea*) Labiatae
Red bay (*Persea borbonia*) Lauraceae
Red buckeye (*Aesculus pavia*) Hippocastanaceae
Red cedar (*Juniperus virginiana*) Cupressaceae
Red maple (*Acer rubrum*) Aceraceae
Red mulberry (*Morus rubra*) Moraceae
Red root (*Lachnanthes caroliniana*) Haemodoraceae
River birch (*Betula nigra*) Betulaceae
Roserush (*Lygodesmia aphylla*) Compositae
Rue anemone (*Anemonella thalictroides*) Ranunculaceae
Ruellia (*Ruellia caroliniensis*) Acanthaceae
Rush-featherling (*Pleea tenuifolia*) Liliaceae
Sabal palm (*Sabal palmetto*) Palmae
Saltbush (*Baccharis halimifolia*) Compositae
Saltgrass (*Distichlis spicata*) Gramineae
Saltmarsh aster (*Aster tenuifolia*) Compositae
Saltwort (*Salicornia bigelovii, S. virginica*) Chenopodiaceae
Sand live oak (*Quercus geminata*) Fagaceae
Sand pine (*Pinus clausa*) Pinaceae
Sand post oak (*Quercus margaretta*) Fagaceae
Sassafras (*Sassafras albidum*) Lauraceae
Saw palmetto (*Serenoa repens*) Palmae
Scarlet basil (see red basil)
Sea lavender (*Limonium carolinianum*) Plumbaginaceae
Sea oat (*Uniola paniculata*) Gramineae
Sea oxeye (*Borrichia frutescens*) Compositae
Seaside pennywort (*Hydrocotyle bonariensis*) Umbelliferae
Sebastian bush (*Sebastiania fruticosa*) Euphorbiaceae
Sensitive briar (*Schrankia microphylla*) Leguminosae
Shoal grass (*Halodule wrightii*) Zannichelliaceae
Showy crotolaria (*Crotolaria spectibilis*) Leguminosae
Silverbell (*Halesia* sp.) Styracaceae
Slash pine (*Pinus elliottii*) Pinaceae
Smilax (*Smilax* sp.) Smilacaceae
Soloman's-seal (*Polygonatum biflorum*) Liliaceae
Sourwood (*Oxydendron arboreum*) Ericaceae
Southern crabapple (*Malus angustifolia*) Rosaceae
Southern magnolia (*Magnolia grandiflora*) Magnoliaceae
Sparkleberry (*Vaccinium arboreum*) Ericaceae
Spatterdock (*Nuphar luteum*) Nymphaeaceae
Spider lily (*Hymenocallis* sp.) Amaryllidaceae

255

Spiderwort (*Tradescantia ohiensis*) Commelinaceae
Spring coral root (*Corallorhiza wisteriana*) Orchidaceae
Spruce pine (*Pinus glabra*) Pinaceae
St. Johns-wort (*Hypericum* sp.) Guttiferae
Staggerbush (*Leucothoe* sp.) Ericaceae
Star anise (see Florida anise)
Stiffcornel dogwood (*Cornus foemina*) Cornaceae
Stinking cedar (see Torreya tree)
Sugarberry (*Celtis laevigata*) Ulmaceae
Sugar maple (*Acer saccharum*) Aceraceae
Sundew (*Drosera* sp.) Droseraceae
Swamp chestnut oak (*Quercus michauxii*) Fagaceae
Swamp coreopsis (*Coreopsis nudata*) Compositae
Swamp cyrilla (*Cyrilla racemiflora*) Cyrillaceae
Swamp lily (*Crinum americanum*) Amaryllidaceae
Sweet pepperbush (*Clethra alnifolia*) Clethraceae
Sweetbay (*Magnolia virginiana*) Magnoliaceae
Sweetgum (*Liquidambar styraciflua*) Hamamelidaceae
Sweetleaf (see horse sugar)
Tape-grass (*Vallisneria americana*) Hydrocharitaceae
Thread dew (*Drosera filiformis*) Droseraceae
Tickseed (*Coreopsis gladiata*) Compositae
Titi (see swamp cyrilla)
Torreya tree (*Torreya taxifolia*) Taxaceae
Trailing arbutus (*Epigaea repens*) Ericaceae
Trillium (*Trillium* sp.) Trilliaceae
Trout lily (*Erythronium umbilicatum*) Liliaceae
Tulip poplar (*Liriodendron tulipifera*) Magnoliaceae
Tupelo (*Nyssa* sp.) Nyssaceae
Turkey oak (*Quercus laevis*) Fagaceae
Turtle grass (*Thalassia testudinum*) Hydrocharitaceae
Verbena (*Verbena brasiliensis*) Verbenaceae
Violet (*Viola* sp.) Violaceae
Wafer ash (*Ptelea trifoliata*) Rutaceae
Wake robin (*Trillium maculatum*) Trilliaceae
Walter viburnum (*Viburnum obovatum*) Caprifoliaceae
Water hickory (*Carya aquatica*) Juglandaceae
Water oak (*Quercus nigra*) Fagaceae
Water tupelo (*Nyssa aquatica*) Nyssaceae
Wax myrtle (*Myrica cerifera*) Myricaceae
White baneberry (see baneberry)

White oak (*Quercus alba*) Fagaceae
White water lily (*Nymphaea odorata*) Nymphaeaceae
White-topped pitcher (*Sarracenia leucophylla*) Sarraceniaceae
Widgeon grass (*Ruppia maritima*) Ruppiaceae
Wild azalea (*Rhododendron canescens*) Ericaceae
Wild columbine (*Aquilegia canadensis*) Ranunculaceae
Wild ginger (*Hexastylis arifolia*) Aristolochiaceae
Wild grape (*Vitis* sp.) Vitaceae
Wild hibiscus (*Hibiscus* sp.) Malvaceae
Wild indigo (*Baptisia* sp.) Leguminosae
Wild olive (*Osmanthus americanus*) Oleaceae
Wild rice (*Zizania aquatica*) Gramineae
Willow (*Salix* sp.) Salicaceae
Wiregrass (*Aristida stricta*) Gramineae
Witch hazel (*Hamamelis virginiana*) Hamamelidaceae
Wood nettle (*Laportea canadensis*) Urticaceae
Woody goldenrod (*Chrysoma pauciflosculosa*) Compositae
Yaupon holly (*Ilex vomitoria*) Aquifoliaceae
Yellow-fringed orchid (*Habenaria* sp.) Orchidaceae
Yellow poplar (*Liriodendron tulipifera*) Magnoliaceae
Yellow-eyed grass (*Xyris* sp.) Xyridaceae

REFERENCES AND SUGGESTED READING

Ashton, Ray E., and Patricia Sawyer Ashton. 1981. *Handbook of Reptiles and Amphibians of Florida. Part One: The Snakes.* Miami, FL: Windward Publishing.

Ashton, Ray E., and Patricia Sawyer Ashton. 1985. *Handbook of Reptiles and Amphibians of Florida. Part Two: The Lizards, Turtles & Crocodilians.* Miami, FL: Windward Publishing.

Ashton, Ray E., and Patricia Sawyer Ashton. 1988. *Handbook of Reptiles and Amphibians of Florida. Part Three: The Amphibians.* Miami, FL: Windward Publishing.

Boyd, Mark F., Ed. 1956. *Florida Place—Names of Indian Derivation Either Obsolescent or Retained Together with Others of Recent Application.* Special Publication No. 1. Tallahassee, FL: Bureau of Geology, Florida Department of Environmental Protection.

Brown, Larry N. 1987. *A Checklist of Florida's Mammals.* Tallahassee, FL: Nongame Wildlife Program, Florida Game and Fresh Water Fish Commission.

Carter, Elizabeth F., and John L. Pearce. 1985. *A Canoeing and Kayaking Guide to the Streams of Florida. Volume 1, North Central Peninsula and Panhandle.* Hillsborough, NC: Menasha Ridge Press.

Cerulean, Susan, and Ann Morrow. 1993. *Florida Wildlife Viewing Guide.* Helena, MT: Falcon Press Publishing.

Clewell, Andre F. 1981. *Natural Setting and Vegetation of the Florida Panhandle.* Mobile, AL: U.S. Army Corps of Engineers.

Florida Natural Areas Inventory. 1990. *Guide to the Natural Communities of Florida.* Tallahassee, FL: Florida Natural Areas Inventory and Florida Department of Natural Resources.

Forested Wetlands of Florida—Their Management and Use. 1976. Gainesville, FL: Center for Wetlands, University of Florida.

Gildersleeve, Nancy B., and Susan K. Gildersleeve, Eds. 1991. *Florida Hiking Trails*. Gainesville, FL: Maupin House.

Godfrey, Robert K. 1988. *Trees, Shrubs, and Woody Vines of Northern Florida and Adjacent Georgia and Alabama*. Athens, GA: University of Georgia Press.

Grow, Gerald. 1987. *Florida Parks: A Guide to Camping in Nature*. Tallahassee, FL: Longleaf Publications.

Hendry, Charles W., Jr., and Charles R. Sproul. 1966. *Geology and Ground-Water Resources of Leon County, Florida*. Bulletin No. 47. Tallahassee, FL: Bureau of Geology, Florida Department of Environmental Protection.

Kurz, Herman, and Kenneth Wagner. 1957. *Tidal Marshes of the Gulf and Atlantic Coasts of Northern Florida and Charleston, South Carolina*. Florida State University Studies, No. 24. Tallahassee, FL: The Florida State University.

Lane, Ed. 1986. *Karst in Florida*. Special Publication No. 29. Tallahassee, FL: Bureau of Geology, Florida Department of Environmental Protection.

Lane, James A. 1984. *A Birder's Guide to Florida*. Denver, CO: L & P Press.

Means, D. Bruce. 1985. The Canyonlands of Florida. *The Nature Conservancy News*, September/October.

Moler, Paul. 1988. *A Checklist of Florida's Amphibians and Reptiles*. Tallahassee, FL: Nongame Wildlife Program, Florida Game and Fresh Water Fish Commission.

Myers, Ronald L., and John J. Ewel, Eds. *Ecosystems of Florida*. Orlando, FL: University of Central Florida Press.

Nelson, Gil. 1994. *The Trees of Florida: A Reference and Field Guide*. Sarasota, FL: Pineapple Press.

Puri, Harbans S., and Robert O. Vernon. 1964. *Special Publication No. 5 Revised: Summary of the Geology of Florida and A Guidebook to the Classic Exposures*. Tallahassee, FL: Bureau of Geology, Florida Department of Environmental Protection.

Rosenau, Jack C., Glen L. Faulkner, Charles W. Hendry, Jr., and Robert W. Hull. 1977. *Springs of Florida*. Bulletin 31 (revised). Tallahassee, FL: Bureau of Geology, Florida Department of Environmental Protection.

Rupert, Frank, and Steve Spencer. 1988. *Geology of Wakulla County, Florida.* Tallahassee, FL: Bureau of Geology, Florida Department of Environmental Protection.

Schade, Carleton J. 1985. *Late Holocene Sedimentology of St. George Island, Florida.* Masters Thesis, Tallahassee, FL: Florida State University.

Soil Conservation Service. 1981. *26 Ecological Communities of Florida.*

Stevenson, Henry M. 1976. *Vetebrates of Florida.* Gainesville, FL: University Presses of Florida.

Stevenson, Henry M. 1988. *Checklist of Florida's Birds.* Tallahassee, FL: Nongame Wildlife Program, Florida Game and Fresh Water Fish Commission.

Tebeau, Charlton W. 1973. *A History of Florida.* Miami: University of Miami Press.

U.S. Department of Agriculture. 1984. *Soils and Vegetation of the Apalachicola National Forest.* Apalachicola National Forest.

Watts, Betty M. 1975. *The Watery Wilderness of Apalach, Florida.* Tallahassee, FL: Apalach Books.

Wolfe, Steven H., Jeffrey A. Reidenauer, and D. Bruce Means. 1988. *An Ecological Characterization of the Florida Panhandle.* FWS Biological Report 88(12). Washington DC: U.S. Fish and Wildlife Service.

Yon, J. William, Jr. 1966. *Geology of Jefferson County, Florida.* Geological Bulletin No. 48. Tallahassee, FL: Bureau of Geology, Florida Department of Environmental Protection.

Zieman, Joseph C., and Rita T. Zieman. 1989. *The Ecology of the Seagrass Meadows of the West Coast of Florida: A Community Profile.* Washington DC: U.S. Fish and Wildlife Service.

OTHER SOURCES OF INFORMATION

DeLorme Mapping Company
P.O Box 298
Freeport, ME 04032
(207) 865-4171
publishes *Florida Atlas & Gazetteer* (detailed road maps with guide to outdoor recreation)

Florida Association of Canoe Liveries & Outfitters
Box 1764
Arcadia, FL 33821
(941) 494-1215
free list of canoe outfitters

Florida Audubon Society
460 Hwy. 436, Suite 200
Casselberry, FL 32707
(407) 260-8300

Florida Board of Tourism
Florida Department of Commerce
126 West Van Buren St.
Tallahassee, FL 32399-2000
(904) 487-1462
free road map of Florida

Florida Department of Environmental Protection
Division of Recreation and Parks
3900 Commonwealth Blvd.
Tallahassee, FL 32399-3000
(904) 487-4784
information on parks, free canoe trail guide, and maps with access points for
36 Florida canoe trails

Florida Game and Fresh Water Fish Commission
620 S. Meridian St.
Tallahassee, FL 32399-1600
(904) 488-4674 for general information
(904) 488-1960 for Florida freshwater fishing handbook

Florida Sierra Club
462 Fernwood Rd.
Key Biscayne, FL 33149
(305) 361-1292

Florida Trail Association, Inc.
P.O. Box 13708
Gainesville, FL 32604
(904) 378-8823
(800) 343-1882 (Florida only)

Florida Wildlife Federation
2545 Blairstone Pines Dr.
P.O. Box 6870
Tallahassee, FL 32314-6870
(904) 656-7113

Northwest Florida Water Management District
Route 1, Box 3100
Havana, Fl 32333
(904) 539-5999

Save the Manatee Club
500 N. Maitland Ave.
Maitland, FL 32751
1-800-432-JOIN

The Nature Conservancy
Florida Field Office
2699 Lee Rd., Suite 500
Winter Park, FL 32789
(407) 628-5887

U.S. Fish & Wildlife Service
6620 S. Point Dr., South
Suite 310
Jacksonville, FL 32216-0912
(904) 232-2580

U.S. Forest Service
Woodcrest Office Park
325 John Knox Rd.
Building F
Tallahassee, FL 32303
(904) 942-9300

INDEX

Note: Citings of wildlife and plant species in this index generally refer to locations with significant information about the cited species. Not all references to plants and animals in the text are cited. Illustrations are indicated by boldface. Photos on color pages are indicated by "CP."

265

INDEX

Morrison Hammock Scenic Area
70–71
Mud Swamp/New River Wilderness
Area 78
Munson Hills Bike Trail 76
Museum of Florida History 189

National Forest System 5
National Wildlife Refuge System 5
Nature Conservancy 134, 197
Naval Live Oaks Area 88–89
New Bridge Road 144
North Line Road 101–102

Oak Hill 20
Ocheesee Pond 179
Ochlockonee Bay 72
Ochlockonee River State Park 104,
145–150
Ochlockonee River Wildlife
Management Area 142
Ochlockonee Units 142–143
Off–Road Cycling 76
Okaloosa Area 90
Okefenokee sea 16
Orange Hill 20
Otter Lake 103
Owl Creek 65, 82, 83

Paleorefugia 197
Panacea Unit 103–105
Perdido Key and Johnson Beach Area
92–93
Pine flatwoods CP2
Pine Log State Forest 150–154, **152**
Plum Orchard Pond Nature Trail 96
Point Washington State Forest and
Wildlife Management Area 150, 209
Poison
ivy **12**–13
oak 12–13
sumac 13
Poison House Road 141
Poisonous Plants 12–13
Poisonous Snakes 7–9
copperhead 8

cottonmouth 7, **8**
dusky pygmy rattlesnake 7
eastern coral 7–8
eastern diamondback rattlesnake 7
Ponce de Leon Spring 155
Ponce de Leon Springs State
Recreation Area 155–156
Porter Lake 65, 75
Puddin Head Lake 161
Puerto Rican Mole Crab 109
Purple pitcher plant CP1

Rainfall 4
Ravines 40–42
Red Cedar Trail 161
Repellant 11
Reptiles 45–48
Revell Landing 75
River Bluff State Picnic Site 156–159
River otter 57–58
River swamps 38, **39**
Rivers
Alapaha 177
alluvial 36–37
Apalachicola 19, 36, 37, 39, 42, 65,
75, 78–86, 145, 179, 184, 185, 187,
197, 198, 202, 206
Aucilla 21, 37, 43, 96, 98, 193–196,
217, CP20, CP21
Big Gully Creek 80
Blackwater 19, 37, 115, 119–120,
123, 213
Brushy Creek 82
Buckthorn Creek 147
Chattahoochee 20, 179
Chipola 20, 37, 81, 130, 206,
214–215
Choctawhatchee 19, 20, 37, 39, 75,
154, 155, 208
Coldwater Creek 117, 120–121, 212
Cypress Creek 207
Dead 104, 146, 147
Depot Creek 207
East 83, 84, 85
Econfina 37, 203
Econfina Creek 214

268